URBAN GEOGRAPHY OF POST-GROWTH SOCIETY

Masateru HINO and Jun TSUTSUMI eds.

Tohoku University Press,
Sendai

Cover photo: Jozenji-Street Jazz Festival in Sendai City, 2009.

Published in 2015 by

Tohoku University Press,Sendai

2-1-1 Katahira,Aoba-ku,Sendai 980-8577, Japan

Tel : +81-22-214-2777

Fax : +81-22-214-2778

Website : http://www.tups.jp/

E-mail : info@tups.jp

Edited by Masateru Hino and Jun Tsutsumi

Copyright © 2015 by Masateru Hino and Jun Tsutsumi

ISBN978-4-86163-254-9

Printed in Japan 2015 by

TOHOKU UNIVERSITY CO-OP

Preface

This book is a collection of articles monitoring urbanization processes in Japanese cities since the 1990s. Two major aspects of this book are notable with respect to the study of urbanization globally.

First, this book examines the depopulation (population decline) phase of cities, whereas most previous discussions of urbanization (e.g. the Klaassen model for urbanization in developed countries) have explicitly or implicitly focused on population increase. Because the number of births has fallen below the number of deaths since 2005, a natural decrease of population is common throughout Japan, and this trend will probably become substantially worse in the future. In this depopulation phase, even though the overall urban population will remain relatively stable, Japanese cities will undergo radical changes as compared to when an increasing population was the dominant trend. Because Japanese cities have only relatively recently begun experiencing these types of structural changes, the studies presented herein are new and will provide a different paradigm of urban studies.

Second, this book focuses on the "shrinking city" phenomenon, which has become a key issue in recent urban studies. Since the 1980s in developed countries, shrinking cities have dominated in some areas. In many eastern European countries, remarkable shrinkage has occurred as a result of social structural changes, causing serious problems and increasing the attention being paid to the relationship between globalization and shrinking cities. In the field of urban planning, the problem of shrinking cities has become an urgent issue under the threat of depopulation. This has resulted in the need for modification of previous planning because most plans were based on a growing population, not a shrinking one. In this context, the concept of the compact city has been proposed and, especially in the field of urban planning, widely accepted. The shrinking city trend is also found in Japan and it is not temporary or unique to one area. Japan's struggle to maintain sustainable development under a depopulation trend is an important challenge. In this sense, monitoring the urbanization processes in Japanese cities will be very informative.

We chose the title *Post-Growth* for several reasons. We don't think that post-growth and growth are mutually exclusive concepts. A Post-Growth society can be conceptualized as one in which sustainable development, which has been a common goal globally since the 1990s, is valued more than simply growth. Even though the population is declining, as long as economic, social and cultural sustainability can still be obtained, the quality of life would be preserved subsequently. In this sense, the prefix "post" is not used negatively, but rather it connotes the potentially positive aspects of our future society.

We would like to introduce the book structure here. Part I consists of 10 chapters. Chapter 1 provides an introduction to the book based on a review of the body of literature about urbanization studies in the Post-Growth society. This chapter was written by Dr. Michael Pacione, a professor at the University of Strathclyde in the United Kingdom. He is also the author of the well-known and widely distributed book, *Urban Geography: A Global Perspective* published by Routledge. This chapter overviews the worldwide trend of shrinking cities, examines trends in Japan, and raises several urban geographical questions related to the Post-Growth society. In this society, investment in infrastructure will not by itself be sufficient, and the ability to identify and solve specific problems will be critically important. In this process, geographical approaches, including fieldwork and map representation will be crucial.

Following 9 chapters identify the cessation of metropolitan expansion as well as the revival of population centralization in two major Japanese metropolitan areas: Tokyo and Keihanshin (Kyoto–Osaka–Kobe). Several phenomena are examined, including the distribution of residents by cohort (Chapter 2), commuting patterns (Chapter 3), the spatial pattern of population change (Chapter 4), regional differences of lifestyle (Chapter 5), and so on. In addition, the problems associated with an aging society are addressed, including the isolation of single elderly people (Chapter 6), the "food-desert problem" (Chapter 7) and the increasing number of vacant houses (Chapter 8). The recent gentrification of areas of Osaka and the subsequent social problems related to discrimination against low-income residents are considered in Chapter 9. Finally, Chapter 10 evaluates how the Great East Japan Earthquake, which occurred on 11 March 2011, seriously influenced land price evaluations in Tokyo and Osaka. In sum, Part I provides a clear and practical image of what has happened in Japanese metropolitan areas since the 1990s.

The 4 chapters that comprise Part II consider Japanese regional cities outside of the Tokyo and *Keihanshin* metropolitan areas. The focus is on four Regional Centre Cities (Sapporo, Sendai, Hiroshima and Fukuoka), all of which have the common characteristic that their growth was strongly driven by the "branch-office economy" (an accumulation of branch offices of major companies) during the period of high economic growth. Commonly, new high-rise buildings and prestigious office buildings occupy the central parts of these cities. After the collapse of the "Bubble" economy (roughly, since the late 1990s), most major Japanese companies have reorganized their management systems. This has resulted in the cessation of growth and, even worse, a decline in the number of branch offices in these cities. The office vacancy rate has risen in these cities since the late 1990s, but new types of activities have been observed. In Sendai, volunteers' activities, supported by local residents, supplement the decline in the branch-office economy and help to revitalize the cities (Chapter 11 and 12). Through these activities, a new model of the Post-Growth society can be found. Chapter 13 looks at examples of how municipality consolidation, strongly encouraged by national policy as a countermeasure for population decline, could threaten the development of local autonomy in small and remote municipalities. In Chapter 14, the focus is on the "knowledge spill-over effect" driven by the accumulation of environment-related industries because this type of phenomenon can be regarded as a type of "qualitative growth" of a city. In the 21st century,

Preface

modern society can be conceptualized as being knowledge based rather than labour or capital based. Knowledge, which can be regarded as a source of innovation, should offer important insights for the future of Japanese cities for which the extent of population concentration or dispersal is yet unknown.

Most of the articles included in this book are based on the presentation held at the Urban Commission of the International Geographical Union, as a part of the Regional Conference of International Geographical Congress in Kyoto, August 2013.

We owe gratitude to many people who gladly supported us in writing this book. Comments from Professor Céline Rozenblat (Chair of the IGU Urban Commission: University of Lausanne, Switzerland), Dr. Daniel O'Donoghue (Vice Chair of the IGU Urban Commission: Canterbury Christchurch University, UK) and colleagues attended at the conference greatly assisted our work. In addition, we owe endless gratitude to Professor Dr. Michael Pacione who willingly agreed with us that we decided to raise his original attractive title to the book title.

The research for this book was financially supported by a Grant-in Aid for Scientific Research from the Japan Society for the Promotion of Science (2012-2015" Restructuring urban geography for the task of reshaping the sustainable urban space"). In addition, the invaluable professional support from the editorial staffs of Tohoku University Press made this publication possible. We would like to express our sincere gratitude for them.

February 2015
Masateru Hino and Jun Tsutsumi

4

Contents

Preface   1

Part I

1. Perspectives on the Post-Growth City   7
    Michael PACIONE

2. Geographical Shrinking of the Tokyo Metropolitan Area: Its Demographic and   31
    Residential Background
    Takashi ABE

3. Urban Shrinkage of the Keihanshin Metropolitan Area in Japan: Changes in   45
    Population Distribution and Commuting Flows
    Tatsuya YAMAGAMI

4. Occupational Structure in the Tokyo Metropolitan Area, 1985-2005:   61
    An Extended Shift-share Analysis of Changing Geographic Patterns
    Ryo KOIZUMI

5. Time Budgets of Working Mothers Living in Central Tokyo: An Analysis on the   77
    Impacts of the Internet
    Naoto YABE

6. The Aged Society in a Suburban New Town: What Should We Do?   91
    Takashi KAGAWA

7. Urban Policy Challenges Facing an Aging Society: The Case of the Tokyo Met-   107
    ropolitan Area
    Tetsuya ITO, Nobuyuki IWAMA and Makoto HIRAI

8. Aging Suburbs and Increasing Vacant Houses in Japan   123
    Tomoko KUBO, Yoshimichi YUI and Hiroaki SAKAUE

9. Gentrification in a Post-Growth Society: The Case of Fukushima Ward,   147
    Osaka
    Yoshihiro FUJITSUKA

Part II

10. Spatial Characteristics of Land Evaluation in the Tokyo Metropolitan Area after the Great East Japan Earthquake
Hirohisa YAMADA ... 159

11. Image of the Post-Growth City: Recent Transformation of Japanese Regional Central Cities
Masateru HINO ... 179

12. The Characteristics of Office Location in Sapporo City, Japan
Jun TSUTSUMI ... 197

13. Spatial Government Systems of Newly Merged Municipalities and Population Changes within Municipalities Impacted by those Government Systems: Under a National Pro-merger Policy of Municipalities in Post-Growth Societies
Jun NISHIHARA ... 207

14. Knowledge Spillover Effects on Agglomerations of Environment-related Industries: A Case in Japan
Jun YAMASHITA ... 225

15. Conclusion ... 247

List of Contributors ... 251

Index ... 253

1. Perspectives on the Post-Growth City

Michael PACIONE

Abstract

The concept of post-growth has emerged recently as a focus for discussion of alternative forms of economic and social development that challenge the dominant growth paradigm of capitalism. The concept of the post-growth city is part of this wider agenda. There are two principal dimensions to the urban geography of post-growth society. The first is seen in the physical manifestations of economic decline and population loss in central cities, most evident in the phenomenon of the shrinking city; while the second is concerned with social and quality of life problems in no growth or shrinking cities. The first of these is a longstanding and well documented process in many advanced nations. The second is a more recent perspective on post-growth that focuses attention more on quality of life than quantity of consumption. The cause and consequences of urban shrinkage for cities and citizens are questions of fundamental importance in post-growth societies, and are attracting increasing research attention as the multi-dimensional character of the process of city shrinkage is manifested more widely. In this discussion we consider both the physical and social perspectives on post-growth urban development. In section 1 we explain the characteristics, causes and consequences of shrinking cities, and consider the implications for urban planning and management; then in section II we examine the 'quality of life' perspective on the post-growth city. Finally, we identify a number of key questions for urban geographical research in the context of the post-growth city, and identify the value of geographical research to enhance understanding of, and planning for the future, of shrinking cities in contemporary post-growth society.

Keywords

Post-growth society, urban shrinkage, quality of life

1.1 Introduction

The concept of post-growth has emerged recently as a focus for discussion of alternative forms of economic and social development that challenge the dominant growth paradigm of capitalism. The concept of the post-growth city is part of this wider agenda. There are two principal dimensions to the urban geography of post-growth society. The first is seen in the physical manifestations of economic decline and population loss in central cities, most evident in the phenomenon of the shrinking city; while the second is concerned with social and quality of life problems in no growth or shrinking cities. The first of these is a longstanding and well documented process in many advanced nations. The second is a more recent perspective on post-growth that focuses attention more on quality of life than quantity of consumption.

In this chapter we consider both the physical and social perspectives on post-growth urban development. In section I we explain the characteristics, causes and consequences of shrinking cities, and consider the implications for urban planning and management; then in section II we examine the 'quality of life' perspective on the post-growth city. We also identify a number of key questions for urban geographical research in the context of the post-growth city, and highlight the value of geographical research to enhance understanding of, and planning for the future, of shrinking cities in contemporary post-growth society.

1.2.1 The physical dimension of the post-growth city - problems, planning and prospect in the shrinking city

For most countries of the world urbanisation is the dominant on-going process. Over the course of the past half-century, a world in which most people lived in rural areas has been transformed into a predominantly urban world (Pacione 2009). However, while urbanisation continues to occur in most of the developing world, in the developed realm the centripetal movement of population has been reversed with cities experiencing suburbanisation, counterurbanisation, and exurbanisation.

Four stages of urban development can be envisaged:

1. Urbanisation: when certain settlements grow at the cost of their surrounding countryside;
2. Suburbanisation or exurbanisation: when the urban ring (commuter belt) grows at the cost of the urban core (physically built-up city);
3. Disurbanisation or counterurbanisation: when the population loss of the urban core exceeds the population gain of the ring, resulting in the agglomeration losing population overall;
4. Reurbanisation: when either the rate of population loss of the core tapers off, or the core starts regaining population with the ring still losing population.

In the context of post-growth society particular attention is focused on the centrifugal movement of population from core cities via the processes of counter-urbanisation, suburbanisation, and exurbanisation (Lucy and Phillips 1997; Champion 1999). In many countries of the developed world one result of these centrifugal population trends has been the emergence of the shrinking city phenomenon. A shrinking city is one that has experienced severe population and job loss, with the result that the 'urban footprint' exceeds the needs of the current and likely future population (Oswalt 2008).

The modern phenomenon of shrinking cities is caused primarily by three main processes of de-industrialisation; suburbanisation and counter-urbanisation; and demographic transition (ageing). In Europe an additional specific factor underlying the emergence of shrinking cities is the post-1989 dissolution of socialist systems in Eastern Europe and Russia that led to population loss in peripheral cities as people migrated in search of employment. Collectively these processes generate a spiral of disinvestment and decline. Over time, these cumulative effects, together with the process of urban sprawl, cause residents to abandon centre city neighbourhoods; a classic example being Detroit.

The major consequences of urban shrinkage are seen in:

1. Declining population densities – leading to reduced feasibility of public transit, greater travel distances, more inefficient energy use, and loss of urban 'vitality'
2. Growing imbalance between the demand for and supply of housing
3. Growing imbalance between the demand for and supply of social infrastructure – schools, transport, utilities.
4. Increased rates of poverty and associated problems
5. Declining demand for local commercial services
6. Emergence of vacant and derelict land and buildings
7. Greater pressure on municipal budgets due to the costs of maintaining old infrastructure designed for a larger population.

Between 1950 and 2000 more than 350 cities worldwide lost a significant number of their inhabitants (Figure 1). Until the collapse of communism in Eastern Europe in 1989, more than 80% of all shrinking cities were in US (Table 1), UK, Germany, Italy, France (Table 2) and Japan (Table 3).

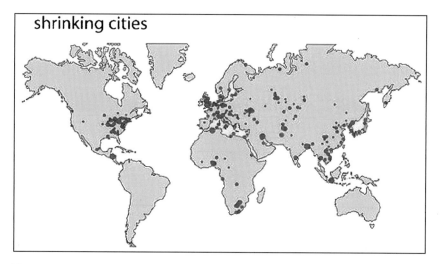

Figure 1   World distribution of shrinking cities
Source: Oswalt 2008

Table 1 Shrinking cites in the US-decline from peak population

City	Peak Population (year)	2010 Population	change (%)
Baltimore	949,708 (1950)	620,961	−34.6
Buffalo	580,132 (1950)	270,240	−53.4
Cincinnati	503,998 (1950)	296,943	−41.1
Cleveland	914,808 (1950)	396,815	−56.6
Detroit	1,849,568 (1950)	713,777	−61.4
Gary	178,320 (1960)	80,294	−55.0
Philadelphia	2,071,605 (1950)	1,526,006	−26.3
Pittsburgh	676,806 (1950)	305,704	−54.8
St. Louis	856,796 (1950)	319,294	−62.7
Toledo	383,818 (1970)	287,208	−25.2
Youngstown	170,002 (1930)	66,982	−60.6

Source: US Census of Population

Table 2 Shrinking cities in Europe-decline from peak population

City	Peak Population (year)	2010 Population	change (%)
Liverpool (UK)	855,000 (1931)	434,900	−49.1
Halle (Ger)	329,625 (1986)	230,900	−30.0
Leipzig (Ger)	713,470 (1933)	515,469	−27.8
Genoa (It)	842,114 (1970)	610,766	−27.5
Bytom (Pol)	239,800 (1987)	183,200	−23.6
Sosnowiec (Pol)	259,600 (1987)	220,400	−15.1
Ostrava (Cz)	331,219 (1990)	306,006	−7.6
Donetsk (Ukr)	1,121,480 (1992)	974,598	−13.1
Makiiva (Ukr)	455,000 (1987)	363,677	−20.1
Timisoara (Rom)	351,293 (1990)	312,113	−11.2

Source: National Censuses of Population

Perspectives on the Post-Growth City

Table 3 Shrinking cities in Japan-population change 2005-2010

City	2005 Population	2010 Population	change (%)
Kyoto	1,474,811	1,474,473	−0.02
Kitakyushu	993,525	977,288	−1.63
Niigata	813,847	812,192	−0.20
Hamamutsu	804,032	800,912	−0.39
Shizuoka	723,323	716,328	−0.97
Hiyashiosaka	513,821	509,632	−0.82
Amagasaki	462,647	453,608	−1.95
Nagasaki	455,206	443,409	−2.58
Yokosuka	426,178	418,448	−1.81
Gifu	413,357	413,239	−0.03
Nagano	386,572	381,533	−1.30
Wakayama	375,591	369,400	−1.65
Nara	370,102	366,528	−0.97
Asahikawa	355,004	347,275	−2.18
Kochi	348,990	343,416	−1.60
Iwaki	354,492	342,198	−3.47
Akiti	333,109	323,363	−2.93
Aomori	311,386	299,429	−3.84
Shimonoseki	290,693	280,987	−3.34
Hakodate	294,264	279,110	−5.15

Source: Statistic Bureau, Japan Ministry of Internal Affairs

1.2.2 Shrinking city – flourishing region

For many shrinking cities the metropolitan region beyond the core city has continued to grow through the suburbanisation that has contributed to the population decline of the city. This is evident in the city of St. Louis (Gordon 2008). In 1950, 44% of the region's population lived in the city of St. Louis; the inner ring counties accounted for another 41% meaning that 85% of the metropolitan region's population lived in the city or inner suburbs. By 2009, the population of the city and inner ring had fallen to 65% of the region. The city of St. Louis reached a population peak in 1950 and has lost over 537,000 people since then (Figure 2).

These changes are reflected in regional migration tends during the 2000s. Between 2000 and 2009:

1. The city of St. Louis lost a net 63,000 migrants (18% of its 2000 population)

2. The inner ring counties lost a net 59,000 (4% of the 2000 population)

3. The middle ring counties gained a net 64,000 migrants (8.7% of the 2000 population)

4. The outer ring counties gained a net 24,000 migrants (16.4% of the 2000 population)

The situation of St. Louis reflects the position in many metropolitan areas across the developed world in which core cities continue to stagnate or shrink while the region remains vibrant.

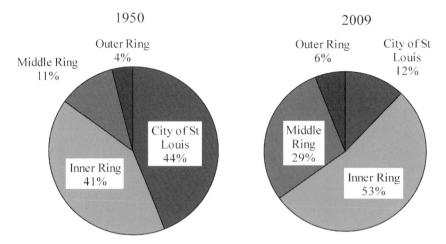

Figure 2 Distribution of population in St. Louis metropolitan region, 1950-2009
Source: Cox 2011

1.2.3 Shrinking cities – policy perspectives

There are essentially three possible policy responses to city shrinkage:
1. Do nothing – either deny there is a problem or recognise the problem but not respond (no strategy).
2. Try to reverse decline and stimulate population growth (growth strategy)
3. Accept decline and manage the consequences (post-growth strategy)

Leaving aside the no strategy option, the conventional growth strategy approach to shrinkage is to:
1. Try to increase the city tax base by redeveloping the downtown area
2. Stimulate development by expanding the public sector
3. Raise revenues through higher property and business taxes
4. Reduce expenditure by curtailing services

The latter two strategies can, of course, also accelerate population decline.

This growth approach typically employs top-down public-private partnership to revitalise declining central cities, using strategies such as Enterprise Zones and Urban Development Corporations (Raco 2005). The main role of government is to attract and accommodate the requirements of private investors without unduly influencing their development decisions. Over the past fifty years in the UK and US these business-government initiatives have produced a range of property-led downtown redevelopments – such as London's Canary Wharf and Pittsburgh's Golden Triangle.

On the other hand, the distributional impact of these projects has been typically uneven with, in most cases, (e.g. Baltimore's Inner Harbour redevelopment) redeveloped downtowns resembling islands of renewal in seas of decay (Levine 1997). A principal reason for this unequal effect is that the new downtown developments based on advanced services and tourism often have only limited links with the local economy, and rarely generate economic development in surrounding neighbourhoods – ie there is no trickle-down effect. In addition, the kinds of jobs created are unlikely to provide employment opportunities for the urban poor; and many of the benefits of redevelopment are taken by suburban commuters (Merrifield 1993). In most cases these central area regeneration strategies have not stemmed population loss from the city.

There is a need, therefore, to consider an alternative policy perspective, in effect a post-growth strategy. This requires several conditions including that:

1. Shrinking cities must accept that they are unlikely to regain their former population size and status

2. Urban planners and managers of shrinking cities must overcome their traditional aversion to the idea of 'creative shrinkage'. They must recognise that a downsized city may be the right-sized city

3. Urban managers must acknowledge that shrinkage is not only a problem for a city but also an opportunity. For example, the absence of growth forces and abundance of vacant land create opportunities to enhance quality of life by setting aside land for green spaces, recreation, and urban agriculture. Such non-conventional urban land uses can benefit existing residents and may attract future investment.

Viewed from the perspective of a post-growth strategy shrinking cities are not seen as 'declining to decay', but rather as moving from one form of urbanism to another different city form.

A post-growth policy of creative shrinkage would focus development efforts on urban islands – areas of denser urbanism concentrated at key nodes within the existing (too large) urban footprint that are determined to be the most viable areas of the depopulating city. Development would be constrained to these 'islands' (eg by means of a targeted provision of housing rehabilitation grants) as a way of maintaining local density and vitality as the city as a whole loses population; with the area around the urban islands scheduled for demolition, relocation of remaining population, and eventually a return to natural conditions.

The resultant 'urban islands' could:

1. Maintain a population density needed to make infrastructure provision more economic

2. Maintain urban vitality and sense of community

3. Reduce transport costs (cf. the compact city model)

4. Provide an opportunity to relieve congestion in older city neighbourhoods

5. Provide desirable single-family housing (similar to that available in the suburbs) and perhaps (re)-attract population

6. Enable vacant land to be used for 'urban greening' (eg parks, recreation, allotments)

7. Allow for vacant land adjacent to the suburbs on the edge of the city to be sold with a condition that it ceases to be part of the city – generating income and reducing costs of infrastructure to the city. Such land free from the burden of city taxes and bureaucracy could be attractive for developers.

Whether the post-growth strategy of creative shrinkage is feasible in practice remains open to debate but it has been employed in a number of US cities (eg Youngstown PA). In practice, the planned downsizing of cities faces several obstacles including the fact that:

1. Most urban planners and managers lack the experience or tools for the task, being traditionally focused on growth strategies rather than planned decline

2. Potential opposition would come from local politicians who would lose their electoral base of power

3. Historic preservation groups could oppose demolition of many old buildings

4. It requires 'responsible relocation' of residents from 'de-selected' areas that are to be abandoned

1.2.4   Shrinking cities – prospective

Whether shrinking cities continue to decline or achieve a sustainable future as smaller but stronger cities is an open question. The answer to this will vary with local context but generally will depend on how city governments, planners, managers, and citizens:

1. Acknowledge the reality of their being a small city

2. Reconfigure the urban environment eg with non-conventional 'green' land uses

3. Re-use (now) surplus land and buildings

4. Target available (reduced) resources – eg to provide viable residential neighbourhoods and communities

5. Balance the need for affordable housing (for remaining poor residents) with a need to retain (and attract) middle-income households (to enhance the tax base)

6. Link to the wider metropolitan region

7. Focus on transformative planning that uses available resources (physical, financial and human) to identify strategies to integrate the city into the post-industrial economy

The shrinking city phenomenon poses some final fundamental questions regarding urban futures. These include:

1. Is population loss a bad thing for a city? According to conventional growth-oriented urban planning the answer is yes. Another answer is – not necessarily. It can be argued that when

Perspectives on the Post-Growth City 15

a city is smaller it is also more 'human' in scale; more liveable; less anonymous; with a more manageable and responsive government.

2. By having to deal explicitly with the problems of shrinking, cities have an opportunity to discuss a paradigm shift from growth-centred urban planning to a more sustainable approach

3. Finally, and fundamentally, the phenomenon of shrinking cities opens a window into a wider debate about post-growth society and prompts us to consider a different kind of city living marked by a greater emphasis on urban liveability and quality of life.

These questions provide the focus for the second part of the discussion.

1.3.1 Mapping urban quality of life in post-growth society

The global economy is an interrelated complex of many different economic systems (subsistence, communist, capitalist). One thing that all of the world's large economies have in common is an absolute dependence on growth. The success of nearly every country in the world is measured by GDP. In essence fast growth is better than slow growth; no growth is bad, and negative growth (recession) is considered a catastrophe if it continues for more than a few months. A post-growth perspective on urban living rejects the capitalist imperative of constant growth and poses a number of questions, three of which are – First, since we inhabit a planet of limited size and resource capacity can (unsustainable), growth continue indefinitely? Second, what good is increased production and consumption if the result isn't increased human satisfaction? Third, is growth always good; and should growth continue to be the unquestioned fundamental goal of human economies and societies?

1.3.2 Alternatives to the paradigm of growth

Many alternative perspectives to the growth paradigm have emerged in recent years. These are evidenced in several ways. For example:

1. Bhutan introduced a measure of gross national happiness (GNH); since copied by cities in USA (eg Seattle) and state level governments in India (e.g. Assam).

2. Academics have focused research attention on concepts of subjective well-being, quality of life, and sustainable urban development

3. Phrases such as 'green growth' (with its intellectual roots in South Korea), 'genuine progress' (and the associated measure of social and economic welfare), 'sustainable society' and even 'de-growth' (a radical thesis of prosperity without growth) appear in policy discussion.

4. The growing number of grassroots and intellectual movements eg the happiness movement; and the downshifting movement (people who choose to work and earn less in exchange for more time).

5. In 2012 the UN High Level Panel on Global Sustainability noted the need for the interna-

tional community to measure development beyond GDP and develop a new sustainable development index.

6. Ethical based critiques of the 'growth paradigm' have championed other 'post-materialistic' values such as equity and altruism, sentiments reflected in the rise of democracy-based protest movements (eg Occupy Wall Street)

7. 'Simple living' movements (from Schumacher's Small is Beautiful) including 'slow food' and 'slow city' movements

8. Emergence of 'new economics' – a body of economic philosophy and theory based on ideas associated more with sufficiency than growth.

However, none of the alternative growth paradigms can be said to have had a transformative impact on the overwhelming dominance of economic growth as the driving force of contemporary civilisation. Despite the rise of (sustainable) alternatives to growth the world is not on the verge of turning its back on economic growth. There is no dispute that (economic and population) growth has benefitted humankind, most of whom live longer, healthier, more prosperous lives as a result of economic growth and development. Growth will (rightly) continue to be the goal for developing countries but a question for richer countries is - can nations that are already wealthy create economies of happiness without economic growth? This raises a related question – how much growth is enough?

It is often said that money cannot buy you happiness. This is not correct – money is essential for well-being: up to a point. Another fundamental question is does happiness/well-being increase continuously with economic growth or is there a point beyond which additional national economic growth does not increase happiness? This question taxed the economist Richard Easterlin (1974) and led to the Easterlin Paradox which suggested that beyond a certain level of national economic growth, ($15,000 - $75,000 per person in GDP terms depending on which country you live in), pursuit of further economic growth did not add to happiness.

1.3.3 Japan : the first post-growth society?

As Figure 3 shows, in 2009 Japan's GDP was essentially the same as it was in 1995. In addition, the country's share of global GDP had fallen over the period from 17% to 4% and in 2011 China overtook Japan to become the world's second largest economy.

In classical economic terms Japan was failing. Yet the country still functions; crime is low; literacy rates are high; life expectancy is better than almost anywhere else (82 years cf to 78 in the US); trains run on time; and unemployment is a fairly low 5% For some this suggests that despite serious problems (e.g. a large national debt), rather than being a failed state Japan is proof that growth is not necessary to deliver a high standard of living for the people. Rather than stagnating it may be that Japan is settling onto a plateau of enough. Japan, through accident or design, may be the world's first post-growth society.

Perspectives on the Post-Growth City

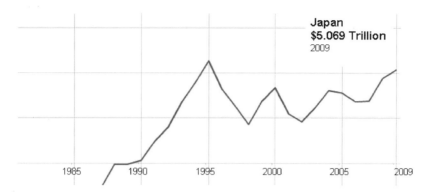

Figure 3 Japan's GDP over recent decades
Source: Statistic Bureau, Japan Ministry of Internal Affairs

As well as the economic dimensions of post-growth, in Japan:
1. Population growth has levelled off since 2005 (at 128 million)
2. Some cities have lost population
3. The population is ageing (with 23% of total population over 65 years of age: the highest in the world.
4. The ratio of dependent population (the sum of the elderly plus younger aged divided by the working age population) is 57%.
5. Average life expectancy at 86 years for women and 80 years for men is the highest in the world
6. The proportion of elderly households is 21%

1.3.4   Quality versus quantity

Post-growth philosophy emphasises a focus on improving quality of life rather than increasing quantity of consumption. Study of socio-spatial variations in quality of life at different scales, (not least the urban), provides opportunities for urban geographical research to engage with the post-growth condition.

The definition of quality of life varies (among individuals, cultures and countries) but a general indication is provided by Maslow's (1943) hierarchy of needs model (Figure 4).

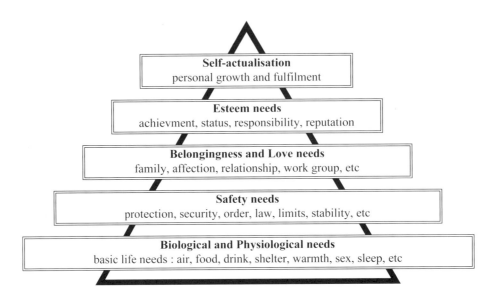

Figure 4 Maslow's hierarchy of needs model
Source: Maslow 1943

1.3.5 Quality of life research in urban geography

Figure 5 illustrates the place of urban quality of life research within human geography. While research into differential quality of life may be undertaken at both inter-urban (for example, comparative evaluations of world cities), and intra-urban scales most research, including much of my own work (Pacione 1980; 1982; 1986; 1993; 1995; 2003; 2004), has focused on the latter.

As Figure 5 indicates geographical research on differential quality of life at the intra-urban scale seeks to identify socio-spatial variations in quality of life, or human well-being, along a number of dimensions including, for example, health, wealth, housing and crime. Mapping of differential quality of life aids identification of urban 'environments of advantage' (elite areas) and 'environments of disadvantage' – characterised by a range of social, economic and environmental problems. The applied or problem-oriented perspective that underlies this work and that is central to the goal of creating a liveable city, (and, of course, liveable neighbourhoods and communities), means that particular attention is focused on the 'environments of disadvantage' within contemporary cities. Study of conditions at the disadvantaged end of the quality of life spectrum forms a key area of research in post-growth urban geography.

Perspectives on the Post-Growth City

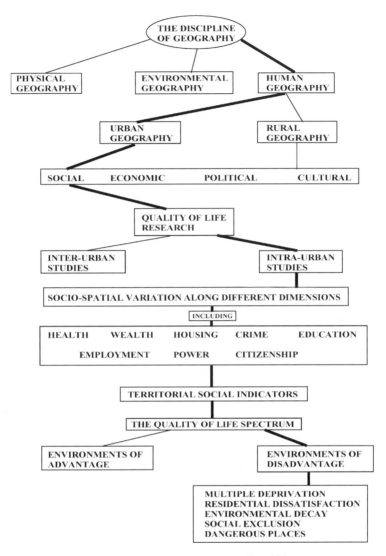

Figure 5 An urban geographical perspective on quality of life
Source: Author

1.3.6 A Conceptual model for quality of life research

In order to analyse socio-spatial variations in quality of life within cities geographers have employed territorial social indicators based on both objective and subjective measures of life quality. Most of the research using territorial social indicators has used objective measures derived either from primary field surveys or from analysis of secondary, normally census-based, data sets. Collectively this line of research has contributed valuable insights into such questions as the extent and distribution of substandard housing, and the differential incidence of deprivation within the city.

The objective perspective has been paralleled, however, by the development of work using subjective social indicators, an approach closely aligned to the concept of urban liveability (Pacione 1990). In contrast to the objective definition of urban life quality the urban liveability perspective views life quality not as an attribute inherent in the environment but as a behaviour-related function of the interaction of environmental characteristics and person characteristics. It is axiomatic that in order to obtain a proper understanding of urban environmental quality it is necessary to employ both objective and subjective evaluations. In other words, we must consider both the city on the ground and the city in the mind.

We can examine some of the key dimensions of a geographical approach to quality of life research with reference to Figure 6 which represents a five-dimensional model for quality of life research.

In addition to the distinction between objective and subjective measures of life quality geographical analyses of quality of life may be structured in terms of level of specificity of the life concern (which can range from satisfaction with one's life as a whole to feelings about particular issues such as the availability of public services in a locality). Clearly, just as quality of life can be assessed at various levels, so society can be assessed at different geographic scales ranging from the individual through the group or local scale to the city, regional, na-

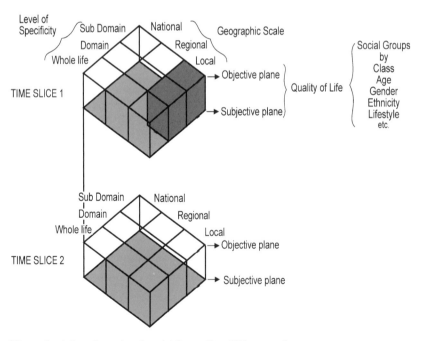

Figure 6 A five-dimensional model for quality of life research
Source: Author

Perspectives on the Post-Growth City

tional and international (Figure 6). Whatever scale is chosen a recurrent problem is that eco-logical correlations do not necessarily reflect the life concerns of all individuals within the area. This is an inherent difficulty for the spatial or territorial approach to the study of quality of life. The larger is the unit of enquiry the greater the potential ignorance of internal varia-tions from the mean position. It follows that, although descriptive pattern identification and mapping at the macro-scale is of value as a pointer to detailed investigation, policy-relevant quality of life indicators are more likely to be derived at the local area scale. Such indicators are also likely to be concerned with specific life domains such as housing conditions, employ-ment or access to public facilities. In addition to different spatial scales, analysis of quality of life may also be undertaken at different points in time to provide measure of changing urban conditions and progress against policy goals. Finally, complementing the four dimensions relating to indicator type, level of specificity, scale of analysis and time a fifth dimension of importance for quality of life research centres on the quality of life experienced by different social groups in the city (Figure 6). Urban populations may be disaggregated along a large number of planes of division including class, age, lifestyle, gender and ethnicity. There are, in addition, groupings based on behaviour (for example public transport riders), and common interest (for example estate residents). To be of real value to both citizens and policy-makers quality of life studies must be directed to the appropriate social groups or constituencies.

1.3.7 The anatomy of disadvantage

As noted earlier, geographical research into differential quality of life within cities has fo-cused particular attention on conditions of people and places at the disadvantaged end of the quality of life spectrum (Figure 5). It is axiomatic that the forces of a capitalist society, if left unchecked, tend to make the rich richer and the poor poorer and thus increase the gap between the two groups. Consequently at any one time certain countries, cities and localities will be in the throes of decline as a result of the retreat of capital investment, while others will be expe-riencing the impact of capital inflows. At the metropolitan scale, the outcome of this uneven development process is manifested in the poverty, powerlessness and polarisation of disad-vantaged people and places.

Disadvantage, or multiple deprivation, is manifested in a variety of forms, many of which are inter-related and mutually reinforcing. As Figure 7 indicates, poverty is a central element in the multi-dimensional problem of deprivation. The root cause of poverty is economic and stems from three principal sources. The first arises from the low wages earned by those em-ployed in declining traditional industries or engaged, often on a part-time basis, in newer service-based activities. A second major cause of deprivation is the unemployment experi-enced by those marginal to the job market such as single parents, the elderly, the disabled, and increasingly never-employed school leavers. A third contributory factor underlying multiple deprivation is related to reductions in welfare expenditure in most Western states as a result of growing demand and ensuing fiscal crisis.

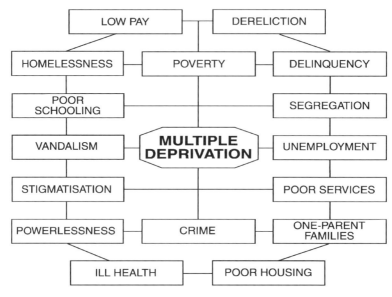

Figure 7 The anatomy of multiple deprivation
Source: Author

Significantly, the complex of poverty-related problems (Figure 7) has been shown to exhibit spatial concentration within cities. This intensifies the overlapping effects of the various forms of deprivation for the residents of particular urban localities. It also underlines the importance of a spatial or geographical perspective in analysing the differential distribution of disadvantage in contemporary society.

We can illustrate the geographical approach to differential quality of life in cities with reference to two case study examples.

1.3.8 Case study 1: The geography of quality of life in Glasgow

The first case study is selected to illustrate the use of objective territorial social indicators to examine differential quality of life in the city of Glasgow, UK. In this research particular attention is focused on conditions at the disadvantaged end of the quality of life spectrum. A combination of statistical and cartographic analysis is employed to identify the nature, intensity and incidence of multiple deprivation in the city.

A set of 64 indicators relating to demographic, social, economic and residential conditions was extracted from the census for each of the 5374 output areas in Glasgow. The data set was subjected first to univariate analysis to examine the distributions of individual social indicators across the city. While examination of each of the 64 indicators is of both academic and

Table 4   Component structure and loadings-multiple deprivation

Component 1: Multiple Deprivation	Loading
male unemployment	0.7511
occupying council (social) housing	0.4896
households with >1.5 persons per room	0.5183
household spaces vacant	0.4906
households with single person < pension age	0.5261
households of single parents	0.6617
travel to work by bus	0.3189
household heads in lowest socio–econ groups	0.3000
young children living in high flats	0.6019
households above the occupancy norm	0.6935

Source: Author

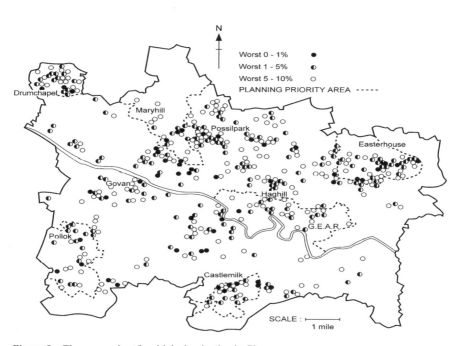

Figure 8   The geography of multiple deprivation in Glasgow
Source: Author

practical utility in its own right, the univariate analyses suggested some degree of statistical and spatial overlap among the revealed patterns. An R-type principal components analysis was used to explore the weave of linkages among the individual distributions, and to provide a conceptually and statistically rigorous composite measure of multiple deprivation. In this study the principal component was readily identified as an indicator of multiple deprivation, with high correlations among measures relating to male unemployment, council/social housing, single-parent households, and overcrowded housing (Table 4).

Calculation of component scores provided a measure of deprivation for each of the 5,374 census output areas in the city. Mapping these scores revealed the spatial expression of multiple deprivation in Glasgow (Figure 8).

This research identified the nature, intensity and incidence of multiple deprivation within the city. In addition identification of the major loci of deprivation ('environments of disadvantage') provides a basis for detailed analyses of particular problems and problem areas. The analytical results also provide a base for critical assessment of policies aimed at alleviating conditions of disadvantage. In addition, longitudinal studies can map the changing geography of multiple deprivation in the city over time.

1.3.9   Case study 2: Landscapes of fear in the city

The second exemplar of the urban geography approach to quality of life illustrates the use of subjective social indicators to gauge gender-differentiated fear of crime at the local level within the city. Fear of crime is a growing social problem, a major policy issue and an important element in the social geography of contemporary cities. For the most vulnerable subgroups of the population living in high-risk environments the impact of fear of crime on daily living patterns and on general quality of life can be profound. A major obstacle to addressing this social stressor is lack of detailed information on fear of crime at the neighbourhood scale.

Table 5   Perceived life problems in the study area (% respondents)

Problem	Males	Females	Total	Overall Rank
Unemployment	83.7	82.9	83.3	1
Poor schooling	26.1	22.0	24.1	8
Bad housing	73.0	70.6	71.8	3
Crime	80.3	79.9	80.1	2
Lack of leisure facilities	53.9	49.9	51.9	4
Lack of play spaces	34.6	38.3	36.5	5
General unfriendliness	32.6	33.0	32.8	6
Bad relations with police	30.4	29.0	29.7	7

Source: Author

Perspectives on the Post-Growth City

Table 6   Perceived risk from different forms of crime in the study area (% respondents)

Nature of risk	Males	Females
Assault	56.7	27.4
Sexual assault	0.0	31.5
Burglary	37.8	29.0
Car theft	4.5	5.2
Street theft	0.0	6.9
Arson	1.0	0.0

Source: Author

Table 7   Perceived danger areas in the study area (% respondents)

Locations	Males	Females
Parks	7.6	19.7
Gang neighbourhoods	34.0	14.9
Bridges and overpasses	0.0	11.9
Playing fields	6.8	9.5
Schools	8.2	7.1
Peripheral roads/spaces	0.0	20.8
Town centre	43.4	16.1

Source: Author

This research was designed to gauge the nature and extent of fear of crime among male and female residents of a deprived social housing estate on the edge of Glasgow, and to identify the geography of fear within the area.

The research employed an interview procedure to determine the relative importance of crime as a social problem on the estate. For both males and females crime was regarded as the second most serious problem in the area (Table 5).

Related social problems were identified in references to the general unfriendliness of the locality and bad relations between residents and the police. Fear of assault and burglary were the most prevalent crime risk reported (Table 6)

Investigation of the fear of crime revealed clear gender-based differences. For most young males the high risk of assault was accepted as part of their lifestyle and living environment. Respondents accepted that they are 'fair game' and an automatic target for local gangs. The relative physical weakness of young females fostered a fear of assault and in particular sexual assault. These perceptions of risk conditioned the daily activity patterns of people living on the estate. Young males took care to avoid known gang territories, and the town centre in the evenings. Females were particularly wary of parks and other open spaces including periphery roads, bridges and over/underpasses (Table 7)

The information on respondents' cognitive maps of fear was used to identify specific 'danger areas' within the study area (Figure 9)

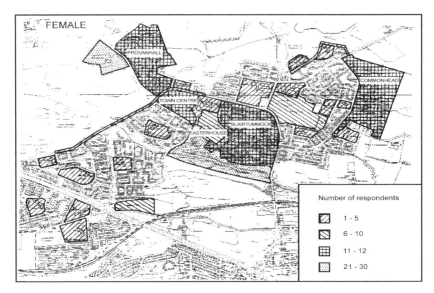

Figure 9 Females geography of fear in the study area
Source: Author

Clearly, analysis of the particular characteristics of these dangerous spaces may contribute to the design of policies aimed at reducing fear of crime in the locality, and to the enhancement of life quality for residents.

These case study examples are but two of the many dimensions of quality of life research that offer research opportunities for urban geography in post-growth society. Some others are shown in Table 8.

1.3.10 The value of quality of life research for the urban geography of post-growth society

The question of the usefulness of measuring quality of life or human well-being is of central importance in the current climate in favour of 'relevant' or applied research, and for studies of the post-growth city. Geographers engaged in quality of life research have identified several outputs of value to social scientists, communities and policy makers. These include:

1. Providing knowledge of how differential quality of life (e.g. on housing or health status) is distributed through society (e.g. social groups) and across space (e.g. neighbourhoods and communities in a city)
2. Producing baseline measures of quality of life/wellbeing in a city, neighbourhood or community against which we can compare subsequent measures and identify trends over time (e.g. improvement in levels of educational attainment)

Table 8 Some urban scale quality of life research questions in post-growth society

Urban Theme	Some Research Questions
Urban economy	• the changing nature of work (e.g. downsizing) • corporate social responsibility (who benefits?) • rise of the 'third sector' (e.g. voluntary agencies)
Local economy	• local exchange trading systems • community businesses
Local communities	• residential segregation (by class, ethnicity, lifestyle etc) • the urban community (relevance today?) • difference and identity in the city (the place of different groups e.g. women, elderly, young, disabled in the city)
Demography	• the increasing dependent population • retirement housing and communities
Collective consumption	• welfare needs and provision (by family – state?) • equity and inequity in access to public services • social justice in the city (who gets what where and how?)
Local democracy	• participation strategies (who decides?) • urban social movements
Sustainable urban development	• rhetoric or reality?
Urban metabolism	• e.g. waste management, energy consumption
Future city form	• e.g. the green city, eco–city, dispersed city, car–free city, informational city, virtual city
Differential quality of life in the city	• mapping and analysis of socio–spatial variations in well–being within the city • urban liveability

Source: Author

3. Identifying problems and problem areas meriting special attention and possible societal action (e.g. high pockets of crime)

4. Identification of normative standards against which actual conditions may be judged in order to inform effective policy formulation (e.g. actual provision versus optimum levels of elderly care provision)

5. Monitoring the effects of policies on the ground (e.g. strategies to address youth unemployment)

6. Achieving a better understanding of the causes and conditions which lead to individuals' feelings of well-being, and of the effects of such feelings on their behaviour.

7. Promoting public participation in the policy making process (e.g. by making the results of academic research available to local people and communities)

1.4 Conclusion – urban quality of life in post-growth society?

Drawing on the foregoing discussion we can offer a number of general conclusions on the question of the urban geography of post-growth society:

1. Post-growth is a phenomenon, challenge, and opportunity of the developed world.
2. Economic growth will remain, rightly, the national goal of poorer countries of the world in which 2 billion people 'live' on less than $2 per day.
3. In the developed world context the rise of democracy movements to protest against the lack of regulation of the financial system and excessive profiteering by key actors may spread the ideas of 'new economics'
4. In practice alternative strategies to the paradigm of growth have had only limited effect in modifying the capitalist growth dynamic.
5. Continued economic growth will remain the driving force of national and global economies.
6. Happiness or quality of life will be seen most likely as parallel and complementary goals, not as replacements for the growth paradigm.
7. The physical and socio-economic reality of post-growth is apparent in some richer countries, (such as Japan). This phenomenon provides research opportunities for urban geographers to map socio-spatial variations in quality of life; provide critical analyses of the human consequences of current economic policy; and inform urban policy and urban management strategy.

Urban shrinkage is a phenomenon of increasing significance in many countries of the world. The causes and consequences of shrinkage for cities and citizens are receiving growing attention as the multi-dimensional physical, social and economic characteristics of the process are manifested more widely. Further research into the evolving phenomenon of post-growth urban society is required to increase understanding of the causes and multiple dimensions of urban shrinkage, and to aid in identifying potential responses to this contemporary urban challenge.

Remedial approaches range from those based on a conventional growth paradigm to more recent perspectives on 'smart shrinking'. As this discussion has demonstrated, urban geographers, with their eclectic view of urban society and change, and focus on space and place, are well positioned to enhance understanding of, and planning for the future of, shrinking cities in contemporary post-growth society.

References

Champion, A. 1999. Urbanisation and counterurbanisation. In *Applied Geography: Principles and Practice,* ed. M. Pacione, 347-357. London: Routledge.

Cox, W. 2011. *Shrinking city, flourishing region: St. Louis region.*
(http://www.newgeography.com/content/002013-shrinking-city-flourishing-region-st-louis-region) (last accessed 28 September 2014)

Easterlin, R. 1974. Does economic growth improve the human lot? In *Nations and Households in Economic Growth*, ed. R. David and R. Reder, 89-125. New York: Academic Press.

Gordon, C. 2008. *Mapping Decline: St. Louis and the Fate of the American City*, Philadelphia: University of Pennsylvania Press.

Levine, M. 1987. Downtown redevelopment as an urban growth strategy: a critical appraisal of the Baltimore renaissance. *Journal of Urban Affairs* 9 (2): 133-138.

Lucy, W. and Phillips, D. 1997. The post-suburban era comes to Richmond: city decline, suburban expansion and exurban growth. *Landscape and urban Planning* 36: 259-275.

Maslow, A. 1943. A theory of human motivation. *Psychological Review* 50: 370-396.

Merrifield, A. 1993. The Canary Wharf debate. *Environment and Planning A* 25: 1247-1265.

Oswalt, P. ed. 2008. *Shrinking Cities volumes I and II*. Ostfildern: Hatje Cantz.

Pacione, M. 1980. Differential quality of life in a metropolitan village. *Transactions of the Institute of British Geographers* 5(2): 185-206.

Pacione, M. 1982. Evaluating the quality of the residential environment in a deprived council estate. *Geoforum* 13 (1): 45-55.

Pacione, M. 1986. Quality of life in Glasgow – an applied geographical analysis. *Environment and Planning A* 18: 1499-1520.

Pacione, M. 1990. Urban liveability: a review. *Urban Geography* 11(1): 1-30.

Pacione, M. 1993. The geography of the urban crisis – some evidence from Glasgow. *Scottish Geographical Magazine* 109: 87-95.

Pacione, M. 1995. The geography of multiple deprivation in the Clydeside conurbation. *Tijdschrft voor Economische en Sociale Geografie* 86 (5): 407-425.

Pacione, M. 2003. Urban environmental quality and human wellbeing – a social geographical perspective. *Landscape and Urban Planning* 65: 19-30.

Pacione, M. 2004. Environments of disadvantage – the geography of persistent poverty in Glasgow. *Scottish Geographical Journal* 120 (1/2): 117-132.

Pacione, M .2009. *Urban Geography: A Global Perspective Third Edition*. London: Routledge.

Raco, M. 2005. A step change or a step back: the Thames gateway and the rebirth of the urban development corporation. *Local Economy*, 20 (2): 141-153.

30

2. Geographical Shrinking of the Tokyo Metropolitan Area: Its Demographic and Residential Background

Takashi ABE

Abstract

Japan has entered the decrease-in-population phase after 2000. The geographical expansion of the Tokyo metropolitan area seems to reach the maximum point and it entered the "shrinking phase". On the other hand, population has been increasing in the central areas of Tokyo. We tried to clarify the demographic and residential mechanism of this "shrinking" phenomenon in the Tokyo metropolitan area. We classified municipalities in the Kanto Region to five types of development; developing zone, recovering zone, shrinking zone, under-developed zone and neutral zone, by using population increasing ratios of 1990-1995 and 2005-2010. Shirinking zone is distributed over the areas which did not receive the benefit of new railroad line: that is, in Saitama, Ibaraki and Chiba prefectures outside of the 40-km circle from the Tokyo station. Although the cohort born in the 1955 and earlier had a strong tendency to move toward the suburbs between their 20s and 40s before 1990, the same will not be seen in 1965-1980 birth cohort. For this generation, it can be said that suburbanization is no longer the dominant paradigm. The background of such population movement pattern can be explained by several demographic factors as well as by effects of the changes of housing preference. A rapid increase in the rate of unmarried people in their 30s and 40s may be one of the key demographic factors behind this population movement. The increase in condominiums in Tokyo and the increase in vacant dwelling units in the suburbs are residential factors contributing to these population movements. "The single family house with the yard in the suburbs" is no longer the ideal living style.

Keywords

geographical shrinking, Tokyo metropolitan area, cohort share analysis, housing preferences, unmarried people

2.1 Introduction

Since 2006, the number of deaths in Japan has exceeded the number of births. There is thus both a shrinking in the overall population and a shift in the age distribution. Geographically, changes in population distribution in Japan depends on internal and international migration. The Tokyo Metropolitan Area has for many decades been the largest urban agglomeration in the world and has attracted a large number of immigrants from non-metropolitan areas in Japan and other countries. Its contiguous area has been steadily expanding; its radius reached over 70 km in 1990. This period of growth in Tokyo and other Japanese cities was characterized by a decrease in population in central areas, due to the conversion of residential land to commercial or business uses. This is called a "doughnut phenomenon", counterbalanced by the rapid increase in population and housing development in the suburbs, and many new suburban new residential areas were developed. However, Japan has entered a phase of decreasing population, and the change in the residential paradigm from single-family detached houses with yards to high-rise condominiums occurred (Miyazawa, 2006). The geographical expansion of megacities seems to reach a maximum point. Some scholars have argued that such cities enter a "shrinking phase" and confirmed the phenomenon of "empty nesters" (i.e., adults whose children have left the home) in the suburbs of the Tokyo Metropolitan Area (Aiba et. al., 2008, Fujii and Oe, 2006). On the other hand, the population in central areas of Tokyo has been increasing. So-called "return migration" has become evident (Miyazawa and Abe, 2005). We tried to clarify the demographic and physical mechanisms of these phenomena in the Tokyo metropolitan area.

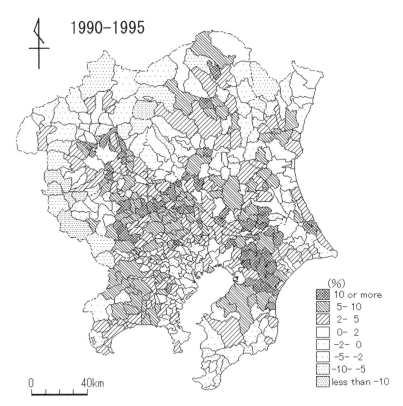

Figure 1 Population Change Ratios from 1990 to 1995 by Municipality (2000 Boundary) in the Kanto Region
Source: Population Censuses 1990, 1995 and 2000

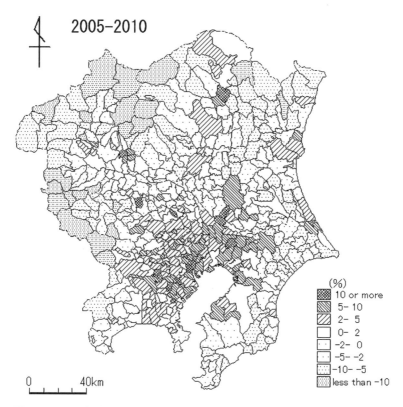

Figure 2 Population Change Ratios from 2005 to 2010 by Municipality (2000 Boundary) in the Kanto Region
Source: Population Censuses 2000, 2005 and 2010

2.2 Population distribution change within the Tokyo metropolitan area

Figure 1 and Figure 2 show the comparison between the population change ratios in 1990–1995 and the population change ratios in 2005–2010 for each municipality in the Kanto Region. Thus, although the decline of a population growth rate in the Kanto Region is remarkable, the central areas of Tokyo have begun to increase after a historic decrease in population since 1965. On the other hand, in cities, towns and villages outside a 1-hour commute to Tokyo station, a decrease in population can be seen, in contrast to the increases in past decades.

Figure 3 shows such change as a two-dimensional scatter chart. We classified municipalities in the Kanto Region, beside municipalities in remote islands, into 5 types of development: developing zone, recovering zone, shrinking zone, under-developed zone and neutral zone, by using population change ratios of 1990-1995 and 2005-2010. Table 1 shows the criteria for each category. Figure 4 shows the distribution of each zone. According to these figures, each zone is distributed over the following areas.

1. Developing Zone: This zone is not continuous. We can find small aggregations in the 40-km radius from the Tokyo station: the Tama foothill area in Tokyo and Kanagawa Prefecture,

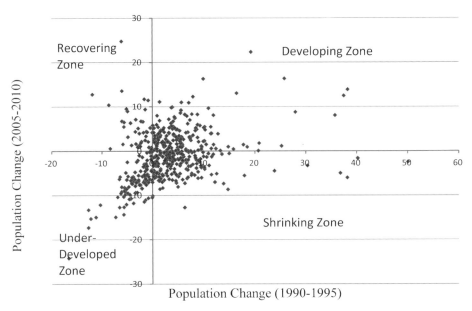

Figure 3 Relationship Between the Population Change (1990-1995) and the Population Change (2005-2010)
Source: Population Censuses 1990, 1995, 2005 and 2010

Table 1 Criteria of Classification

Zone Category	Population Growth Rate (1990-1995) (A) %	Population Growth Rate (2005-2010) (B) %	ABS(A)+ABS(B) %
Developing Zone (D)	+	+	>=10
Recovering Zone (R)	–	+	>=10
Shrinking Zone (S)	+	–	>=10
Under-developed Zone (U)	–	–	>=10
Neutral Zone (X)	+or–	+or–	<10

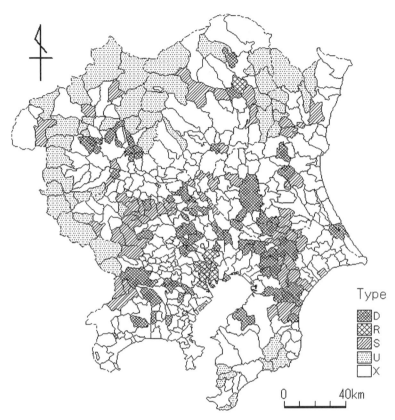

Figure 4 Types of Development in the Kanto Region
D: Developing Zone   R: Recovering Zone   S: Shrinking Zone
U: Under-Developed Zone   X: Neutral Zone
Source: Population Censuses from 1990 to 2010

and northern part of Saitama Prefecture. Developing zones in Ibaraki Prefecture and Chiba Prefecture are served by several new railroad lines leading to Tokyo, but they do not contribute to form a doughnut-shaped developing zone.

2. Recovering Zone: This zone is distributed in the 23 Special Wards of Tokyo and Yokohama City and in Kizuregawa Town of Tochigi Prefecture.

3. Shrinking Zone: This zone is distributed over the areas which did not receive the benefit of new railroad line: that is, in Saitama, Ibaraki and Chiba prefectures outside of the 40-km circle.

4. Under-developed Zone: This zone is distributed over the mountainous areas in Saitama,

Gumma, Tochigi and Ibaraki Prefectures, and remote coastal areas of Chiba Prefecture.

2.3 Cohort share analysis of the Tokyo metropolitan area

The net migration of each generation can be estimated by using the cohort share analysis method used by Oe (1995). Assuming that the influence of regional differences in the sex- and age- specific death rate are negligible, the change in the cohort share occupied by one area out of all of Japan is determined only by net migration from this area to other areas in Japan and abroad. Figure 5 and Figure 6 show changes in the share of several birth cohorts in central (the 23 special wards) and suburban (Saitama, Chiba, and Kanagawa) areas in the Tokyo metropolitan area after 1970. Table 2 shows the rates of change in cohort share in central and suburban areas at five-year intervals. By using these figures and this table, we estimated net migration patterns in central and suburban areas in the Tokyo metropolitan area since 1970 as follows.

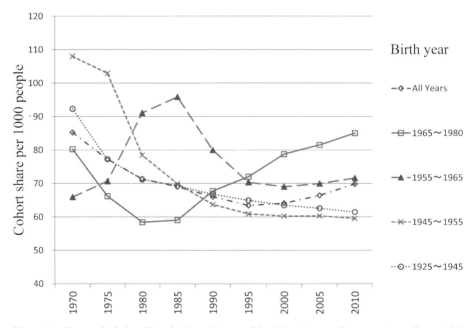

Figure 5 Changes in Cohort Share in Central Areas of the Tokyo Metropolitan Area According to Birth Year
Source: Population Censuses from 1970 to 2010

Geographical Shrinking of the Tokyo Metropolitan Area: Its Demographic and Residential Background

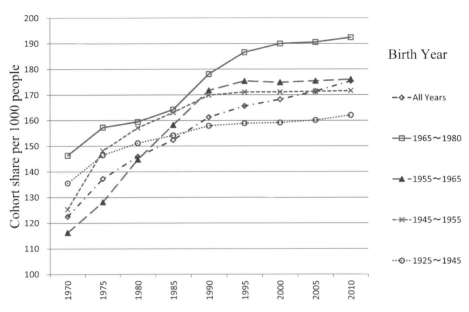

Figure 6 Changes in Cohort Share in Suburban Areas of the Tokyo Metropolitan Area According to Birth Year
Source: Population Censuses from 1970 to 2010

Table 2 Changes in Cohort Share According to Birth Year

Periods	All Year Central	All Year Suburbs	1965~1980 Central	1965~1980 Suburbs	1955~1965 Central	1955~1965 Suburbs	1945~1955 Central	1945~1955 Suburbs	1925~1945 Central	1925~1945 Suburbs
1970~1975	−9.4%	12.1%	−17.5%	7.5%	7.1%	7.5%	−4.7%	18.2%	−16.3%	8.1%
1975~1980	−7.6%	6.3%	−11.7%	1.4%	28.9%	1.4%	−23.8%	6.1%	−7.8%	3.2%
1980~1985	−3.3%	4.4%	1.1%	3.0%	5.2%	3.0%	−10.9%	3.8%	−2.7%	2.0%
1985~1990	−4.3%	5.9%	14.7%	8.4%	−16.6%	8.4%	−8.8%	4.1%	−3.6%	2.4%
1990~1995	−3.9%	2.7%	6.3%	4.8%	−12.0%	4.8%	−4.4%	0.7%	−2.7%	0.7%
1995~2000	1.0%	1.6%	9.4%	1.8%	−1.8%	1.8%	−1.1%	0.0%	−2.3%	0.2%
2000~2005	3.7%	1.9%	3.5%	0.3%	1.4%	0.3%	0.1%	0.1%	−1.4%	0.6%
2005~2010	5.1%	2.3%	4.4%	1.0%	2.3%	1.0%	−1.3%	0.1%	−1.8%	1.2%

Increase Rate   <−5%   −5%~5%   5%<

*The cohort share increase rate from year t to year t+5=
((cohort share in t+5) - (cohort share in t))/(cohort share in t)

Source: Population Censuses from 1970 to 2010

1. 1970s: The shares of all cohorts in suburban areas increased. We estimated that there was a large-scale positive net migration to suburban areas of the Tokyo metropolitan area in the 1970s. In central areas, only one cohort from 1955 to 1965 substantially increased in share; this generation was considered to exhibit a large-scale positive net migration to central areas. All other cohort shares decreased greatly in central areas. In other words, there was a large-scale migration from central areas to suburban areas within the Tokyo metropolitan area in this period. This large-scale migration can be ascribed to the suburbanization of a generation of baby boomers and was accompanied by a decrease in the share of children's cohorts from 1965 to 1980 in central areas. This movement of children may be thus termed "accompanied migration." Furthermore, the increase in cohort share from 1955 to 1965 in central areas might have resulted from large-scale positive net migration from outside of the Tokyo metropolitan area.

2. 1980s: In the 1980s, the tendency in the 1970s toward the increase of cohort shares in suburban areas continued. In central areas, the tendency toward the decrease in cohort shares for cohorts composed of people born before 1955 became slower. Although the share of the 1955–1965 cohort increased during the first half of the 1980s in central areas, it decreased in the latter half of the 1980s. In other words, it can be said that this generation underwent suburbanization. However, this generation began to be suburbanized later than were older generations. One of the reasons for this delay is the progression of the tendency toward late marriage and the increase of unmarried young people; this is described in the following chapter. During the so-called "bubble economy" period that occurred in the latter half of the 1980s in Japan, the share of the 1965–1980 cohort increased greatly in both central and suburban areas. It may be said that a substantial portion of the generation composed of the children of baby boomers has migrated to central areas. This may have resulted from the unipolar population concentration in Tokyo.

3. 1990s: With the collapse of the bubble economy, the positive net migration to suburban areas of the Tokyo metropolitan area decreased quickly in the 1990s. Although cohorts composed of people born before 1965 have continued to exhibit a negative net migration from central areas, cohorts composed of people born from 1965 to 1980 have continued to exhibit increases in central areas; this younger generation has not yet been suburbanized.

4. 2000s: Since 2000, remarkably, no generation has exhibited significant positive net migration in suburban areas. Cohorts composed of people born in 1955 and afterwards have exhibited a positive net migration to central area. The most remarkable changes in migration pattern can be observed in regard to cohorts composed of people born in 1965 and later. Cohorts composed of younger people who were born after 1965 in central areas exhibited suburbanization until 1980, as they accompanied their parents in migrating to the suburbs. On the other hand, people in the same generation who were born outside of the Tokyo metropolitan area began to migrate to central areas after 1985. Unlike previous generations,

these people did not become suburbanized; rather, they have stayed in central areas since 2000. In addition, a part of same generation who once went to suburban areas to live with their parents returned to central areas in this period. As a result, the total number of people in central areas of this generation increased after 2000. Changing housing preferences are thought to be the backdrop for this phenomenon – people once preferred single detached houses but now prefer high-rise condominiums. Furthermore, the increase in the rate of unmarried people in younger generations and the tendency toward late marriage might serve as demographic backdrops to changes in migration pattern. We will discuss these factors in the following chapter.

2.4 Demographic and physical background of the shrinking phenomenon

2.4.1 Increase of unmarried people

Figure 7a and Figure 7b show changes in the percentage of unmarried people according to age and region during the past 30 years. Figure 7a shows that the percentage of unmarried people between 40 and 44 years old has increased rapidly in recent years and now exceeds 30% in the central areas of Tokyo. The percentage of unmarried people in the central areas of Tokyo is notably higher than in the Kanto Region and the whole country. Interestingly, from 2005 to 2010, the percentage of unmarried people aged 30 to 34 years decreased in central areas whereas it increased slightly in the Kanto Region and the whole country (Figure 7b). These statistics may partly reflect actual changes in the central areas. However, the rate of unknown marital status increased rapidly from 2005 to 2010, and its influence should also be considered.

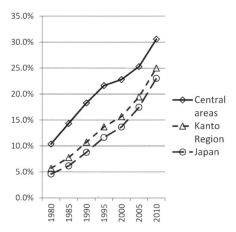

Figure 7a Percentage of Unmarried People Aged 40–44 years
Source: Population Censuses from 1980 to 2010

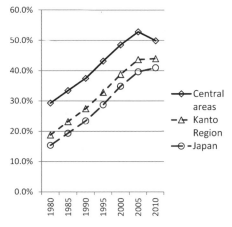

Figure 7b Percentage of Unmarried People Aged 30–34 years
Source: Population Censuses from 1980 to 2010

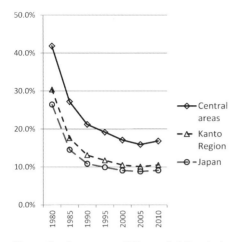
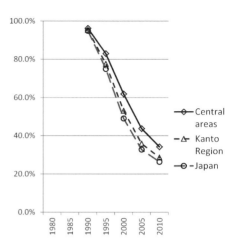

Figure 8a Percentage of Unmarried People in the 1945–1955 Birth Cohort
Source: Population Censuses from 1980 to 2010

Figure 8b Percentage of Unmarried People in the 1965–1975 Birth Cohort
Source: Population Censuses from 1980 to 2010

Figure 8a and Figure 8b show changes in the percentage of unmarried people by birth cohort from 1945 to 1955 and from 1965 to 1975, respectively. Although the percentage of unmarried people in the central areas is higher than in the Kanto Region and the whole country, for younger cohorts, the regional gap is becoming less distinct.

The increase in the above mentioned percentage of unmarried people has slowed the movement of people into suburban single-family homes with yards — the setting that is often held up as ideal for raising children. Unmarried people are more likely to stay in the central areas, where other unmarried people live. Consequently, differences in marriage patterns by cohort directly affect patterns of migration.

2.4.2 Residential development in central areas

The increase in condominiums can be identified as one of the forces behind the increase in the residential population in central areas in Tokyo. Figure 9 shows the construction years for the total number of dwellings in various areas in the Kanto region based on the results of the Housing and Land Survey in 2013. Figure 10 shows the construction years for concrete dwelling units, most of which are condominiums, based on the same statistics. Geographically, the number of dwelling units in the suburbs of Tokyo is larger than the number of dwelling units in Tokyo in every construction period. However, concrete dwelling units do not exhibit this trend. Regarding concrete dwelling units built before 1980, there are more dwelling units in Tokyo than in the Tokyo suburbs. From 1981 to 2000, which is inclusive of the so-called "bubble period," the number of concrete dwelling units constructed in the Tokyo suburbs increased compared with in Tokyo. After 2001, again, slightly more concrete dwelling units in

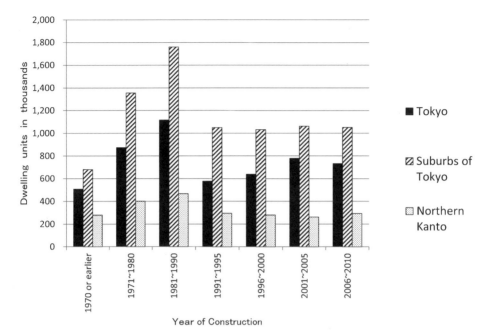

Figure 9 Dwelling Units by Year of Construction (Total Units)
Suburbs of Tokyo: Saitama, Chiba, Kanagawa
Northern Kanto: Ibaraki, Tochigi, Gunma
Source: Housing and Land Survey 2013

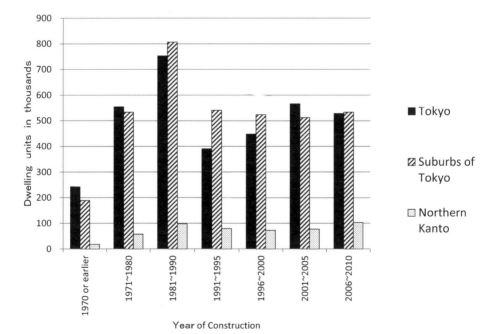

Figure 10 Dwelling Units by Year of Construction (Concrete Units)
Data: Housing and Land Survey 2013

Tokyo may be observed. The percentage of dwelling units made from concrete out of the total number of dwelling units built in Tokyo was 63.1% until 1995 and increased to 71.7% after 1996. Thus, out of the entire number of dwelling units, the percentage of dwelling units made from concrete (i.e., the ratio of condominiums) is high. Thus, the construction of condominiums is increasing in Tokyo. This is also a cause of changes in the population distribution and it may also be a result of such changes.

2.4.3 Increase of vacant houses in exurban areas

Figure 11 shows changes in the number and percentage of vacant dwelling units for zones comprising successive 10-km-radius concentric circles from Tokyo Station based on the Housing and Land Survey of 2008. In 1998, the 0-to-10-km zone showed the highest vacancy rate. In 2008, however, the highest vacancy rate appeared in the 50-km-and-beyond zone. As shown in Figure 4, this zone is also the area in which "Shrinking Zone" of the Tokyo metropolitan area is distributed. In other words, with the decrease of the population, the residential vacancy rate in this zone has also increased.

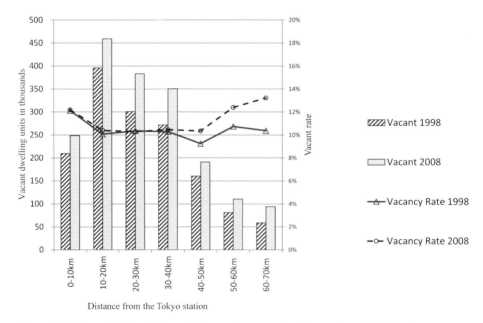

Figure 11 Vacant Dwelling Units and Vacancy Percentage by Distance from Tokyo Station
Source: Housing and Land Survey 2008

2.5 Concluding remarks

1. In the Tokyo metropolitan area, in areas outside of a 40-km concentric circle from Tokyo Station, where no new railway lines have been developed, the population began to decline in the 1990s after increasing for several decades, whereas the opposite is true for central areas of the Tokyo metropolitan area.

2. Based on cohort share analysis, the population movement of the Tokyo metropolitan area can be estimated as follows. In the 1980s and prior, a positive net migration of all birth cohorts into suburban areas was observed. In central areas, the birth cohort between 1955 and 1965 increased in share until 1985. When people who comprised this cohort were aged older than 20 years old, they underwent suburbanization in the latter half of the 1980s. Since the 2000s, no generation has exhibited a significant positive net migration to suburban areas. Cohorts composed of younger people who were born after 1965 did not suburbanize, in contrast to previous generations; rather, they have stayed in central areas since 2000.

3. The background of this population movement pattern can be explained by several demographic factors as well as by the effects of changes in housing preference. A rapid increase in the percentage of unmarried people in their 30s and 40s may be one of the key demographic factors behind this population movement. The increase in condominiums in central areas and the increase in the vacancy rate in the concentric zone 50-km-and-beyond from Tokyo Station are the results of changes such as in the distribution of population; this has also caused the formation of zones in which shrinkage is occurring.

References

Aiba, S., Sawada, M., Kawahara, S., Kuwata, H., and Maki, N. 2008. Urban design method in age of shrinking city: Measures by government and feature of the field. *Summaries of technical papers of Annual Meeting Architectural Institute of Japan, F-1, Urban planning, building economics and housing problems* 2008: 405-406. (J)

Fujii, T. and Oe, M. 2008. A study on generational changes in the suburbs of the Tokyo metropolitan area: A comparative analysis from 1980 to 2020 among cohorts by GBI. *Journal of architecture and planning* 605: 101-108. (J)

Miyazawa, H. 2006. The changing face of suburban new towns in large metropolitan areas: The case of Tama New Town, Tokyo. *Annals of the Japan Association of Economic Geographers* 52: 236-250. (J)

Miyazawa, H. and Abe, T. 2005. Recovery and changes in the socioeconomic composition of population in the central area of Tokyo during the period from 1995 to 2000: Analysis of small-area census data. *Geographical Review of Japan* 78: 893-912. (J)

Oe, M. 1995. Cohort analysis of population distribution change in Japan: Processes of population concentration to the Tokyo Region and its future. Journal of population problems 216: 1-19.(J)

(J) means "written in Japanese" (with an English summary, in some cases).

3. Urban Shrinkage of the Keihanshin Metropolitan Area in Japan: Changes in Population Distribution and Commuting Flows

Tatsuya YAMAGAMI

Abstract

The purpose of this article is to report the results of a preliminary analysis of the urban shrinkage of the Keihanshin metropolitan area in Japan. The article focuses on changes in population distribution and commuting flows from 1990 to 2010. An analysis of population redistribution confirms a shift from decentralisation to re-concentration around 2000. This trend was derived from both population recovery around the city centres of Kyoto, Osaka, and Kobe and a strong decrease in population in distant peri-urban municipalities. In addition, a mosaic pattern of population redistribution is also suggested. Next, from the analysis of commuting flows into the central cities, the number of municipalities where the ratio of commuters to central cities exceeded 10% decreased, especially those with the ratio over 30%. Furthermore, it was confirmed that the hypothetical urban fringe where the ratio of commuters falls below 5% has shifted closer to the central cities. These results show narrowing of the spatial extent of the Keihanshin metropolitan area in terms of densely populated areas and central cities' commuting zones. It is possible that these trends will induce distinctive urban shrinkage in the future.

Keywords

urban shrinkage, population distribution, commuting flows, Keihanshin metropolitan area

3.1 Introduction

Japan experienced rapid urbanisation throughout the 20th century. The main feature of urbanisation processes until the 1960s was population concentration in the central parts of the three largest metropolitan areas, namely Tokyo, Kyoto-Osaka-Kobe (Keihanshin), and Nagoya. Following Japanese migration system changes in the 1970s, a substantial decrease in net population inflow into the metropolitan regions was observed (Tsuya and Kuroda 1989). After the 1980s, unipolar population concentration in the Tokyo Metropolitan area became prominent, fluctuating according to economic conditions (Ishikawa and Fielding 1998). However, the correlation between metropolitan size and population growth remained positive until 2000 (Yamagami 2003a).

With regard to the spatial structure of metropolitan areas after the 1960s, population dispersion from central cities to suburbs had advanced exponentially. This population decentralisation process was brought about by notable population growth in the suburbs and spatial expansion of urbanised areas (Yamada and Tokuoka 1991). The centrifugal movement of the population growth peak had been under way in large metropolitan areas (Yamagami 2003b). At the same time, the areas of depopulation around the city centre were expanding, this known as the doughnut phenomenon.

In the late 1990s, after the collapse of the bubble economy in Japan, drastic changes in population redistribution trends within metropolitan areas were evident. Population recovery around the central parts of large cities became prominent. On the other hand, population growth peaks arising from population dispersion disappeared, and in the outer suburbs the population stagnated. These trends denote a shift in population redistribution from decentralisation to re-concentration (Yamagami 2003b).

By the mid-2000s, Japan had entered an era of depopulation consequent to declining birth rates and population ageing. In the early 2000s, population growth was evident in major metropolitan areas as before, while a decreasing population became more noticeable in many local areas (Matsubara 2007). The rural depopulation trend deepened and broadened (Matanle and Sato 2010), and the wave of population ageing and consequent depopulation gradually undermined major metropolitan areas.

For example, suburban municipalities, especially distant peri-urban areas, now face strong population losses in the Osaka metropolitan area (Buhnik 2010). In the distant suburban areas of the Tokyo metropolitan area, it is predicted that population declines owing to rapid ageing are unavoidable. Consequently, social problems such as the loss of social infrastructure and an increase in the number of empty houses and vacant spaces will emerge (Naganuma et al. 2006). These population shrinkages in suburbs generate a sharp decline in the working-age population and in the number of railway commuters to the central cities (Sakanishi 2006). Similarly, the number of suburb-to-central city commuters has decreased in the three largest metropolitan areas because of weakening population dispersion from the metropolitan centre (Tani 2007). It seems that a shift in population redistribution from decentralisation to re-concentration leads to a decreasing number of suburb-to-central city commuters.

Japan has entered an era of depopulation. The major metropolitan areas in Japan, most of which manage to sustain population growth, are experiencing a partially shrinking population. Considering the declining birth rate and ageing population, it is inevitable that major metropolitan areas in Japan also face longstanding depopulation. Thus, urban shrinkage in Japan deserves careful attention, especially 'slow-burn' shrinking cities where population decline has been a steady process over time (Großmann et al. 2013).

The purpose of this article is to report the results of a preliminary analysis of urban shrinkage in Japan. The article focuses on changes in population distribution and commuting flows. The narrowing of the spatial extent of both densely populated areas and commuting zones of central cities are discussed because these trends will induce distinctive urban shrinkage in the future. The study period ranges from 1990 to 2010. Around 1990 in Japan, a sharp increase in land prices in the bubble economy led to marked population dispersion in metropolitan areas.

The study area is the Keihanshin metropolitan area, the second largest agglomerated region in Japan. Data is based on the population census of Japan, which is conducted every five years.

3.2 Study area

3.2.1 Overview of the Keihanshin metropolitan area

The Keihanshin metropolitan area lies in the Kansai (Kinki) region, which is located in the central part of western Japan and includes Shiga, Kyoto, Osaka, Hyogo, Nara, and Wakayama prefectures (Figure 1). The northern and southern parts of the Kansai region are mountainous areas. Flatlands comprising basins and plains are distributed along the rivers and seacoast. In the Kansai region, most built-up areas stretch from Kyoto basin to the Osaka-Kobe bay area. This area comprises the main part of the Keihanshin metropolitan area.

The name Keihanshin derives from the Kanji readings of the three core cities: Kyoto, Osaka, and Kobe. Of these core cities, Osaka is the second largest economic centre in Japan and the main city of the Kansai region. Both JR (West Japan Railway Company) and private train lines provide extensive services in the Keihanshin metropolitan area. It takes about 30 minutes from Osaka station to Kyoto or Kobe station via the JR lines. These three cities maintain competitive and mutually dependent relations with each other and organise a unified metropolitan region. The Keihanshin metropolitan area is ranked the third largest economic region based on an analysis of night-time satellite images, and also the ninth largest region by population in the world (Florida et al. 2012). The Keihanshin metropolitan area is one of the largest urban agglomerations worldwide.

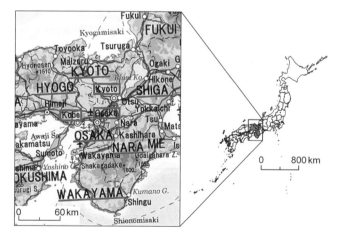

Figure 1 Overview of the Kansai region
Note: Underlined place names are the prefectures included in the Kansai region. Place-names surrounded by a rectangle denote the core cities of the Keihanshin metropolitan area.
Source: Geospatial Information Authority of Japan website.

3.2.2 Delineation of the Keihanshin metropolitan area

The units of analysis in this study are municipalities (cities, towns, and villages). The merger of municipalities across Japan was strongly promoted in the 2000s. To compare the results of different periods more precisely, the borders between municipalities are fixed as those of 2010.

Early versions of the definition of metropolitan areas, such as the Standard Metropolitan Statistical Area (SMSA) of the US, consider a metropolitan area to comprise a central city and suburbs. Based on this concept, delineation of the Keihanshin metropolitan area proceeds in two steps.

The first step is to define the central cities. As mentioned, the Keihanshin metropolitan area comprises three core cities, and therefore its spatial structure is polycentric. The ratios of the daytime to night-time population of these cities are greater than 1, showing a certain level of independence. However, the three cities maintain close relations and form an integrated urban agglomeration. Therefore, these three cities are classified as central cities.

Next is to determine how to identify outlying municipalities as suburbs. When identifying suburbs, the index value is the ratio of workers commuting to central cities to the total residential working population in each municipality. The value adopted in Japan varies according to the researcher, for example 10% (Yamada and Tokuoka 1991), 7.5% (Osada 2003), and 5% (Kawashima et al. 1993). In this study, to investigate commuting flows over the wide area around the three central cities, a municipality qualifies as a suburb if the total ratio of workers living in the municipality commuting to one of the three central cities is greater than 5% once during the study period.

Figure 2 shows the distribution of the municipalities where the maximum values of the commuting ratio to central cities were greater than 5% during the study period, and thus the spatial extent of the Keihanshin metropolitan area. As a result, 111 municipalities are regarded as suburbs. As indicated on the map, the distance decay effect of the maximum values of the commuting ratio to the central cites is evident, and the values between Kobe and Kyoto and in a southward direction from Osaka are high. Figure 2 also shows the year when each municipality recorded the maximum value of the commuting ratio. Many municipalities recorded maximum values in the 1990s, whereas a scattered distribution of municipalities where maximum values were recorded after 2000 is evident. Figure 3 shows population distribution in the Keihanshin metropolitan areas in 1990. As this map shows, the population is concentrated around Osaka city and along the line between the south part of Kyoto and Kobe.

Before the analysis, it may be helpful to examine population change in the Kansai region (Table 1). The Kansai region's population was around 21 million in 2010, constituting approximately 16% of Japan's population. The Keihanshin metropolitan area's population is around 17.5 million, accounting for more than 80% of the Kansai region. As shown in Table 1, the population in the Kansai region is growing slightly as a result of the growth of the Kei-

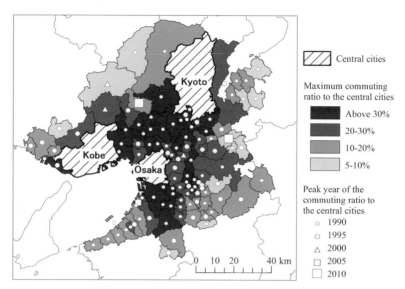

Figure 2 Spatial extent of the Keihanshin metropolitan area
Note: Central cities are Kyoto, Osaka, and Kobe city. Suburban municipalities are the municipalities where the maximum values of the commuting ratio to the central cities were greater than 5% during the study period.
Source: Population census of Japan

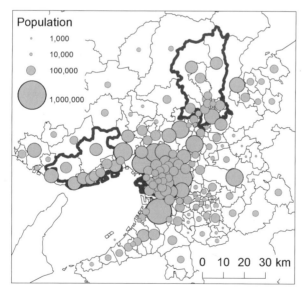

Figure 3 Population distribution within the Keihanshin metropolitan area in 1990
Note: Thick lines indicate the boundaries of the central cities.
Source: Population census of Japan

Table 1 Population changes in the Kansai region

		1990	1995	2000	2005	2010
population (in thousands)	Kansai region	20,414	20,627	20,856	20,893	20,903
	Keihanshin MA	16,998	17,195	17,445	17,556	17,657
	rural areas	3,486	3,512	3,494	3,419	3,327
growth rate (% per 5 years)	Kansai region		1.04%	1.11%	0.18%	0.05%
	Keihanshin MA		1.16%	1.45%	0.64%	0.57%
	rural areas		0.77%	−0.51%	−2.15%	−2.70%
population ratio to Kansai region	Keihanshin MA	83.26%	83.36%	83.64%	84.03%	84.47%
	rural areas	17.07%	17.03%	16.75%	16.36%	15.91%

Note: The Kansai (Kinki) region comprises Shiga, Kyoto, Osaka, Hyogo, Nara, and Wakayama prefectures. Although Nabari city in Mie prefecture is included in the Keihanshin metropolitan area (Keihanshin MA), the population in that city is excluded.

Source: Population census of Japan

hanshin metropolitan area. On the other hand, the remote areas of the central cities, signified as 'rural areas' in the table, began decreasing in the late 1990s, after which this depopulation intensified. On this account, it is almost impossible to consider counterurbanisation or exurbanisation as major trends in the Kansai region.

3.3 Spatial narrowing of densely populated areas

In this section, patterns of population redistribution after 1990 are examined. The question is whether densely populated areas are narrowing spatially in the Keihanshin metropolitan area. The first step is to examine the patterns of population redistribution based on maps and basic statistics. Then, the relation between the distances from central cities and population densities are analysed with the urban density function.

As illustrated in Figure 3, the population in 1990 is concentrated around Osaka city and along the line between the south part of Kyoto and Kobe. The population redistribution pattern after 1990 can be described as follows (Figure 4). In the first half of the 1990s, population dispersion was the dominant trend. A decrease in the population in the Hanshin area was a severe consequence of the Great Hanshin-Awaji Earthquake. In the late 1990s, the population dispersion trend became partial, and the population around city centres showed signs of moderate recovery. After the year 2000, population dispersion became more partial, highlighting population recovery around city centres. In addition, steep population losses in distant peri-urban areas were evident after mid-1990. Although Buhnik (2010) discussed peri-urban shrinking in the first half of the 2000s, it is confirmed that this trend intensified afterwards.

To examine these population redistribution patterns in light of the hypothesis of the urban

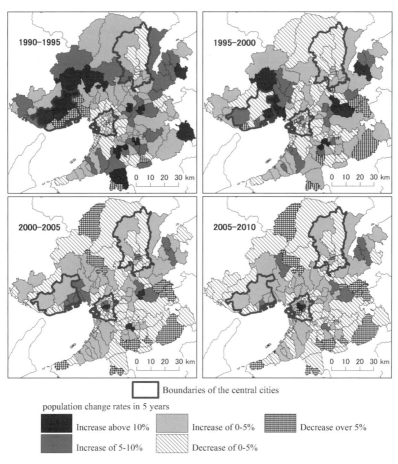

Figure 4 Patterns of population redistribution within the Keihanshin metropolitan area from 1990 to 2010
Source: Population census of Japan

development stage model (Klaassen et al. 1981, van den Berg et al. 1982), the population growth rate of central cities and suburbs are described in Table 2. Table 2 shows great population dispersion to the suburbs until the mid-1990s. After the late 1990s, the population recovery of central cities was prominent, and population growth rates of central cities exceeded that of suburbs. When we see these trends in the urban development stage model, the patterns of population redistribution shift from the absolute decentralisation of suburbanisation stage to the relative decentralisation of suburbanisation stage and more to the relative centralisation of urbanisation. These shifts indicate a contrasting phenomenon to the hypothesis, similar to the trends observed in many European urban agglomerations (Kabisch and Hasse 2011).

Next, the relation between distances from central cities and population densities are examined with the urban population density function. Density function relates population density to distance from the city centre. It is well known that population density is shifting exponen-

Table 2 Population growth rates and urban development stage in the Keihanshin metropolitan area

	Keihanshin metropolitan area	central cities	suburbs	urban development stage	type of population redistribution
1990-95	1.16%	−1.30%	2.36%	Suburbanisation	absolute decentralisation
1995-00	1.45%	1.26%	1.54%	Suburbanisation	relative decentralisation
2000-05	0.64%	1.12%	0.41%	Urbanisation	relative centralisation
2005-10	0.57%	0.97%	0.39%	Urbanisation	relative centralisation

Note: The urban development stage follows van den Berg et al. (1982).
Source: Population census of Japan

tially from the city centre to the outer suburbs in urbanised areas (Clark 1951). This relationship can be represented as:

$$D(d) = D_0 e^{-ad}$$

or in logarithmic form,

$$\ln D(d) = \ln D_0 - ad \quad (1)$$

where $D(d)$ is the population density d kilometres away from the city centre, e is the base of natural logarithm, and D_0 and a are parameters to be estimated. D_0 is the hypothetical density at the city centre and a is the density gradient, denoting the rate at which density declines as one moves out from the centre.

Although this function assumes a monocentric structure of urbanised areas, the Keihanshin metropolitan area has three core cities. Thus, its spatial structure is polycentric. For this reason, the weighted mean distances to the three central cities are used here. Because the number of workers employed in Osaka city is three times more than Kyoto and Kobe, the weighted mean distances are calculated as follows.

$$x_i = (d_{i1} + 3d_{i2} + d_{i3})/5 \quad (2)$$

where d_{i1}, d_{i2} and d_{i3} are the distances in kilometres from i municipality to Kyoto, Osaka, and Kobe respectively. By using these weighted mean distances, the model applied here is the same equation as (1), such that

$$\ln D_x = \ln D_0 - ax$$

Parameters are estimated by the method of least square technique.

In addition, the hypothetical urban fringe is calculated based on the obtained parameters. This urban fringe denotes a weighted mean distance from central cities to the point where population density falls below 200 people per square kilometre. Although 200 people per square kilometre is low for the density of urbanised areas regarded as densely-populated areas, the Kansai region is mountainous terrain, and thus peri-urban municipalities are widely occupied by mountains. The value of 200 people per square kilometre is adopted as an approximate figure of the urban fringe to fit the actual situation in the Keihanshin metropolitan area. Wards in the central cities are included in the analysis.

Table 3 shows the results of the regression analysis. Table 3 shows the constants indicating rising hypothetical central densities after 1995, reflecting population recovery around the city centres. On the contrary, the absolute value of x parameters decreased until 2000, although these increased again after this period. This means that density gradients became flatter until 2000, but then became steeper after that. Similarly, the hypothetical urban fringe gradually moved away from the city centres until 2000, and then shifted closer to the central cities. These results confirm that the pattern of population redistribution shifted from decentralisation to re-concentration around 2000, and then the spatial extent of the densely populated areas narrowed.

Furthermore, the values of R-square decreased during the study period. This trend implies the mosaic pattern of population redistribution in the Keihanshin metropolitan area, where higher density regions recorded population growth and lower density regions experienced population decline irrespective of the distances from central cities. It is likely that regional differences in population growth are expanding, and the degree of inequality of population density becomes greater in the Keihanshin metropolitan area.

3.4 Narrowing of the commuting zone of central cities

In this section, the decreasing ratio of commuters to central cities in suburban municipalities is presented based on the maps. Then, the relation between the distances from central

Table 3 Results of the applications of urban population density functions

	density function	R^2	urban fringe
1990	$\ln D_x = 10.2514 - 0.0738x$	0.443	67.11
1995	$\ln D_x = 10.2168 - 0.0722x$	0.442	68.12
2000	$\ln D_x = 10.2284 - 0.0721x$	0.440	68.38
2005	$\ln D_x = 10.2574 - 0.0729x$	0.440	68.03
2010	$\ln D_x = 10.2902 - 0.0739x$	0.439	67.55

(n=155)

Note: x is the weighted mean distance to the central cities, D_x is the population density at x, and urban fringe is the weighted mean distances in kilometres from central cities to the point where the population density falls below 200 people per square kilometre. Wards in the central cities are included in the analysis.
Source: Population census of Japan

cities and the ratio of commuters to central cities are analysed through simple linear regression analysis.

Figure 5 shows the distribution of the ratio of commuters to the central cities in 1990 and 2010, and changes over these 20 years. As mentioned before, the higher commuting areas were spread around central cities and the distance decay effect of the commuting ratio to central cites is evident. After the 1990s, the number of municipalities showing more than a 30% commuting rate decreased, while those showing less than a 10% commuting rate increased in the outer suburbs. Looking at the distribution of changes in the commuting ratio during this period, few municipalities recorded an increase, while most municipalities indicated decreasing commuting ratios to the central cities.

Figure 6 summarises the characteristics of these maps. As shown, there was little change in the number of municipalities where the ratio of commuters to central cities exceeded 5%. On the contrary, municipalities with the ratio over 10% decreased, especially those with the ratio over 30%. If the value 10% or more is adopted as a criterion for identifying suburbs, then the number of suburban municipalities decreased. Consequently, the spatial extent of the Keihanshin metropolitan area narrowed.

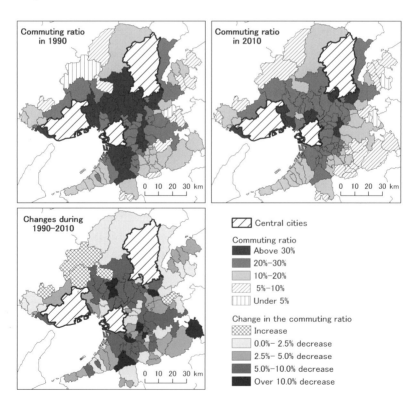

Figure 5 Distribution of the commuting ratio to central cities within the Keihanshin metropolitan area from 1990 to 2010
Source: Population census of Japan

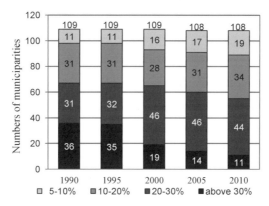

Figure 6 Changes in the numbers of municipalities classified according to the commuting ratio to central cities
Source: Population census of Japan

As clearly illustrated in the maps, distance decay effects in the commuting flows into central cities were evident. To clarify, simple linear regression analysis is used to examine the relation between the distances and ratio of commuters to central cities. The dependent variable TCR_x is the total commuting ratio to central cities at distance x. Independent variable x is the weighted mean distance to central cities calculated from the equation (2) in the previous section. Moreover, from the parameters obtained in the analysis, the weighted mean distance from central cities to the point where the ratio of commuters falls below 5% can be calculated. This value can be regarded as the hypothetical urban fringe because the value 5% is the criterion for identifying suburbs. Wards in the central cities are excluded from the analysis.

Results of the regression analysis are summarised in Table 4 and depicted as graphs in Figure 7. It was found that absolute values of the parameter x and the constants decreased, meaning that the distance decay effect was weakening and the ratio of commuters to central cities at $x = 0$ was decreasing respectively. In addition, paying attention to the urban fringe confirmed that the hypothetical urban fringe moved away from the city centres until 1995, and then sifted closer to central cities. These results mean that the influence of the overall decrease of commuters to central cities was greater than the impact of the attenuation of the distance decay effect on commuting flows to central cities. The 5% commuting zone is used here and frequently as the definition to delineate the suburbs of the metropolitan area. Therefore, these results show the narrowing of the spatial extent of the Keihanshin metropolitan area.

In summary, there is little change in the number of municipalities where the ratio of commuters to central cities exceeded 5%. On the contrary, municipalities with the ratio over 10% decreased, especially those with the ratio over 30%. The regression analysis of the relation

Table 4 Results of regression analysis on the commuting flows to central cities

year	regression expression	R^2	urban fringe
1990	$TCR_x = 0.4820 - 0.0065x$	0.471	66.46
1995	$TCR_x = 0.4696 - 0.0062x$	0.480	67.68
2000	$TCR_x = 0.4396 - 0.0059x$	0.482	66.03
2005	$TCR_x = 0.4200 - 0.0057x$	0.494	64.91
2010	$TCR_x = 0.4201 - 0.0055x$	0.489	63.65

($n=111$)

Note: x is the weighted mean distance to the central cities, TCR_x is the total commuting ratio to central cities, and urban fringe is the weighted mean distances in kilometres from central cities to the point where the total commuting ratio of commuters to central cities falls below 5%. Wards in the central cities are excluded in the analysis.
Source: Population census of Japan

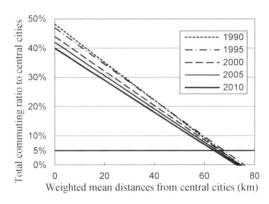

Figure 7 Distance decay of the commuting flows to central cities
Source: Population census of Japan

between the distances and ratio of commuters to central cities confirmed that the hypothetical urban fringe has shifted closer to central cities. These results show the narrowing of the spatial extent of the Keihanshin metropolitan area.

3.5 Discussions and conclusion

This chapter has reported the results of a preliminary analysis of the urban shrinkage of the Keihanshin metropolitan area. The focus was on changes in population distribution and commuting flows from 1990 to 2010.

The analysis of population redistribution confirms a shift from decentralisation to re-concentration around the year 2000. This trend was derived from both population recovery around the city centres of Kyoto, Osaka, and Kobe and the strong population losses in the distant peri-urban municipalities. In other words, the densely populated areas in the Keihanshin metropolitan area gradually narrowed. Considering intensified depopulation in remote areas from central cities in the Kansai region, the wave of population ageing and consequent depopulation that began in the rural areas is gradually undermining the distant peri-urban municipalities in the Keihanshin metropolitan area. It is possible that this depopulation wave will shift the suburbs closer to central cities, thus leading to population shrinkage in the Keihanshin metropolitan area.

In addition, the results of urban density functions suggest a mosaic pattern of population redistribution. In other words, higher density regions record population growth, while lower density regions experience population decline regardless of the distances from central cities. This trend possibly derives from and leads to deepening inequalities in various aspects of urban society in geographical terms. It may be safe to say that various social problems associated with urban shrinkage are about to become significant in the Keihanshin metropolitan area.

Next, the analysis of commuting flows into the central cities verified little change in the number of municipalities where the ratio of commuters to the central cities (Kyoto, Osaka, and Kobe) exceeded 5%. On the contrary, municipalities with the ratio over 10% decreased, especially those with the ratio over 30%. Furthermore, the regression analysis of the relation between the distances and ratio of commuters to the central cities confirmed that the hypothetical urban fringe where the ratio of commuters falls below 5% has shifted closer to the central cities. These results clearly show the narrowing of the sphere of influence of central cities in the matter of commuting flows in the Keihanshin metropolitan area.

Possible factors causing this spatial narrowing of the central cities' commuting zone are the growing independence of suburbs from central cities and the emergence of a multinucleated structure of the metropolitan area (Fujii 1990). It is true that decreasing numbers of commuters to the central cities was nearly equivalent to increasing numbers of commuters to other suburban municipalities. However, considering that the main aspect of population dispersion from central cities to the suburbs was migration to obtain only housing in suburbs while working in the central cities, it seems probable that the decrease in the ratio of commuting to the central cities resulted from both weakening population dispersion to the suburbs and population recovery in the central cities. The drastic change in the population redistribution pattern also causes spatial narrowing of the central cities' commuting zone. This trend will further progress population ageing and lead to population shrinkage in suburban municipalities. Based on these results, it can be said that major metropolitan areas in Japan are about to enter the slow-burn shrinking cities where population loss has been a steady process over time

(Großmann et al. 2013).

The first remaining issue to tackle is an analysis of the relationship between changes in population redistribution and commuting flows. Furthermore, detailed investigations need to be attempted in future research on the social conditions affecting the decision-making processes of individuals and families, current status, and the influence of urban inequalities, as well as the relevance of the abovementioned results to the discussions of urban shrinkage in Europe, North America, and other countries.

Acknowledgements

An early version of this article was first published in Japanese in the *Urban Geography of Japan* 8, 40-51, 2013.

References

Berg, L. van den, Drewett, R., Klaassen, L. H., Rossi, A., and Vijverberg, C. H. T. eds. 1982. *Urban Europe: a study of growth and decline*. Pergamon: Oxford.

Buhnik, S. 2010. From shrinking cities to *toshi no shukusho*: identifying patterns of urban shrinkage in the Osaka metropolitan area. *Berkeley Planning Journal* 23: 132-155.

Clark, C. 1951. Urban population densities. *Journal of Royal Statistical Society A* 114: 490-496.

Florida, R., Mellander, C., and Gulden, T. 2012. Global metropolis: assessing economic activity in urban centers based on nighttime satellite images. *The Professional Geographer* 64: 178-187.

Fujii, T. 1990. Review of recent studies in the structure of the metropolitan area. *Japanese Journal of Human Geography* 42: 522-544. (J)

Großmann, K., Bontje, M., Haase, A., and Mykhnenko, V. 2013. Shrinking cities: notes for the future research agenda. *Cities* 35: 221-225.

Ishikawa, Y. and Fielding, A. J. 1998. Explaining the recent migration trends of Tokyo metropolitan area. *Environment and Planning A* 30: 1797-1814.

Kabisch, N. and Hasse, D. 2011. Diversifying European agglomerations: evidence of urban population trends for the 21st century. *Population, Space and Place* 17: 236-253.

Kawashima, T., Hiraoka, N., Okabe, A., and Ohtera, N. 1993. Metropolitan analyses: boundary delineations and future population changes of Functional Urban Regions. *Gakushuin Economic Papers* 29: 205-248.

Klaassen, L. H., Bourdres, J. A., and Volmuller, J. 1981. *Transport and reurbanisation*. Aldershot: Gower.

Matanle, P. and Sato, Y. 2010. Coming soon to a city near you! Learning to live 'beyond growth' in Japan's shrinking regions. *Social Science Japan Journal* 13: 187-210.

Matsubara, H. 2007. Reorganization of Japanese urban systems and internal structures of urban areas in a globalized economy and a declining population society. *Annals of the Japan Association of Economic Geographers* 53: 443-460.

Naganuma, S., Arai, Y., and Esaki, Y. 2006. The ageing population in the suburbs of metropolitan Tokyo. *Japanese Journal of Human Geography* 58: 399-412. (J)

Osada, S. 2003. The Japanese urban system 1970-1990. *Progress in Planning* 59: 125-231.

Sakanishi, A. 2006. Commuting patterns in the Osaka metropolitan area: a GIS-based analysis of commuter rail passengers. *Review of Urban and Regional Development Studies* 18: 41-59.

Tani, K. 2007. Changes in migration and commuting flows in Japan's Major metropolitan areas since the Taisho Era. *The Annals of Japan Association for Urban Sociology* 25: 23-36. (J)

Tsuya, N. O. and Kuroda, T. 1989. Japan: the slowing of urbanisation and metropolitan concentration. In *Counterurbanization: the changing pace and nature of population deconcentration*, ed. A. G. Champion, London: Edward Arnold.

Yamada, H. and Tokuoka, K. 1991. A study of the urbanization process in post war Japan. *Review of Urban and Regional Development Studies* 3: 152-169.

Yamagami, T. 2003a. The relation between population size and population increase in metropolitan areas in Japan. *The Journal of Population Studies* 33: 73-83. (J)

Yamagami, T. 2003b. Spatio-temporal structure of population growth in major metropolitan areas in Japan. *Geographical Review of Japan* 76: 187-210. (J)

(J) means "written in Japanese" (with an English summary, in some cases).

4. Occupational Structure in the Tokyo Metropolitan Area, 1985-2005: An Extended Shift-share Analysis of Changing Geographic Patterns

Ryo KOIZUMI

Abstract

This study examines the geographic patterns of the Tokyo metropolitan area (TMA) in terms of employment and occupation and its transformation after the collapse of the bubble economy. In TMA of the study period, the overall change in the occupational structure after the bubble economy period is characterized by growth of the service sector and increasing participation of women in the workforce. To overcome the technical problems of previous studies on urban distribution of labor, this paper adopts grid square unit data and performs extended shift-share analysis using spatial autocorrelation indices with geographic information systems. In addition, the auther added gray-collar jobs, which consist of sales and service jobs, and examined differences between male and female workers, considering especially the growth of female labor participation. The extended shift-share analysis enables us to assess the relative importance of different components in regional growth or decline. The auther divided the study period (1985-2005) into four 5-year intervals and examined the change in workers by occupational group. The findings revealed that the population of white-collar workers increased remarkably in the inner area of Tokyo, where housing provision accelerated after the 1990s. Moreover, in the suburbs, where white-collar workers moved during the bubble economy period, gray-collar and blue-collar workers increased remarkably after its collapse. In other words, "social polarization" advanced in the inner area, but "social mix" advanced in the suburbs. These changes have become evident after 2000; as a result, it has become difficult to grasp segregation by occupational groups as a simply concentric or sectoral pattern.

Keywords

Occupational structure, Shift-share analysis, Spatial pattern, GIS, Tokyo

4.1 Introduction

The social structure built in Japan after World War II has changed drastically since the 1990s. Comparing Japan with Western countries, the change in Japanese society is characterized by its temporal compression with simultaneous changes in the industrial and educational sectors (Machimura 2009). Although industrialization led to the leveling of the social structure, the movements of social structure by the change job has declined after the rapid period of economic growth in the 1970s and 1980s. This change is reflected in expanding disparities in household incomes since the late 1980s. In addition, particularly in Tokyo, the bubble economy in the late 1980s brought both soaring land prices and large-scale outmigration from the inner area to the suburbs.

The aim of this study was to clarify the spatial patterns of employment in the Tokyo metropolitan area (TMA) after the bubble economy's collapse in the early 1990s, by considering three aspects of change: deepening social polarization, changing demographic structure, and the trend of housing provision. In this study, grid square unit data was adopted and analyses were performed using spatial autocorrelation indices with GIS (geographic information systems) to overcome the technical problems of the previous studies on the urban spatial structure of TMA.

4.2 Background of the recent changes of urban spatial structure

As a topic of urban geography and urban sociology, the spatial patterns of the Tokyo metropolitan area (TMA) have mainly been studied in terms of the residential patterns. However, the structural changes in the TMA can be described in terms of three types of trends: globalization, changing demographic structure, and the trend of housing provision.

After the 1980s, globalization and the service economy brought considerable change to industry and employment in world cities, including Tokyo. A typical example is the decrease in the number of skilled workers because of the declining manufacturing industry and an increase in the number of highly specialized workers involved in the new global economy and financial systems. In addition, low-paid service jobs that do not require any specialization have increased. These changes have been summarized as the "dual city" phenomenon by Mollenkopf and Castells (1991) and "social polarization" by Sassen (2001). Empirical studies in North America and Europe revealed that these changes happened particularly in cities with many multinational enterprises and immigrants (Hamnett 1994, Baum et al. 1997). Mizuno (2010) reviewed the reorganization of large cities, focusing on the principle of financial capital, the global city, and the creative class. In particular, he indicated that the unfettered movements of investment money intend to accelerate Tokyo's financial activities as a "Global Cities" led to globalization of risk by the securitization of real estate.

As for the changing trends in demographic distribution and in housing provision, the first baby boomers' movement into the metropolitan area caused housing problems in Tokyo's inner area during the period of high economic growth. Watanabe (1978) developed a migration model of this process by which the baby-boom generation first rented narrow apartments in the central area and then bought houses in the suburbs as their life stages progressed. The goal of acquiring a house necessarily pushed people to the suburbs, where land was cheaper. Housing provision expanded to Tokyo's outskirts, with rising land prices accompanying economic growth. Figure 1 shows the extensive expansion of the densely inhabited district (DID) in the Tokyo metropolitan area between 1965 and 1970. This trend continued until the 1990s, although its pace slowed temporarily in the early 1980s. In this way, the first baby boomers'

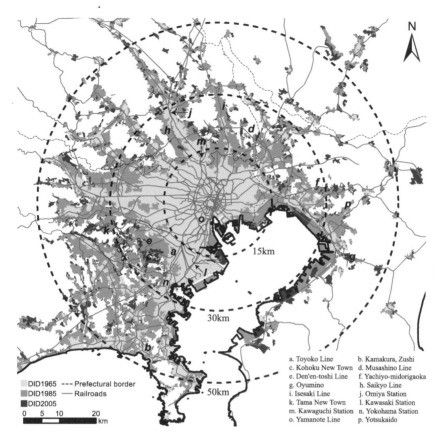

Figure 1 The expansion of the densely inhabited district (DID) in the Tokyo Metropolitan Area (1965-2005)
Source: National land numerical information

housing demands produced a metropolitan area that was spreading horizontally.

However, diversified housing demands reflected variegated family status since 1990s were not satisfied by expansion of residences beyond commuting distance, but by vertical expansion in built-up inner areas. Such a new housing provision necessarily entails rebuilding and redevelopment, and these changes cope with the demographic changes. The centripetal population movement (Toshin-Kaiki) and "the end of suburbanization" describe this process. However, whether these changes affect social polarization associated with the social status dimension needs to be examined.

4.3 Data and methods

Previous studies of the urban spatial structure of TMA have had several technical problems. First, a number of previous studies employed factor analysis or cluster analysis to analyze residential structure of cities. Nevertheless, it is difficult to compare factors or clusters obtained from different input variables. For example, Kurasawa and Asakawa (2004) gave similar names to regional clusters obtained from different time periods. However, factor composition and clusters depend on the input variables as indicated by Yano and Kato (1988) and Machimura (2005). The solution to this problem is the separate analysis of spatial patterns of the variables used in factor analysis.

To avoid these problems, variables representing main factors of the social area analysis should be adopted so that their spatial patterns can be examined separately and in detail. Since Sonobe's (2001) three hypotheses about the social polarization of the city, viz., a world city hypothesis, a deindustrialization hypothesis, and a public policy hypothesis, are commonly based on the notion that transformation of the industrial structure led to change of the occupation structure, the present study adopted variables representing socioeconomic status. The number of workers by occupational group from the national population census was used because occupation can be regarded as a direct index of social status in Japan, where income data for small-area units are not available.

The study area for this research was the TMA within a 50-km radius from central Tokyo (Tokyo Station). This area approximately covers the municipalities where 5% or more workers commute to Tokyo's 23 Wards (Koizumi 2010). The change in occupational structure after the bubble economy's collapse between 1985 and 2005 was mainly analyzed using population census data. The occupational structure is captured by classifying jobs into white-collar, gray-collar and blue-collar. The white-collar ratio is defined as the proportion of the sum of "administrative and managerial workers," "professional and engineering workers," and "clerical workers" to the total number of workers. The gray-collar ratio is defined as the proportion of the sum of "sales workers" and "service workers" to the total number of workers. The blue-collar ratio is defined as the proportion of the sum of "transport and machine operation workers" and "manufacturing process workers" to the total number of workers.

A second problem with previous studies is that they have tended to interpret the spatial patterns appearing on maps according to subjective rather than objective categories. Hence, the findings obtained were likely to depend on the representation of the maps and affected by arbitrary interpretation. To understand the spatial patterns objectively, this study employed the spatial autocorrelation index of Moran's I and its local version (Anselin 1995; Fotheringham et al. 2000). The value that typically range from approximately +1, representing complete positive spatial autocorrelation, to approximately -1, representing complete negative spatial autocorrelation. If I is close to 0, there is very little spatial autocorrelation. The value wij is defined whether they shared boundary or not (when shared boundary +1, not shared 0).

Third, many previous studies have used the administrative unit as a unit area. Though analysis using the administrative unit has some advantages in terms of the abundance of information available, it has the disadvantage of misunderstanding of spatial patterns owing to the shape of the administrative unit. The areal units should be as homogeneous as possible,

Occupational Structure in the Tokyo Metropolitan Area, 1985-2005: An Extended Shift-share Analysis of Changing Geographic Patterns

Table 1   Changes in occupational composition in TMA (1985-2005)

	1985	1990	1995	2000	2005
Male workers	8,519,837	9,280,468	9,557,977	9,195,504	8,785,642
Male white-collar	3,044,519	3,410,206	3,545,820	3,369,248	3,257,678
Male gray-collar	1,934,347	2,150,075	2,297,214	2,339,912	2,210,947
Male blue-collar	3,240,602	3,418,269	3,401,720	3,177,510	2,997,841
Female workers	4,660,319	5,340,090	5,708,611	5,778,474	5,854,134
Female white-collar	2,344,116	2,843,462	3,033,091	3,060,869	3,113,381
Female gray-collar	1,265,521	1,410,197	1,618,579	1,686,142	1,765,067
Female blue-collar	953,654	1,001,537	976,171	961,433	911,092

Source: Population Census

with equal size and shape. This problem is related to the Modifiable Areal Unit Problem (MAUP): the influence of scale and zoning of the unit area on spatial analysis. To reduce the effect of these problems, the grid square unit (3rd level, Japanese geodetic reference system) was employed as a unit area. In the analysis of TMA using grid square statistics, the author used the Third Grid Square (Japanese geodetic reference system) within 50 km from Tokyo Station, where 200 or more people reside per areal unit.

From 1985 to 2005, the occupational structure throughout TMA changed considerably (Table 1). However, analysis of change in the ratio of occupations in each unit area cannot distinguish between change of the occupation composition as a whole and local change. Therefore, the author employed a shift-share analysis that has been used in economic geography to assess the relative importance of different components in regional growth or decline.

Nagao (1996) proposed an extended shift-share analysis for dividing "the differential effect" that indicates a local change different from the trend of the total region into "competitive effect" (C_{ij}) and "allocation effect" (A_{ij}) as follows:

$$\Delta E_{ij} = G_{ij} + M_{ij} + C_{ij} + A_{ij} \qquad (1)$$

$$\Delta E_{ij} = E_{ij}^{t+1} - E_{ij}^{t} \qquad (2)$$

$$G_{ij} = E_{ij}^{th} \cdot (\frac{E_i^{t+1}}{E_i^t} - 1) \qquad (3)$$

$$M_{ij} = (E_{ij}^{t} - E_{ij}^{th}) \cdot \left(\frac{E_i^{t+1}}{E_i^t} - 1 \right) \qquad (4)$$

$$C_{ij} = E_{ij}^{th} \cdot \left(\frac{E_{ij}^{t+1}}{E_{ij}^{t}} - \frac{E_i^{t+1}}{E_i^{t}} \right) \qquad (5)$$

$$A_{ij} = (E_{ij}^t - E_{ij}^{th}) \bullet \left(\frac{E_{ij}^{t+1}}{E_{ij}^t} - \frac{E_i^{t+1}}{E_i^t} \right) \quad (6)$$

where

ΔE_{ij}: the change in the number of workers of sector i in area j,

E_{ij}^t: the number of workers of sector i in area j at t the start of the period year

E_i^{t+1}: the number of workers of sector i in area j at $t+1$ (the next part of the period year),

E_{ij}^{th}: the same dimensional scaling (defined as follows)

$$E_{ij}^{th} = E_j^t \bullet \frac{E_i^t}{E^t} \quad (7)$$

E_j^t: the number of workers in area j at t,

E_i^t: the number of workers of sector j in study area at t,

E^t: the number of workers in study area at t,

G_{ij}: growth effect,

M_{ij}: mix effect,

C_{ij}: competitive effect, and

A_{ij}: allocation effect.

The competitive effect is attributable to differences in growth rate between an areal unit and the whole region. Hence, we can clarify the local trend as strong or weak by analyzing the spatial pattern of the competitive effect.

4.4 Spatial patterns of the occupational structure by gender and time period: an extended shift-share analysis

4.4.1 Spatial patterns of occupation constitution in terms of gender difference

This section examines the process of forming spatial patterns of occupation structure in TMA using grid square statistics. To this end, the author chose 1985, when the bubble economy had begun, as the beginning of the study period and 2005 as the end of the period. Since the number of female workers increased remarkably during this period, the following analysis considers gender difference.

Figure 2 and Figure 3 show areas having a significantly high ratio of three occupational categories as of 1985 and 2005, based on the local version of Moran's I statistic. The map shows only areas with significant p-values of the Local Moran statistic below 0.05. Colored areas show spatial units plotted in the upper right quadrant of the Moran scatterplot. Hence, these areas represent high values surrounded by high values.

Within 15 km of Tokyo station, a predominance of white-collar workers in the western part

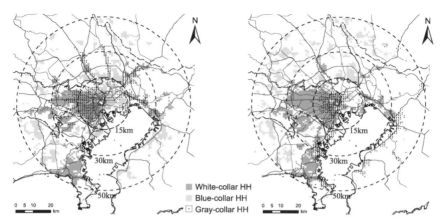

Figure 2 Spatial units with significantly high ratios of the three occupational categories for males (left) and females (right) (1985)
Source: Population Census

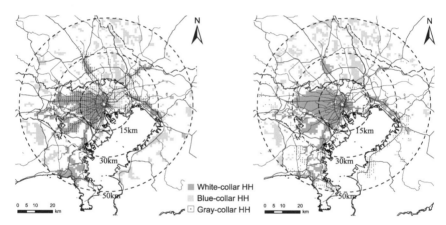

Figure 3 Spatial units with significantly high ratios of the three occupational categories for males (left) and females (right) (2005)
Source: Population Census

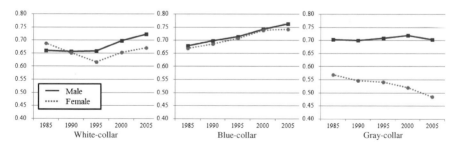

All Moran's I values are significant at the 5% level.

Figure 4 Moran's I statistics for three occupational categories (1985-2005)
Source: Population Census

is common to men and women while a predominance of blue-collar workers in the inner-eastern belt is found only for males. In contrast, a contiguous distribution of gray-collar workers is found in inner Tokyo. Outside the 15-km zone from central Tokyo, a white-collar district extends to the west, while gray-collar belts are found along railroad lines in the eastern radius from central Tokyo. A gender difference is observed in the southern part around Kawasaki Station and on the east side of Tokyo Bay, in Chiba Prefecture; both show a predominance of blue-collar jobs among males and gray-collar jobs among females.

Although the basic spatial patterns of 2005 resemble those of 1985, some notable changes appear. In 2005, values of Moran's *I* statistic indicating the degree of uneven distribution become larger, except for gray-collar workers and female white-collar workers (Figure 4).

Thus, comparing changes in the spatial patterns of occupational structure between 1985 and 2005 revealed that white-collar workers accumulated in the inner area of TMA and existing white-collar districts. An accumulation of the gray-collar workers is observed in the areas surrounding the white-collar's dominant districts. In contrast, the blue-collar belt shifts almost exclusively to the outer area of TMA.

4.4.2 Decomposition of the elements of change in occupational structure and their spatial patterns

To examine in detail the process of the changes mentioned above, extended shift-share analysis was employed, dividing the study period into four 5-year intervals. The periods used in this section are as follows: Period I from 1985 to 1990, Period II from 1990 to 1995, Period III from 1995 to 2000, and Period IV from 2000 to 2005. By measuring the competitive effects, an extended shift-share analysis could be applied to the change in workers by occupational group between the beginning and end of each period.

The extended shift-share analysis breaks down factors affecting change in the occupational structure into four types of effect as shown in Equations (1 to 7): growth effect (GE), mix ef-

Table 2 Moran's I statistics for the competitive effects of change in
the ratio of each occupa-tional category (1985-2005)

	Period I	Period II	Period III	Period IV
White-collar (Male)	0.43	0.32	0.19	0.32
Blue-collar (Male)	0.47	0.36	0.31	0.41
Gray-collar (Male)	0.44	0.35	0.21	0.33
White-collar (Female)	0.58	0.43	0.24	0.33
Blue-collar (Female)	0.48	0.36	0.29	0.27
Gray-collar (Female)	0.52	0.40	0.32	0.51

Source: Population Census
All Morans I values are significant at the 5% level.

fect (ME), competitive effect (CE), and allocation effect (AE). GE is calculated by assuming that the increasing rate of an occupational category in a unit area is proportional to that of the entire region. ME is calculated by supposing that the growth of the differences between a value for a unit area and the value for the whole area depends on the rate of change in the number of workers in an occupational category for the whole area. CE is the local element of change specific to an areal unit because CE shows the amount of change removing the effects of the occupational shift common to the whole study area. AE is a value multiplying the differences in the rate of an occupational category between an areal unit and the whole region by differences in the growth of workers for all occupational categories between unit area and the whole study area. Hence, the grand total of GE for all unit areas equals the employment change; the grand total of ME, CE and AE for all unit areas is 0. Measuring the effect for the whole area requires evaluation of an absolute value or its sum of squares.

Hence, CE is regarded as the local element of the change specific to an areal unit because it shows the amount of change with the effects of the occupational shift common to the whole study area removed. Biased distribution of the competitive effect's value indicates some regularities in the change of spatial structure. On the other hand, fragmented distribution of CE values represents a random pattern of change. The Moran's *I* statistic as a spatial autocorrelation index distinguishes between these spatial patterns.

The value of the Moran's *I* revealed that the spatial distribution of CE values for occupational groups was uniforms from Periods I to III, except for female blue-collar workers. Segregation by occupation was strengthened during Period IV (Table 2). Gender differences for each occupation show uneven distribution of female white-collar and gray-collar workers compared to male workers: the spatial cohesiveness of female workers was greater than that of male workers. For blue-collar workers, the differences of ratio between male and female lessened from Periods I to III. During Period IV, the spatial distribution of female workers lessened, but that of male workers increased.

4.4.2.1 Period I

Figure 5 shows the area where Local Moran values for CE of each occupational group were significantly positive at the 0.05 level in Period I.

In Period I, highly positive values of CE are observed for white-collar workers in the zone 10-30 km from central Tokyo and for blue-collar workers in the 20-40 km zone. This implies that each occupational group has increased significantly in these areas. For gray-collar workers, relatively large positive CE values are found in the 30-40 km zone for both men and women. In addition, the areas with large positive CE values for three occupational groups overlap in the 20-30 km zone. These areas commonly underwent large-scale land development, for instance, in the area along the JR Musashino Line between Kawaguchi and the former Urawa City as well as in Tama New Town. Concerning male gray-collar and both

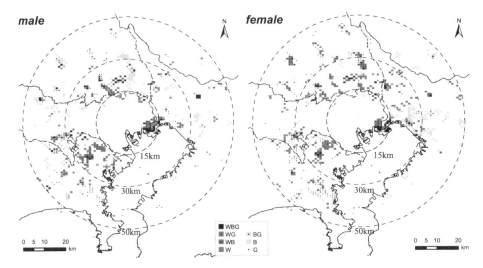

Figure 5 Spatial units with significantly positive local Moran values in 1985-1990 for CEs of white-collar, gray-collar and blue-collar ratios (grid square statistics unit) by gender.
Source: Population Census

genders of white-collar workers, positive CE values can be observed in the area along the JR Saikyo Line (opened in 1985) and the Tokyu Den'en-toshi Line. In addition to these areas, highly positive CE values for male gray-collar workers are seen in the southern part of Yokohama City along the Yokohama Municipal Subway, and the JR Musashino Line. In contrast, large CE values for female gray-collar workers are found in the areas along the Negishi Line (southern part of Yokohama City) and around Tsurugashima Station of the Tobu Tojo Line. For blue-collar workers, a highly positive CE was obtained in the area along the Tobu Isesaki Line, around Yotsukaido, along the Keisei Line, and the JR Musashino Line.

4.4.2.2 Period II

As a whole, positive CE values can be observed in the suburbs (Figure 6), similar to the result in Period I. Positive CE values appeared around Higashi-Urawa Station; Kohoku New Town; and the eastern part of the former Omiya City, common to the three occupational groups. Male white-collar and gray-collar workers showed positive CE values in Kohoku New Town and Tama New Town, and the eastern part of Edogawa Ward. For male gray-collar workers, positive CE values are found in the area along the Tobu Tojo Line. Positive CE values for male gray-collar and white-collar workers are also found in the vicinity of Yotsukaido and Shonandai stations. For blue-collar workers, areas near Sakura Station and along the Tobu Isesaki Line and Tobu Noda Line show a positive CE, although the extent of areas with positive values is relatively small. However, areas in and around the Konandai and Takane-Kohdan Stations show negative CE values for male gray-collar and white-collar workers despite

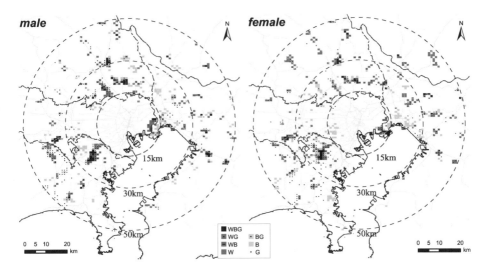

Figure 6 Spatial units with significantly positive Local Moran values 1990-1995 for CEs of white-collar, Gray-collar and blue collar ratios (grid square statistics unit) by gender
Source: Population Census

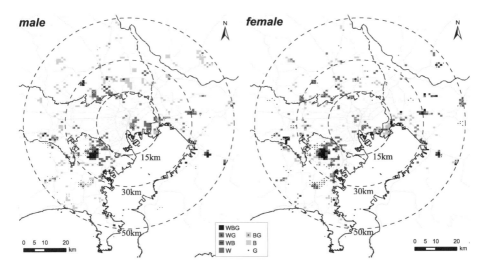

Figure 7 Spatial units with significantly positive Local Moran values in 1995-2000 for CE of white-collar, gray-collar and blue collar ratios (grid square statistics unit), by gender
Source: Population Census

the suburban location.

4.4.2.3 Period III

In Period III, spatial patterns of positive values of CE become complicated, and the changes in white-collar workers show a gender difference (Figure 7). In the inner area where negative CE values were observed in preceding periods, positive CE values for white-collar workers are observed in Chuo Ward along the Sumida River. An increase in white-collar workers' highly positive-CE-value is found in the 10-20-km zone for males and around the 20-30-km zone for females. Moreover, increases in the suburbs are also observed. As a result, in some suburban areas, both blue-collar and gray-collar or both blue-collar and white-collar workers show an increase.

In contrast, negative CE values expanded into the suburbs. Both men and women in Misato Park in Misato City and Izumino Station of the Sagami Railway Line and white-collar men in the area surrounding Hanamigawa estate in Chiba City and Tamadaira estate in Hino City show negative CE values.

4.4.2.4   Period IV

In Period IV, the number of male gray-collar workers also shows a decline; only female gray-collar and female white-collar workers increase. However, even though the total number of workers declines, there exist areas with positive CE values. In particular, Period IV has a spatial pattern different from those of the preceding periods (Figure 8). A notable feature of Period IV is the increase in white-collar workers within 10 km of central Tokyo. Male gray-collar workers also show a significant increase in the 10-30 km area. On the other hand, an increase of blue-collar workers is found prominently in the zone beyond 20 km from central Tokyo, similar to the other time periods. Positive CE values common to the three occupational groups are observed in limited areas, such as Oyumino Station of the Keisei Chiba Line and along the Odakyu Tama Line, where residential development progressed rapidly.

Similar to Period III, positive CE values for white-collar workers are observed in central Tokyo. In Period IV, the central part of Yokohama City and Koto Ward (east side of the Sumida River) and part of Edogawa Ward also show highly positive CE values for male white-collar workers. In addition, CE values changed from negative to positive in some parts inside the Yamanote Line. For gray-collar workers, the areas with positive CE values spread to the area surrounding the Yamanote Line. Moreover, positive CE values for gray-collar workers are also observed in the areas around Tamagawajosui, Tachikawa, Omiya, and Higashi-totsuka Stations, and in a wide range along the Den'entoshi Line. In addition, the areas around Yachiyo-midorigaoka Station, the north side of Kohoku New Town, around Chuorinkan and Katakura, and Kakio Stations show positive CE values for blue-collar workers. However, compared with other occupational groups, a notable feature of blue-collar workers is the significant CE values in areas that are not near railroad stations, but along main roads, such as the Higashiomiya and Hino Bypasses.

These areas with positive CE values in Period IV can be divided into two types: central Tokyo and newly developed suburbs. The number of white-collar workers remarkably increased in central Tokyo; however, blue-collar and gray-collar workers increased prominently in the suburbs. These data show how different types of occupational groups have contributed

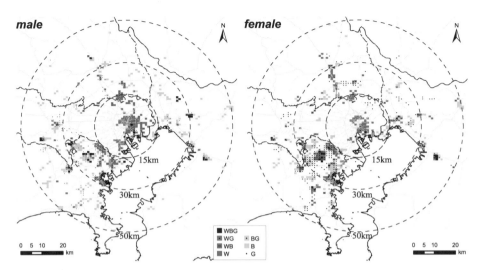

Figure 8 Spatial units with significantly positive Local Moran values in 2000-2005 for CEs of white-collar, gray-collar and blue collar ratios (grid square statistics unit)
Source: Population Census

to the population growth and decline according to the location of each area.

4.5 Discussion and conclusion

As shown, the post-1985 spatial patterns of occupation structure in the Tokyo metropolitan area changed dramatically over time. Gender difference became apparent after the 1990s. The number of white-collar workers increased around Urawa, Kashiwa, and Chiba Stations and along the Toyoko Line throughout the target period. After 2000, an agglomeration of white-collar workers was observed in central Tokyo. This implied that population growth in these areas was comprised mainly of white-collar workers. On the other hand, in the areas around Zushi and Kamakura Cities, located on the fringe of the white-collar belt, the number of white-collar workers has decreased. Since the proportion of managerial workers is relatively high, their retirement may be the cause of the decline in white-collar workers in these areas.

For blue-collar workers, the agglomeration in the districts of the eastern part of the 15-km zone has disappeared; however, the number of blue-collar workers continuously increased in the 20-km zone and beyond. It is believed that the commuting distance for blue-collar workers is shorter than that for white-collar workers. Relocation of factories to the suburbs may have caused the change in the spatial pattern of the blue-collar workers.

The spatial pattern of the gray-collar workers shows a large gender difference. In particular, the spatial extent of the agglomerated district of female workers is narrower than that of male workers. An explanation may lie in commuting distance: female workers tend to choose workplaces near their homes.

Findings reveal that in the suburbs, where white-collar workers moved during the bubble economy period, gray-collar and blue-collar workers increased remarkably after its collapse, by contrast the population of white-collar workers increased remarkably in the inner area of Tokyo. In other words, "social polarization" advanced in the inner area while "social mix" advanced in the suburbs. These changes have become evident after 2000, and as a result, it has become difficult to grasp segregation by occupational groups as simply a concentric or sectoral pattern.

To explain the background of these changes, two factors can be noted. The first factor is the land use change. New construction or movement of factories within the metropolitan area and their reorganization may have led to extinction of the blue-collar belt within the 15-km zone and the inland expansion of the blue-collar belt. These trends were accelerated by the Act on Special Measures Concerning Urban Renaissance in 2002, which promoted urban renewal in the metropolitan core through private companies' capital investment. In addition, building regulations were eased in this era. Housing provision in the inner area was induced by the relocations and closing of factories and warehouses in the built-up area after the bubble economy's collapse.

The second factor is the filtering process of the housing market. Since the housing market is divided by price range, residents are filtered through housing cost. As a result, homogeneous residents tend to live in districts supplying the same quality of housing. The 1960s and 1970s were a time of suburbanization, when large numbers of similar-quality houses were built in the suburbs. In the downtown vicinity, a large number of condominiums were built after the late 1990s. Although the breadth of housing choices increased, housing prices were not necessarily cheap. By conducting a questionnaire survey with the residents of a super high-rise condominium in the Tokyo Bay area, Koizumi et al. (2011) clarified that the residents are primarily white-collar workers earning relatively high incomes. In addition, the form of acquisition of a house changed from a one-time purchase to a ladder upward, toward a better house, as public assistance for housing acquisitions was reduced (for example, the abolition of the Housing Loan Corporation). In other words, residents in these newly developed condominiums are generally limited to white-collar workers who earn high incomes. In addition, the majority of residents moving into the downtown vicinity are 30-40 years old, corresponding to the life stage of first-time homebuyers. This population change will probably affect not only the spatial patterns of the occupational structure of the metropolitan area but also the spatial patterns of age structure of the residents.

These results are revealed by adopting grid square unit data and perform extended shift-share analysis using spatial autocorrelation indices. To clarify the changing geographic patterns of occupational structure, the influences of population increase (or decrease) should be removed. In the era of the growth of female labor participation, moreover, the analysis by gender is useful. These analyses enable us to understanding of the changes in occupational structure, critical to understanding and guiding urban development in the Tokyo Metropolitan

Area but also useful for other cities undergoing rapid change.

References

Anselin, L. 1995. Local indicators of spatial association - LISA. *Geographical Analysis* 27: 93-115.

Baum, S. 1997. Sydney, Australia: a global city? Testing the social polarisation thesis. *Urban Studies* 34: 1881-1902.

Fotheringham, S. Brunsdon, C. and Charlton, M. 2000. *Quantitative geography: Perspectives on spatial data analysis*. London: Sage publication.

Hamnett, C. 1994. Social polarization in global cities: Theory and evidence. *Urban Studies* 31: 401-424.

Koizumi, R. 2010. Spatial patterns of occupational structure and their changes in Tokyo Metropolitan Area. *Quarterly Journal of Geography* 62: 61-70. (J)

Koizumi R., Nishiyama, H., Kubo, T., Kukimoto, M. and Kawaguchi, T. 2011. New dimensions of housing acquisition in the Tokyo bay area: Skyscraper condominium residents in Toyosu. *Geographical review of Japan* 84: 592-609. (J)

Kurasawa, S. and Asakawa, T. ed. 2004. *New social atlas of metropolitan Tokyo: 1975-90*. Tokyo: University of Tokyo Press. (J)

Machimura, T. 2005. Book Review: Kurasawa, S. and Asakawa, T. ed. New social atlas of metropolitan Tokyo: 1975-90. *The Annals of Japan Association for Urban Sociology* 23: 195-203. (J)

Mizono, M. 2010. Economic geographies of urban restructuring in the 2000s: financial capitalism, global cities, and the creative class. *Japanese Journal of Human Geography* 62: 426-444. (J)

Mollenkopf, J. and Castells, M. 1991. *Dual city: Restructuring New York*. New York: Russell Sage Foundation.

Nagano, K. 1996. Regional Employment Changes in Japanese Manufacturing Industry, 1970-1990: An Extended Shift-Share Analysis. *Geographical review of Japan* 69: 303-326. (J)

Sassen, S. 2001. *The global city: New York, London, Tokyo*. 2nd edition. Princeton University Press.

Sonobe, M. 2001.*Contemporary metropolitan society: dual city?* Tokyo: Toshindo Publising Co., Ltd.

Watanabe, Y. 1978. The residence in megacity and the population movement within urban area. *Comprehensive urban studies* 4: 11-35. (J)

Yano, K. and Kato, F. 1988. Canonical trend surface analysis of residential structure in the Tokyo City Area. *Japanese Journal of Human Geography* 40: 20-39. (J)

(J) means "written in Japanese" (with an English summary, in some cases).

5. Time Budgets of Working Mothers Living in Central Tokyo: An Analysis on the Impacts of the Internet

Naoto YABE

Abstract

In recent years, population recovery or "gentrification" has become increasingly common in city centers in most developed countries. The emergence of relatively new gender relations, such as single female households or DINK families, has also been observed. This study sought to examine factors that enable working mothers living in city centers to simultaneously manage their jobs and households, focusing especially on the impacts of the Internet. An activity diary survey conducted with working mothers who lived in central Tokyo revealed that such mothers allocated more time to work than their counterparts who lived in the suburbs of Tokyo. Thus, working mothers who lived in the city center had tight time budgets. The survey also showed that reducing time devoted to housekeeping tasks was crucial to balancing jobs with housekeeping. Housekeeping time was scrutinized under different conditions to determine factors that contributed to its reduction. Results indicated that Internet services like e-commerce did not contribute to a reduction in housekeeping time over a single day. Whether Internet services reduce housekeeping time over longer periods of a week or month should be examined. Allocating tasks to husbands definitely reduced housekeeping time. The amount of housework shared by husbands in the city center was larger than that of husbands in suburban areas, suggesting that living in the city center reorganizes the time budgets of households. For husbands, living in the city center could reduce commuting time and increase time devoted to housekeeping. For working mothers, living in the city center could increase the time devoted to work. These results indicate that comparatively new "quality of life" models are emerging in central Tokyo.

Keywords
Internet, activity diary, gender, Tokyo

5.1 Background

Early studies investigating suburban women focused especially on constraints regarding their employment. The spatial-entrapment thesis, which argued domestic responsibilities of suburban women restricted their employment prospects and job search area, was a typical example. On the one hand, England (1993) studied an American suburb and found that the spatial-entrapment thesis was not necessarily appropriate for the late 1980s and early 1990s. On the other hand, time budget analyses of a Tokyo suburb indicated that suburban women experienced difficulty in finding full-time jobs because of domestic responsibilities, lack of

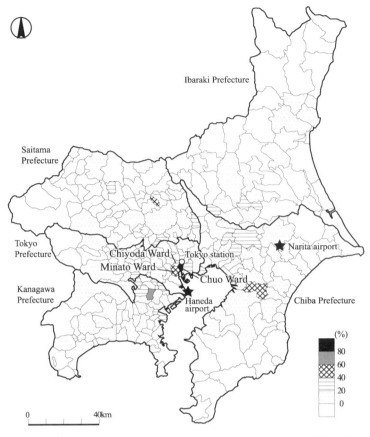

Figure 1 Population increase in the Tokyo Metropolitan Area from 1995 to 2010
Source: Population census

support from their husbands and lack of employment opportunities in the suburban area (Okamoto 1995; Kawase 1997; Sugiura and Miyazawa 2001).

Some cities in the developed world, however, have moved beyond suburbanization. In recent years, population recovery or "gentrification" has become increasingly common in city centers in most developed countries (Smith 2002). The Tokyo metropolitan area is not an exception (Miyazawa and Abe 2005; Yabe 2003; Yamagami 2003). Central Tokyo, which consists of 3 wards — Chiyoda, Chuo and Minato — has experienced population increases since the late 1990s (Figure 1). The population of central Tokyo in 1995 and 2010 was 243,588 and 375,008, respectively. Unlike the city center, the population in suburban Tokyo indicates stagnation or decline. In observing these data, Esaki (2006) insisted that the suburbanization process in the Tokyo metropolitan area had reached an end.

The back-to-the-city movement may challenge conventional wisdom about suburban women, like the spatial-entrapment thesis, because living in city centers offers women plenty of job opportunities and could ease some constraints on employment. Yui et al. (2003) and Wakabayashi et al. (2002) focused on single women living in central Tokyo, but there are few studies about working mothers living in central Tokyo. Miyazawa (1998) employed time budget analysis and found that working mothers living in the Nakano Ward, which is located at the periphery of sub-central Tokyo, had difficultly working full-time jobs because of time consumed by picking up children at nursery schools. His work revealed that the time budget analysis is quite an effective method for investigating the constraints of working mothers.

The present study is a report on time budget data from an activity diary survey of working mothers living in central Tokyo. Other time budget studies in recent years have put an emphasis on the impact of the Internet (Couclelis 2009; Ren and Kwan 2009; Ren et al. 2013), Because Internet activities such as online shopping have the potential to ease space-time constraints (Farag et al. 2007; Rotem-Mindali and Salomon 2007), this study also included this factor. As for factors that eased constraints, an earlier study suggested that support from working mothers' families was important (Sugiura and Miyazawa 2001). In short, this study examined the time budgets of working mothers living in central Tokyo, with a special focus on the impact of the Internet and the support of families. The results of this paper can contribute to the description of the differences in "quality of life" between suburbs and city centers, especially for mothers.

In the following sections, we describe the methods used to collect time budget data on working mothers living in central Tokyo, and outline the time budget data. This is followed by a detailed analysis of the data. The paper concludes with a discussion of findings.

5.2 Activity diary survey

5.2.1 Methods

First, survey respondents were recruited through a research firm. Respondents had to meet the following four conditions to be eligible for the survey: (1) married woman; (2) living in central Tokyo or sub-central Tokyo; (3) not a student; and (4) has a child under 18 years of age. For the purposes of condition two, central Tokyo was defined as the Chiyoda Ward, Chuo Ward and Minato Ward, while sub-central Tokyo was defined as the Shinjuku Ward and Shibuya Ward. A total of 646 participants were identified who matched the four conditions.

Questionnaires were sent to the respondents through the Internet. Participants filled out the form online. The questionnaires asked respondents to record their activities in 30-min intervals for the most recent weekday. Options for activities were presented in advance, and respondents could select an activity from 11 categories. The categories were selected by referencing previous work concerning time budget analysis (Yano 1995). The 11 categories were as follows: (1) Sleep; (2) Meals; (3) Personal care; (4) Travel; (5) Work; (6) Housework; (7) Socializing; (8) Education/Leisure; (9) Mass media; (10) Rest; (11) Other. For the categories of Work, Housework, Socializing, Education/Leisure and Mass media, women recorded whether the activities were conducted with or without the Internet. In addition to the activity diary, the employment status of working mothers and the housekeeping tasks assigned to each family member were recorded. The questionnaires were sent to participants on Tuesday January 17, 2012 and responses were accepted until Monday January 23, 2012. In total, 336 replies were collected; of these, 305 were valid replies for a response rate of 47%.

Because the survey was conducted over the Internet, respondents were limited to working mothers with Internet access. It is widely recognized that Internet surveys frequently exclude older respondents and may cause a sampling bias. In the present study, however, subjects were working mothers with a child under age 18. As mothers with young children are considered middle aged rather than elderly, the sampling bias associated with the Internet was not thought to play a critical role here.

5.2.2   Attributes of respondents

The majority of respondents were in their 30s (N=112; 37%) or 40s (N=142; 47%). There were no respondents in their 60s. This was mainly due to the age requirement for children; 43% of respondents had children under 5 years, and 30% had children ages 6–12. This means that almost 73% of respondents had children in preschool or primary school. Based on these data, it can be said that the sampling bias of Internet surveys had little effect on this study.

Among the 305 respondents, 39% were working mothers (N=120) and 61% were non-working mothers (N=185). Employment status was calculated for working mothers (Table 1). The percentage of working mothers who held full-time jobs was considerably higher than that found for the suburbs in an earlier study (Sugiura and Miyazawa 2001). As to place of residence, 45% of respondents lived in central Tokyo, while 55% lived in sub-central Tokyo.

Table 1   Employment status of working mothers

	N	%
Full time	46	38.3
Temp staff	16	13.3
Part time	38	31.6
Independent	15	12.5
Homemaker	3	2.5
Other	2	1.7
Total	120	100.0

Source: Questionnaire survey (Yabe 2014)

5.2.3 Outlook of the time budget

Time budgets were aggregated to clarify differences between working mothers and non-working mothers (Table 2). The highlighted difference is the time for work. Working mothers spent seven hours daily, on average, on work activity, which no doubt accounts for the constraint on time spent on other activities compared to non-working mothers. This relatively long work activity time compared to the suburban results reflected that many of the working mothers held full-time jobs.

Almost all activities of working mothers showed less time, on average, than those of non-working mothers. The exception was travel: 85.8% of working mothers traveled on a weekday, spending an average of 92 minutes on this activity. In contrast, only 34.2% of non-working

Table 2 Weekday time budget of housewives

	Working mothers		Non-working mothers	
	Share of participation (%)	Average time	Share of participation (%)	Average time
Sleep	100.0	6h 40m	100.0	6h 59m
Meals	96.7	1h 38m	97.8	1h 48m
Personal care	91.7	1h 44m	88.0	2h 24m
Work with Internet	58.3	5h 44m	-	-
Work without Internet	61.7	5h 35m	-	-
Housework with Internet	26.7	1h 17m	43.5	2h 15m
Housework without Internet	90.8	3h 13m	96.2	5h 43m
Travel	85.8	1h 32m	34.2	1h 15m
Socializing with Internet	10.0	1h 2m	9.8	1h 38m
Socializing without Internet	20.0	1h 10m	38.0	1h 49m
Education/Leisure with Internet	33.3	1h 24m	45.7	2h 7m
Education/Leisure without Internet	20.8	1h 15m	31.0	2h 15m
Mass media with Internet	19.2	1h 11m	29.3	2h 8m
Mass media without Internet	32.5	1h 38m	45.1	2h 29m
Rest	55.8	1h 16m	62.5	1h 58m
Other	20.8	1h 6m	25.0	2h 43m
Total Work	100.0	6h 47m	-	-
Total Housework	95.8	3h 24m	98.4	6h 35m
Total Socializing	25.8	1h 18m	43.5	1h 57m
Total Education/Leisure	46.7	1h 34m	58.2	2h 52m
Total Mass media	41.7	1h 49m	58.2	3h 1m

Source: Questionnaire survey (Yabe 2014)

mothers traveled on a weekday. This difference reflected working mothers' commuting time. Considering that the majority of Travel consisted of commuting, then the average one-way commute time was 46 minutes. This commute time for working mothers in our study was thus equivalent to that of the working mothers living in the Tokyo suburbs (Sugiura and Miyazawa 2001). It then follows that for working mothers, time budget differences between city center and suburbs will be found not in commuting time but in work time.

Housekeeping was an activity that revealed a large difference between working mothers and non-working mothers. In contrast to working mothers, non-working mothers spent six and a half hours daily, on average, on housework. Meanwhile, average housekeeping time for working mothers was only three and a half hours. Because working mothers had to make time for work, they had to significantly cut back on housekeeping. This hard constraint affected other activities as well. For the categories Education/Leisure and Mass media, non-working mothers spent one hour more on these activities on a weekday than working mothers. Percent of engagement in those two activities revealed more than a 10% difference between working mothers and non-working mothers. Sleep and Meals were activities that almost all respondents had to engage in. The difference between the two groups was 19 minutes for Sleep and 10 minutes for Meals. Thus, constraints for working mothers were found not only in leisure activities but also for basic activities.

5.3 Results

The findings discussed in the previous section point to a need to investigate ways for working mothers to better budget their time. The most important action for better time budget management is reducing time for housework (Table 3). As much as 74.2% of working mothers had reduced the amount of time they spent on housekeeping tasks. This result indicated that doing housework in short time periods is extremely important in allowing working mothers to balance their jobs and their domestic responsibilities. In reducing housework, Internet services, used by 40.8% of working mothers, definitely played an important role. Support from husbands (19.2%) and parents (14.2%) were also effective in reducing housework.

The data also showed that working mothers cut other activities to generate time for housework, including leisure (35.8%) and sleep (30.0%). Sometimes they reduced time spent eating/drinking with colleagues (29.2%), which might have improved their work environments. Unlike countries that deregulate housekeeping labor to take advantage of the low-cost labor of immigrants, working mothers could not afford to employ housekeepers in Japan. Only 5.8% of the respondents had hired housekeepers. In contrast, it is noteworthy that 34.2% of working mothers took their children to nursery schools. Because a lot of nursery schools in central Tokyo are operated with public subsidies, mothers could use those facilities at a relatively low cost.

For the rest of section 3, we will examine the factors that reduced housework. These factors

Time Budgets of Working Mothers Living in Central Tokyo: An Analysis on the Impacts of the Internet

Table 3 Working mothers' engagement in order to work

	N	%
Reducing housework	89	74.2
Using nursery school	41	34.2
Using the Internet	49	40.8
Increasing housework done by husband	23	19.2
Increasing housework done by live-in parents	17	14.2
Increasing housework done by parents living in neighborhood	11	9.2
Hiring housekeeper	7	5.8
Reducing leisure time	43	35.8
Reducing sleep time	36	30.0
Reducing eating/drinking with colleagues	35	29.2
Other	4	3.3
Nothing special	9	7.5
Total	120	100.0

Source: Questionnaire survey (Yabe 2014)

included use of the Internet, and support from the husband or other family members. We will examine each factor in turn.

5.3.1 Impacts of the Internet

Internet services for consumers first appeared in the late 1990s in Japan. Various services are provided over the Internet, including banking and shopping. In recent years, fresh foods such as vegetables and meat can be purchased at an Internet super market and delivered to consumers' houses on the day of purchase. Such Internet services can reduce time spent traveling to shops and provide more flexible scheduling for working mothers, who can shop online even if they are in their offices.

Table 4 lists the goods and services that working mothers accessed through the Internet. Of the items included, processed foods/daily commodities (56.7%) and fresh foods (51.7%) were stand out. Working mothers also shopped for clothing (47.5%) and books/DVDs (45.0%) online. Results of a chi-squared test, however, indicated that there was no statistically significant difference between working mothers and non-working mothers in terms of Internet use.

The impact of the Internet on reducing housework was measured in the following manner. First, working mothers were subdivided into two groups: the first used the Internet for housework and the second did not. The average time for housework was then compared between the two groups (Table 5).

Table 4 Internet services used in the past month

	Working mothers		Non-working mothers	
	N	%	N	%
Shopping for fresh foods	62	51.7	89	48.1
Shopping for processed foods/daily commodities	68	56.7	97	52.4
Shopping for clothing	57	47.5	89	48.1
Shopping for books/DVDs	54	45.0	70	37.8
Reservations for travel	30	25.0	46	24.9
Reservations for event	22	18.3	20	10.8
Banking	53	44.2	66	35.7
Trading	4	3.3	12	6.5
SNS	30	25.0	59	31.9
Blogging	12	10.0	22	11.9
Other	1	0.8	2	1.1
Not using Internet	11	9.2	17	9.2
Total	120	100.0	185	100.0

Source: Questionnaire survey (Yabe 2014)

Table 5 Average housework time of working mothers by using Internet

	Used the Internet N=32	Did not use the Internet N=88	t test
Housework with Internet	1h 17m	-	
Housework without Internet (Physical housework)	2h 14m	3h 10m	*
Total Housework	3h 32m	3h 10m	

*: significant at the 5% level

Source: Questionnaire survey (Yabe 2014)

The results showed that the group who used the Internet for housework spent less time on "housework without Internet (Physical housework)" than the other group. The first group spent about two hours on physical housework, which was one hour less than working mothers who did not use the Internet for housework. By t test, the difference between the two groups was significant at the 5% level. Interestingly, however, the difference for "housework total" was not statistically significant between the two groups. These data suggest that some percentage of physical housework was simply substituted by the Internet. Internet services did

Time Budgets of Working Mothers Living in Central Tokyo: An Analysis on the Impacts of the Internet

not contribute to a time reduction for individual housework activities. Mothers spent almost equivalent amounts of time shopping in virtual shops as in real shops. Thus, the total amount of housework did not change based on whether they used the Internet or not. The Internet impact was not a reduction in total housework time, but an increase in working mothers' flexibility of schedule.

5.3.2 Impacts of husbands' support

Working mothers' share of housekeeping tasks is calculated in Table 6. Wives performed a larger percentage of all housekeeping tasks than husbands. The presence of husbands was most noticeable for "child care (48.3%)" and "take out garbage (45.8%)". A gendered division of labor is still in effect in central Tokyo at the beginning of the 21st century. The overall share of housekeeping tasks performed by husbands, however, is increasing in central Tokyo com-

Table 6 Division of housework in the households of working mothers

	Wife (%)	Husband (%)
Preparing breakfast	94.2	13.3
Clearing breakfast	91.7	15.0
Preparing dinner	98.3	15.0
Clearing dinner	92.5	19.2
Laundry	95.8	15.0
House cleaning	92.5	27.5
Shopping	97.5	30.0
Take out garbage	72.5	45.8
Child care	99.2	48.3

Source: Questionnaire survey (Yabe 2014)

Table 7 Average total housework time in the household of working mothers

Housekeeping tasks	Supported by husband		Not supported by husband	
	Average time	N	Average time	N
Preparing breakfast	2h 4m	16	3h 27m	104
Clearing breakfast	2h 10m	18	3h 28m	102
Shopping	2h 41m	36	3h 31m	84
Take out garbage	2h 39m	55	3h 48m	65

Source: Questionnaire survey (Yabe 2014)

pared to the suburbs of Tokyo (Sugiura and Miyazawa 2001). For husbands, living in central Tokyo makes for short commuting times. This may influence their time budgets, having room for housekeeping tasks. Other time use surveys have revealed that husbands are increasingly doing more housework all over Japan (Kobayashi et al. 2011).

The impact of husbands' support in reducing housework was analyzed. For each type of housekeeping task, respondents were subdivided into two groups. In the first, the husband shared the housekeeping task; in the second, the husband did not share the task. The average total housework time was then calculated for the two groups to ascertain the impact of husbands' housework on the reduction of housework for working mothers.

A t test showed that four housekeeping tasks indicated statistically significant differences between the two groups at the 5% level (Table 7). When husbands offered support for these tasks, working mothers saved over an hour on total housework time. In particular, this time saving effect was clear for "prepare breakfast" and "clear breakfast". Despite husbands' share of those two tasks being low—13.3% and 15.0%, respectively—such support was quite valuable during a busy morning.

5.3.3 Impacts of parents' support

It was not necessary for parents of working mothers to live in the same house or neighborhood for them to support housekeeping tasks. Among the working mothers, only 8.3% were living with their parents (Table 8). Notice that in this case, parents means specifically the parents of wives, not of husbands. The households of working mothers did tend to live in the neighborhood of the wife's parents. Unlike non-working mothers, 28.7% of working mothers lived close to or with their parents. Working mothers may expect that their parents will support them, causing them to live within 30 minutes of their parents' house.

The impact of parents' support in reducing housework was measured as follows. Working mothers were subdivided into two groups: the first was supported in housekeeping tasks by

Table 8 Distance to the house of wife's parents

	Working mothers		Non-working mothers	
	N	%	N	%
Living with parents	9	8.3	3	1.8
Within 30 min	22	20.4	23	13.8
30 min to 1 hour	24	22.2	53	31.7
1 to 2 hours	22	20.4	45	26.9
More than 2 hours	31	28.7	43	25.7
Total	108	100.0	167	100.0

Source: Questionnaire survey (Yabe 2014)

Time Budgets of Working Mothers Living in Central Tokyo: An Analysis on the Impacts of the Internet

parents living with them; the second was the rest of the respondents. The difference in average total housework time was then checked by *t* test. There was no significant difference between the two groups. An additional test was then conducted. Working mothers were again subdivided into two groups: the first was supported in housekeeping tasks by parents living within 30 minutes of their houses; the second was the rest of the sample. This test also found no statistically significant difference between the two groups. We evaluated this result carefully, taking into account the small sample size: the group supported by parents living with them represented only 17 respondents, while the group supported by parents living in the neighborhood represented only 11 respondents (see Table 3). Nevertheless, the impact of parents in reducing housework was limited in this study. It is thought that parents who support working mothers do not necessarily do so every day. Women may live with or in the same neighborhood as their parents in case of the sudden need for child care.

5.4   Conclusion

Working mothers living in central Tokyo are working longer than suburban counterparts; many are working full-time jobs. This long work time functions as a constraint on time budgets. Reducing housekeeping time is critical in order for working mothers to keep their jobs. To reduce housekeeping tasks, working mothers consider three factors to be important: the Internet, support from their husbands, and support from their parents. Among the three factors, the Internet does not reduce housekeeping tasks, but rather substitutes for physical housework. This finding indicates that the flexibility of working mothers' schedule is increased by online shopping. Working mothers can buy fresh foods anywhere, anytime using smart phones. Husbands' share of housework is still low, reflecting a gendered division of labor. However, compared to findings for the suburbs in an earlier study, husbands' share of housework is increasing. Husbands' support definitely functions to reduce the amount of time that working mothers spend on housework, especially when husbands support them by "preparing breakfast" or "clearing breakfast". As to parents' support, the impact on reducing housework is not clear, due in part to small samples.

In short, living in the city center reorganizes the time budget of households. For husbands, living in the city center may reduce commuting time and increase time devoted to housekeeping tasks. For working mothers, living in the city center could increase the time devoted to jobs. The aforementioned reorganization indicates that comparatively new "quality of life" models are emerging in central Tokyo.

The present study has some limitations, of course. The impact of the Internet on housework is analyzed only for a single day in this paper. Therefore, whether Internet services reduce housekeeping time over longer periods of a week or a month should be examined. In addition, suburban data that is compared with central Tokyo are incorporated in the earlier study. Those data are not ideal for comparison with contemporary situations. Thus, an activity diary survey in the Tokyo suburbs is needed to assure the robustness of the comparison.

Acknowledgements

The author would like to thank the participants of the Urban Geography Commission on the IGU Kyoto regional conference for their helpful comments. The map in this paper was made by MANDARA, a free GIS software. This work was supported by JSPS Grant-in-Aid for Scientific Research (KAKENHI: Grant Number 23720407 and 24242034) and Fukutake Science and Culture Foundation.

Some parts of this paper were first published in Japanese in the *Journal of Geography* 123, 269-284, 2014.

References

Couclelis, H. 2009. Rethinking time geography in the information age. *Environment and Planning A* 41: 1556-1575.

England, K. 1993. Suburban pink collar ghettos: The spatial entrapment of women? *Annals of the Association of American Geographers* 83: 225-242.

Esaki,Y. 2006. *Future Vision of the Metropolitan Population: Population Geography of Urban and Suburban Areas.* Tokyo : Senshu Daigaku Shuppankyoku. (J)

Farag, S., Schwanen, T., Dijst, M., and Faber, J. 2007. Shopping online and/or in-store? A structural equation model of the relationships between e-shopping and in-store shopping. *Transportation Research Part A* 41: 125-141.

Kawase, M. 1997. Changes in married women's commuting activity in terms of life-stage in Kashiwa, Chiba prefecture. *Geographical Review of Japan* 70A: 699-723. (J)

Kobayashi, T., Morofuji, E., and Watanabe, Y. 2011. Sleeping time keeps decreasing, male housework time is increasing: from the 2010 NHK Japanese time use survey. *The NHK Monthly Report on Broadcast Research* 2011 (4): 2-21. (J)

Miyazawa, H. 1998. Investigating time-space constraints on accessibility to day nursery facilities in Nakano Ward, Tokyo. *Geographical Review of Japan* 71A: 859-886. (J)

Miyazawa, H. and Abe, T. 2005. Recovery and changes in the socioeconomic composition of population in the central area of Tokyo during the period from 1995 to 2000: Analysis of small-area census data. *Geographical Review of Japan* 78: 893-912. (J)

Okamoto, K. 1995. The daily activities of metropolitan suburbanites and the urban daily rhythm: The case of Kawagoe, a suburb of Tokyo, and Nisshin, a suburb of Nagoya. *Geographical Review of Japan* 68A: 1-26. (J)

Ren, F. and Kwan, M. P. 2009. The impact of the Internet on human activity–travel patterns: Analysis of gender differences using multi-group structural equation models. *Journal of Transport Geography* 17: 440-450.

Ren, F., Kwan, M. P., and Schwanen, T. 2013. Investigating the temporal dynamics of Internet activities. *Time and Society* 22: 186-215.

Rotem-Mindali, O. and Salomon, I. 2007. The impacts of E-retail on the choice of shopping trips and delivery: Some preliminary findings. *Transportation Research Part A* 41: 176-189.

Smith, N. 2002. New globalism, new urbanism: Gentrification as global urban strategy. *Antipode* 34: 427-450.

Sugiura, Y. and Miyazawa, H. 2001. Are housewives living at Utsukushigaoka happy?: From the time use survey of the housewives in the Minami-osawa district in Tama New Town. *Notes on Theoretical Geography* 12: 1-17. (J)

Wakabayashi, Y., Kamiya, H., Kinoshita, R., Yui, Y., and Yano, K. 2002. *Urban Spaces of Single Women in Tokyo*. Tokyo: Taimeido. (J)

Yabe, N. 2003. Population recovery in inner Tokyo in the late 1990s: A questionnaire survey in Minato Ward. *Japanese Journal of Human Geography* 55: 277-292. (J)

Yabe, N. 2014. Time budgets of working mothers living in central tokyo: An analysis of the impacts of the Internet. *Journal of Geography* 123: 269-284. (J)

Yamagami, T. 2003. Spatio-temporal structure of population growth in major metropolitan areas in Japan. *Geographical Review of Japan* 76: 187-210. (J)

Yano, M. 1995. *Sociology of Time Budgets*. Tokyo: University of Tokyo Press. (J)

Yui, Y., Kamiya, H., Wakabayashi, Y., and Nakazawa, T. 2003. *Urban spaces of working women in Tokyo*. Tokyo: Kokon Shoin. (J)

(J) means "written in Japanese" (with an English summary, in some cases).

6. The Aged Society in a Suburban New Town: What Should We Do?

Takashi KAGAWA

Abstract

This study explains the current condition and the issues of developed communities in a post-growth society. The Osaka area's Senri New Town, the oldest planned post-war community in Japan, was used as a model for this study. The main subject of this study was to understand the living circumstances of the aging population in Senri New Town. To gain a sense of the daily lives of the residents, particularly of the elderly residents and any inconveniences that they feel, questionnaire surveys were given to residents of rented public condominium areas where the elderly population is prominent. Through analysing the results of the study, I propose how geographical researchers should respond to achieve sustainable development in this community. Supposing that the Private Financial Initiative Act (1999) was actively implemented in the Senri New Town, and many new condominiums were to be supplied in this new town. It is presumed that there would be new families migrating to the area, and many of them would have younger children. Therefore, it would be desirable for such communities to have facilities where residents of all age groups could enjoy comfortable living. Also, barrier-free living facilities for elderly residents should have a universal design to provide convenience to other age groups at the same time.

Keywords

elderly residents, rental public condominium, sustainable development,
Private Financial Initiative Act, universal design, Senri New Town

6.1 Supply and demand of housing during the rapid economic growth period

With several successions of an abundant workforce as a foundation, Japan was able to recover after the war and entered into a period of rapid economic growth. From an international perspective, the recovery was due to an abundant and inexpensive workforce. On the other hand, the increase in production led to a demand for workers, mainly in urban areas. At the same time, due to the mechanization of agriculture, a rural workforce surplus emerged. These factors combined and caused a large population movement from rural to urban areas.

Upon moving into urban areas for work opportunities, new migrants needed houses. Despite the fact that middle-class condominiums were available in urban areas during the early years of rapid economic growth, low-cost housing such as detached houses and apartments became mainstream. There were virtually no high-rise apartments as are seen in urban centres nowadays. Urban land area therefore expanded horizontally, resulting in urban sprawl, a chaotic form of urbanization. The development of urban infrastructure could not cope with such rapid urbanization. Lack of housing basically led to other problems concerning urban areas.

Eventually, a time of sound urban development came, in which residents had housing supply with improved living conditions, open space where they could enjoy life, and freedom from traffic congestion due to increased traffic flow. Researchers and city planners used the "garden city" ideology of Howard (1898) and Perry (1929) as a guide to forming new cities and suburbs in a planned manner and providing an adequate supply of housing to meet the increased demand. This model became the foundation for constructing new towns.

6.2 Main new towns and Senri New Town in Japan

6.2.1 Main new towns of Japan's three major metropolises

There are various new towns, large and small, in each area of Japan. Among these new towns, some are developed independently by private establishments, and some are comprehensively developed with research-related facilities. Among the latter, the Tsukuba Science City located in the Tokyo Metropolitan area, and Kansai Science City located in the Keihanshin Metropolitan area are the most famous.

However, there were only a few large-scale new towns that were actively funded by the government. Typical examples of these new towns situated in the three major metropolitan areas are Tama (founded 1971; estimated population around 2010, 216,000 residents; developed land area, 22.3 km²), Chiba (1979, 94,000, 25.3 km²), and Kohoku (1983, 200,000, 25.3 km²) in the Tokyo Metropolis, Kozoji (1968, 48,000, 7.0 km²) in the Chukyo area, and Senri (1962, 89,000, 11.6 km²), Senboku (1967, 142,000, 15.6 km²), Rakusai (1976, 28,000, 2.6 km²), Hokusetsu Sanda and Kobe Research Park (1981, 56,000, 12.0 km²) and Seishin (1982, 92,000, 5.8 km²) in the Keihanshin area. For the new towns established before the 1970s, several issues have emerged recently including that of an aging population, beginning in the late 1990s (Fukuhara 1998, 2001; Kagawa 2001, etc.).

6.2.2 Overview of Senri New Town

Among the new towns mentioned above, Senri New Town was the very first new town established in Japan, and it celebrated its 50th anniversary in 2012. One of the frequently mentioned advantages of Senri New Town is its efficient traffic flow. As shown in Figure 1, Senri New Town is located approximately 10km from downtown Osaka and has excellent access to Shinkansen (bullet train), domestic flights and the expressways. However, after reaching a peak of 130,000 in 1975, the population dropped continuously to 89,000 in 2010: only approximately 68% of its peak population.

In recent years, Senri New Town has shown signs of population stabilisation due to new migration of people into the town, as evidenced in the increased supply of condominiums. In other words, the positive evaluation of the town in terms of its efficient traffic flow and favour-

The Aged Society in a Suburban New Town: What Should We Do?

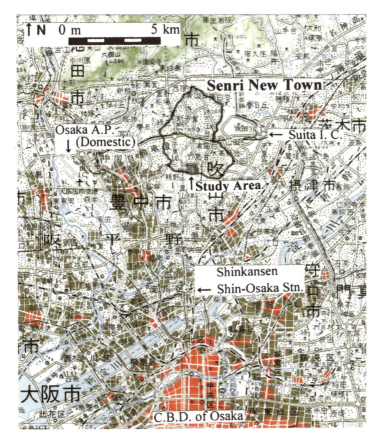

Figure 1   Study area
Source: Topographic map 1/200,000 "Kyoto and Osaka" (2012)

able environment, as mentioned above, has led to a construction boom for new residences, responding to the demand of migrants for a new home. New development is divided into two categories – those that utilize green hillsides and surplus lands, and others that rebuild and redevelop old condominiums. For the latter, a number of developments and redevelopments have taken place since the Private Financial Initiative Act (PFI) was promulgated in 1999.

6.2.3   Aging of population in Senri New Town

There are two factors that have caused an aging population in Senri New Town. One is the absolute population aging in which the elderly population (population above 65 years old) increases as residents get age. The other is the relative population aging, which occurs when second-generation residents (children of the first residents) leave their parents' home for university, work or marriage etc., leading to an increase in the ratio of the first-generation residents or parental generation (Kagawa 2006). Since both of these aging factors have been ex-

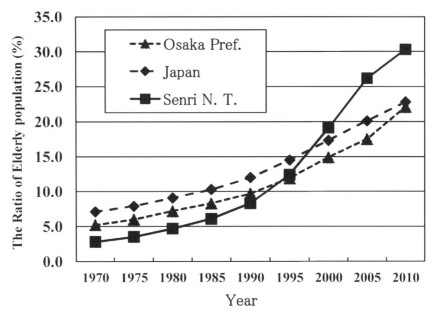

Figure 2 The ratio of elderly population in Japan, Osaka Prefecture and Senri New Town
Source: Population Census

perienced in Senri New Town, the percentage of the elderly population is higher even when compared to the total elderly population of Japan and that of Osaka, as shown in Figure 2. The census data of 2010 shows that the elderly population of Senri New Town has reached 30.3%.

If such population shift is occurring in the oldest large-scale new town in Japan, other "new towns" developed in the same concept will sooner or later experience a similar phenomenon. In fact, Tama New Town, which is the oldest and largest new town in the Tokyo Metropolis, is experiencing a similar situation as in Senri, and various projects have been implemented to address the social changes (Miyazawa 2004a, 2004b, 2006, 2010; Ueno and Matsumoto 2012). There are similar reports about Senri New Town (Narumi and Yamamoto 2005; Suguta 2005).

It is not unusual to hear stories about new towns becoming old towns. In the coming years, it is all the more important to have an attitude that seeks sustainable development of new towns in a post-growth society. While meeting the needs of the remaining first generation residents, it is also necessary to aim for a new town where young families can find condominiums in a comfortable environment. The aim of this study is to understand, from a geographical perspective, where we should focus our efforts, and how development should be done to accommodate a diverse population over his/her lifespans.

6.3 Aging of population in Momoyamadai district
6.3.1 Aging of population according to housing types

The aging population of Senri New Town, as mentioned in the previous section, is not a universal phenomenon within this new town. The author already described in full detail the aging of the population according to the housing types in Momoyamadai District of Senri New Town (Kagawa 2001). In this study, the national census data after 2001 is taken into account and the results are interpreted in the same manner for the same district.

Momoyamadai District is located at the southernmost part of Senri New Town, with Minami-Senri station of the Hankyu Railway in the east, and Momoyamadai Station of the Kita-Osaka Kyuko Railway, directly connected to Midosuji line operated by Osaka Municipal Subway, in the west. Both of these stations are located within approximately a 10-minute walk from the south entrance of Momoyamadai Elementary School, which is close to the heart of the Momoyamadai District. The houses in this district are clustered according to type and arranged in a mosaic-like pattern (Figure 3). For the national census data before 2000, when the census data was not yet released in a simplified form, the population can be analysed according to age group and gender for each housing type.

Using the national census from 1970 onwards, when Senri New Town was established,

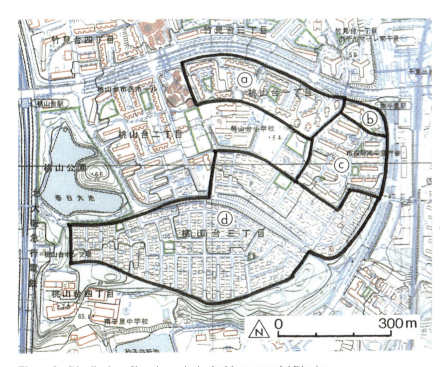

Figure 3　Distribution of housing units in the Momoyamadai District
　　　　　Source: Topographic map 1/10,000 "Suita" (2005)
　　　　　ⓐ: Public housing (rented, 5-storey)
　　　　　ⓑ: Semi-public housing (rented, 12-storey)
　　　　　ⓒ: Semi-public housing (owner-occupied, 5-storey)
　　　　　ⓓ: Detached houses (owner occupied)
　　　　　Note: ⓑ changed to high-rise private condominiums (owner-occupied)

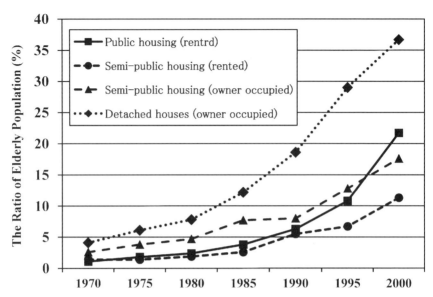

Figure 4 The ratio of elderly population in the Momoyamadai District by housing type
Source: Population Census

Figure 4 shows the progress of the aging of population for each housing type of Momoyamadai District indicated on Figure 3. From Figure 4, it can be observed that the aging of the population had progressed from the earliest period in detached houses, which has become a more expensive type of housing than others since the 1970s. Judging from the latest data (in 2000) found in the figure, the ratio of the elderly population can be estimated to exceed 40% at present. However, in recent years, aging of the proportion of elderly has progressed most rapidly in rented public condominiums.

6.3.2 Aging of population in rented public condominiums

Public housing in Momoyamadai District is made up of 5-storey condominiums (Figure 5) with no elevator. Within one of in the first block of Senri New Town as shown in Figure 3 (ⓐ), there are 613 housing units that were first occupied in 1967. Each of the housing units has a floor area no greater than 50m^2 but has 2-3 rooms, which are mainly in a unique Japanese style. However, the room plan of these housing units is not suitable for an extended family with three generations.

In this chapter, the population structure will be compared in four stages, in four decades from 1970 to 2000 using the national census. In 1970, immediately after the first occupation (Figure 6), it is apparent that the population structure consisted of couples around age 30 with children. This age structure continued shifting upwards, even in 1980 (Figure 7) and 1990 (Figure 8). However, by 2000 (Figure 9), it can be understood that the second generation residents (children of the first residents) had begun to move out from the town. In other words, the

The Aged Society in a Suburban New Town: What Should We Do?   97

Figure 5 Public housing in the Momoyamadai District
Source: Kagawa photographed (2012)

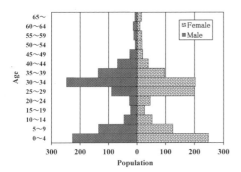

Figure 6 Population structure of public housing in the Momoyamadai District, 1970
Source: Population Census

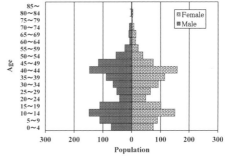

Figure 7 Population structure of public housing in the Momoyamadai District, 1980
Source: Population Census

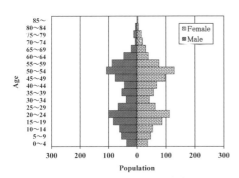

Figure 8 Population structure of public housing in the Momoyamadai District, 1990
Source: Population Census

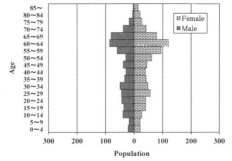

Figure 9 Population structure of public housing in the Momoyamadai District, 2000
Source: Population Census

second generation residents began to live independently from their parents in the 1990s, leaving for university, employment, marriage, and etc., while most of the first generation residents continued to age, joining the elderly population. Thus, absolute population aging and relative population aging, occurred at the same time.

6.4 Inconveniences experienced by elderly residents

In rented public condominiums where aging of population is rapidly progressing, it is supposed that elderly residents may experience great inconvenience due to the unavailability of elevators in the buildings. Also, these residents are most likely to have difficulties in filling out questionnaires or answering interviews as they get older. With these considerations in mind, questionnaires were distributed in August 2012, and collected through the postal mail after being filled out. The author asked those respondents who would agree to be interviewed

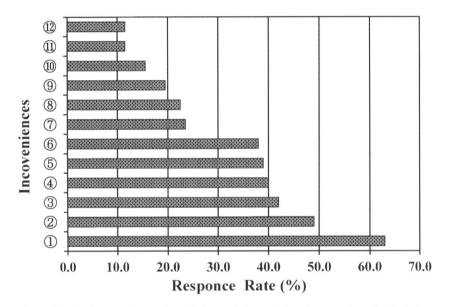

Figure 10 The inconveniences that elderly people in public housing experience inside their house
Source: Questionnaire survey
① Wall and window condensation during winter
② Bathroom step
③ Door defects inside the home
④ Toilet
⑤ Balcony and room step
⑥ Bathtub height
⑦ Inconvenience in use of gas and water
⑧ Drying clothes
⑨ Step at the main door
⑩ Step at the room entrance
⑪ Inconvenience in use of gas in the bathroom
⑫ Others in home

to indicate this on their questionnaire.

The questionnaires were distributed to housing units except those that were clearly vacant. Out of 580 questionnaires distributed to the residents, 200 or 34.5% of them were answered. The main results of the survey are summarized as follows.

Among the questionnaire items, multiple choices were recorded regarding the inconveniences that are likely to affect elderly residents were provided for these areas: inside the home, areas surrounding the home (stairs and around the building), and in and out of the district. Respondents were asked to indicate which features were indeed inconveniences. Furthermore, they were also asked to state the clear reason behind the inconveniences.

Figure 10 shows the inconveniences that they reported experiencing inside the home. The areas of inconvenience respondents indicated with the greatest frequency were "Wall and window condensation during winter" with more than 60%; "Bathroom step", "Door defects inside the home" and "Toilet" with some 40%; "Balcony and room step" and "Bathtub height" with around 30%; and "Inconvenience in use of gas and water" and "Drying clothes" with around 20%. From these results, it became clear that the elderly respondents experience a lot

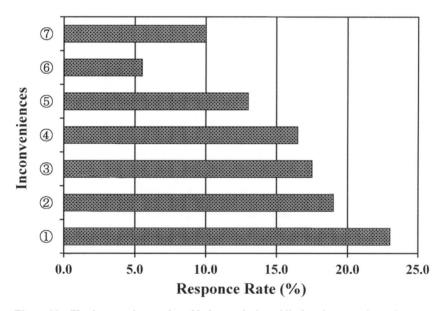

Figure 11 The inconveniences that elderly people in public housing experience in areas surrounding their home
Source: Questionnaire survey
① Height of each stair step
② Step between the building stair hall and house door
③ Mailbox access located at the ground floor
④ Long stairs within the district
⑤ Small step between the road and the outdoor staircase
⑥ Handrail at the stairs
⑦ Others in areas surrounding home

of barriers in their immediate living space. Thus, it is very important to plan and improve the housing units in line with the results from housing studies.

Figure 11 shows the inconveniences that they experience in areas surrounding their home. Starting from the highest to the lowest, the areas of inconvenience felt most frequently were "Height of each stair step" with more than 20%; and "Step between the building stair hall and house door", "Mailbox access located at the ground floor", "Long stairs (within the district)" and "Small step between the road and the outdoor staircase" with around 10%. As shown in Figure 12 and Figure 13, those towns developed on hillsides have long flights of stairs throughout the areas. On the other hand, when the abovementioned result is compared with the barriers that these elderly residents experience in their own homes, the inconveniences in areas surrounding the home are relatively few. Thus, it can be considered that elderly residents do not frequently go out of their homes.

Figure 13 shows the inconveniences that they experience in and out of the district. Starting from the highest to the lowest, the areas of inconvenience most frequently "Difficulty of access of the neighbourhood centres" and "Frequent usage of stairs or frequent walking up hills" both with more than 20%; and "Difficulty using Momoyamadai Station", "Fear of the possi-

Figure 12 Long stairs within the district
Source: Kagawa photographed (2012)

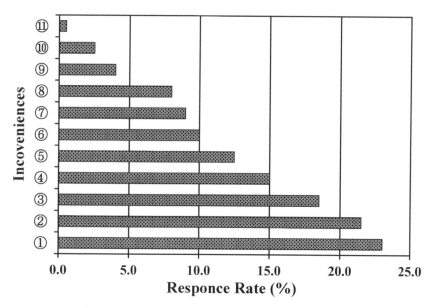

Figure 13 The inconveniences that elderly people in public housing experience in and out of the district
Sauce: Result of questionnaire
① Difficulty of access of the neighbourhood centres
② Frequent usage of stairs or frequent walking up hills
③ Difficulty of using Momoyamadai Station
④ Fear of the possibility of getting hit by car
⑤ Difficulty of getting around areas within Momoyamadai Station
⑥ Difficulty of using Minamisenri Station
⑦ Difficulty of access to the hospital
⑧ Difficulty of using area centre (Minami Centre)
⑨ Difficulty of using Central Osaka (Umeda District)
⑩ Difficulty of using central area of new town (Senri Chuo)
⑪ Difficulty of using Central Osaka (Namba District)

bility of getting hit by a car", "Difficulty in getting around areas within Momoyamadai Station" and "Difficulty in using Minami-senri Station", each with around 10%. The reason behind the inconveniences experienced by many elderly respondents in using and getting around Momoyamadai Station is that, the station has a complex structure, built between the inbound and outbound Shin-Midosuji main road that is parallel to the train line and has ground-level service roads on both sides. In other words, the users of Momoyamadai Station need to go down the stairs under the service road, up the stairs to reach the lobby over the Shin-Midosuji main road, and go back down the stairs again from the ticket gate to reach the platform. Although a separate ticket gate was recently established to make the station barrier-free, this access requires traversing a longer distance. Among various discussions regarding the barriers in public transportation, it is worth mentioning the statement by Aoki (2011), who suggested that organization and system should be considered for sustainable development aside from its structural material aspects. Based on the percentage of answers, it is considered that elderly residents rarely leave home to go out of town, just as they rarely leave their homes.

As for those elderly residents who prefer to be interviewed, most of them experienced inconvenience due to the unavailability of a lift. Installation of a lift seems difficult considering the fact that it has been 45 years since the completion of the condominiums when this research was conducted, and the structure of the building also prevents such installation. Osaka Prefectural Housing Corporation, which manages this public housing, is hesitant to provide a lift due to lack of sufficient financial resources. They do, however, provide a service that allows elderly residents living on the third and fourth floors to transfer to the ground floor or first floor. As long as it is difficult to implement structural material improvements, it may be necessary to continue efforts of improvement through such non-structural means.

6.5   Conclusion: Towards sustainable development for new towns

Although there are numerous elderly residents in Senri New Town, services should not be focused solely on elderly residents. Otherwise, too much focus on welfare for elderly residents may lead to the risks of making the community less appealing to the younger generation. As seen in the questionnaires and interviews of most elderly respondents, they have a strong wish to co-exist with the younger generation in Senri New Town. To realize their hope, it is necessary to devise plans to attract the younger generation who want to settle in Senri New Town. Furthermore, considering the fact that, in an aging society, it is not unusual to see the first generation residents (parents) and the second generation residents (their children) living near each other's houses (Kagawa 2011), there is a need to devise plans to keep the second generation residents within the new town when they leave their parents' house careers and families of their own.

One such plan is the development of houses to meet the second generation's demand, and another is the development of the community's environment. These measures should apply not only to Senri New Town, but also to other new towns and all mature residential areas of the aging society.

Supposing that the Private Financial Initiative Act as mentioned in section 2.2 was actively implemented, and many new condominiums were to be supplied in Senri New Town. It is presumed that there would be new families migrating to the area, and many of them would have younger children. Therefore, it would be desirable for such communities to have facilities where residents of all age groups could enjoy comfortable living. Also, barrier-free living for elderly residents should have a universal design to provide convenience to other age groups at the same time. Among several attempts that have been observed, a traffic device that regulates the speed of bicycles as mentioned in Figure 14 is an excellent example of a purposefully built barrier. Since riding a bicycle on the pavement is allowed in Japan, it is important to take proactive measures in order to prevent collisions between bicycle riders and pedestrians.

Figure 14 A traffic device (barrier) that regulates the speed of bicycles (Takemidai District next to the Momoyamadai District)
Source: Kagawa photographed (2012)

Besides facilities achieving universal design, it is possible to develop communities in a way that residents of all generations can live in comfort by promoting intergenerational exchange through the establishment of nurseries and kindergartens alongside senior care centres, and by providing a wide range of goods in supermarkets and convenience stores.

Since Senri New Town is the oldest new town in Japan, it is highly likely that several attempts in Senri will be adopted in other new towns. To say the least, observations and records of the attempts made for the improvement of Senri New Town should be referenced when conducting a study about the new towns in Japan.

Acknowledgements

This study made use of the Grant-in-aid for Scientific Research 2012-14 (Basic Research Program C "Geographical Research on the Environmental Management for the Sustainable Development of Mature Residential Area", Principal Researcher: Takashi Kagawa, Issue No.: 24520887).

This paper is corrected by D.W. Edgington at the University of British Columbia. A part of this study is included in 'The Necessity for the Universal Design to the New Town in the Mature Period: A Case Study of Public Housing Units in the Momoyamadai, Senri New Town, Osaka Prefecture' (in Todokoro, T. 2014 *"Compact City and Town Planning"*, Kokon-Shoin Press, Tokyo. In Japanese, and in printing.).

I offer this paper to Dr. Takeo Tanioka, the former President of Ritsumeikan University who died in June, 2014. Dr. Tanioka enacted the sectional leader of IGU historical geography commission, and had built the base of internationalization of Ritsumeikan University.

References

Aoki, M. 2011. For sustainable public transport: The need for three kinds of seamless service. Bulletin of Commerce and Economics (Kinki University) 57 (3): 667-676. (J)

Fukuhara, M. 1998. *The present condition of New Towns: Reality and dream for fortieth anniversary*. Tokyo: Tokyo Shimbun Publishing. (J)

Fukuhara, M. 2001. *Let's revive New Towns: For the revival by people's exchange*. Tokyo: Kokon-Shoin. (J)

Howard, E. 1898. *To-Morrow: A peaceful path to real reform*. London: Swan Sonnenschein and Co. Ltd. (Digitally printed version: Cambridge University Press, New York, 2010).

Kagawa, T. 2001. Aging of new town a case of Senri new town. In *Human activity and environmental change*, ed. A. Yoshikoshi, 139-154. Tokyo: Kokon-Shoin. (J)

Kagawa, T. 2006. Shrinking population and the society of metropolitan region: Decrease in population and aging in Senri New Town, Osaka. *Toukei* 57 (1): 2-9. (J)

Kagawa, T. 2011.The separation of parents and their adult children in an aging society with below replacement fertility: A case study of Senri New Town in the northwest part of Suita City, Osaka Prefecture. *Japanese Journal of Human Geography* 63: 209-228. (J)

Kagawa, T. 2015. The necessity of the universal design for new town in the mature period: A case study of public housing units in the Momoyamadai District, Senri New Town, Osaka Prefecture. In *Compact city and town planning*. ed. T. Todokoro, in press. Tokyo: Kokon Shoin. (J)

Miyazawa, H. 2004a. The urban built environment and inaccessibility: A case of study on the early developed area of Tama New Town, Tokyo. *Japanese Journal of Human Geography*, 56: 1-20. (J)

Miyazawa, H. 2004b. Living environment evaluation by persons with lower-limb impairment and their strategies to access activity opportunities in the early developed area of Tama New Town, Tokyo, Japan. *Geographical Review of Japan*, 77 (3): 133-156. (J)

Miyazawa, H. 2006. The changing face of suburban New Towns in large metropolitan areas: The case of Tama New Town, Tokyo. *Annals of the Japan Association of Economic Geographers*, 52: 236-250. (J)

Miyazawa, H. 2010. The present condition and the future of suburban New Town: The case of Tama New Town, Tokyo. Research on Household Economics 87: 32-41. (J)

Narumi, K. and Yamamoto, S. 2005. Some problems of New Town in the society of shrinking population: A case of Senri New Town. Urban Housing Science 49: 3-8. (J)

Perry, C. A. 1929. *The Neighborhood unit in regional survey of New York and its environs*. Committee on regional plan of New York and its environs, New York.

Suguta, H. 2005. *Machizukuri* activities in Senri New Town and its social capital. *Urban*

Housing Science 49: 15-21. (J)

Ueno, J. and Matsumoto,M. 2012. *Legend and topics on Tama New Town.* Tokyo : Kajima Institute Publishing Co., Ltd. (J)

(J) means "written in Japanese" (with an English summary, in some cases).

106

7. Urban Policy Challenges Facing an Aging Society: The Case of the Tokyo Metropolitan Area

Tetsuya ITO, Nobuyuki IWAMA and Makoto HIRAI

Abstract

This study examined socio-economic reconfiguration in urbanized areas experiencing population decrease through a case study of the northwestern part of the Tokyo Metropolitan Area (TMA), and discussed urban policy challenges for an aging society. The results indicated that the population has tended to decline in the TMA fringe area beyond 50 kilometers from the central TMA. Analysis of the study area in the TMA fringe area revealed that the population has just begun to decline around urban centers together with natural and social population decline. In particular, the aging of the population has exerted a strong influence over population decline in urban centers. The elderly in urban centers have not yet faced the problem of low accessibility of retail stores, but we can assume from the fact that many of the elderly went shopping primarily on foot or by bicycle that they will face those problems in the near future. Social connections of some elderly residents were also weakening, and they may become isolated from local community in the urban centers. According to the results of our survey questionnaire, inhabitants rated three types of issues as the most important urban policy challenges: countermeasures to population aging, urban policies to counteract economic decline in urban centers, and countermeasures to the falling birth rate.

Keywords

Tokyo metropolitan area, Fringe area, Population decline, Population aging, Urban policy challenges

7.1 Introduction

The number of in-migrants into metropolitan areas increased during the period of rapid economic growth following WWII in Japan. Rapid population growth, mainly due to in-migrants from rural areas with high birth rates, expanded metropolitan areas, including the three major areas of Tokyo, Nagoya and Osaka. This growth also expanded the fringe along the outside edge of the metropolis, which had historically had social or economic connections with large city centers through economic or daily life activities.

After peaking in 2005, the Japanese total population began to decline; fewer children were born, and the elderly population continued to grow. The National Institute of Population and Social Security Research ed. (2002) has estimated that by 2035, Japan's population will have decreased to 92.1% of its 2005 peak of 127 million. In the metropolitan area as a whole, while there is expected to be an increase in mortality of the elderly and lower birth rates, changes in population are expected to be slight due to the in-migration of young people from others region of Japan (Esaki 2006).

It is true that population changes in metropolitan areas are likely to be much smaller than in rural areas. When we look more closely at the areal pattern of demographic change, however, population changes from place to place mainly due to the distance from the center of the metropolitan area to the suburbs. In this study we use the case of the Tokyo Metropolitan Area (TMA) as an example. In the area around the TMA that consist largely of the municipalities in the Tokyo Metropolitan Government and three prefectures—Chiba, Saitama and Kanagawa—, the decreases in population of the suburban cities along the fringe are a stark contrast

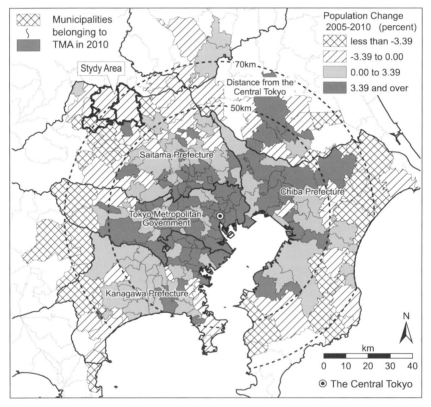

Figure 1 Population changes in the Tokyo Metropolitan Area, 2005-2010
Source: Population census 2010
Note: The Tokyo Metropolitan Area consists of 23 wards called "Tokubetsu-Ku" in Tokyo metropolitan government, 5 government-ordinance-designated cities called "Seirei-Shi" that include 44 administrative districts or "Gyosei-Ku", and 192 cities, towns and villages or "Shi-Cho-Son". This figure illustrates 259 municipalities (23 wards, 44 "Gyosei-Ku," 192 "Shi-Cho-Son"), excluding the "Seirei-Shi" in the TMA.

to the population increases occurring in the central part of the TMA (Figure 1). This population decline will lead to shrinking metropolitan areas on one side. On the other, it will also lead to a stagnation of economic and social activities (Ito et al. 2012). The elderly are likely to be isolated from their local communities and families in the urbanized area (Iwama ed. 2011). Moreover, the local economy is likely to gradually decline because consumption patterns of the elderly population are much lower than those of younger people.

The purpose of this study was to examine socio-economic reconfiguration in urbanized areas experiencing population decreases through a case study of the northwestern part of the TMA, and to discuss the urban policy challenges of an aging society. We focused on demographic changes by municipality and small areas based on statistical analysis; we also considered socio-economic changes through the analysis of daily activities based on a survey questionnaire administered by the authors in sample areas. Finally, the pressing urban policy challenges of an aging society are discussed based on the results of the questionnaire.

The study area was composed of three municipalities—Kumagaya City, Fukaya City and Yorii Town in the Saitama Prefecture—located on the northwestern fringe of the TMA beyond a radius of approximately 60 kilometers from the TMA center (Figure 1). According to the 2010 census, these cities had the following populations: Kumagaya, 203,180; Fukaya, 144,618; Yorii, 35,774. Together, the total population of these municipalities was 383,576, corresponding to 5.3% of the population of the Saitama Prefecture (7,194,556). Historically, these municipalities were characterized as a center of transportation and commerce in the northern part of the Kanto Region. They were modernized by the textile industry during the late 19th century, and then continued to experience development through the machine industry like automobile parts production and electrical industry like television production during the period of rapid economic growth. The people living in these areas can now easily reach central Tokyo by rail or highway. Using the well-developed public transportation infrastructure, many commuters make the daily round trip to the central TMA for school or work. These municipalities are defined as a northwestern part of the Kanto Metropolitan Area by the Japanese Statistics Bureau on the basis of commuting flows using census data. This study defines the Kanto Metropolitan Area as a part of the TMA that has socio-economic ties with Tokyo, and consists of 23 wards called "Tokubetsu-Ku" in the Tokyo metropolitan government, 5 government-ordinance- designated cities called "Seirei-Shi" that include 44 administrative districts or "Gyosei-Ku," and 192 cities, towns and villages or "Shi-Cho-Son".

7.2 Regional characteristics of population change

This chapter first explains regional patterns of population change by municipalities in the TMA between 2005 and 2010. It then considers demographic changes and the spatial distribution of the elderly through a case study of a sample area on a small scale.

7.2.1 Population change of three municipalities

Figure 1 illustrates the population changes in the TMA between 2005 and 2010, according to the census data. In this subsection, we discuss the population changes in the figure that shows 259 municipalities (23 wards, 44 administrative districts or "Gyosei-Ku," 192 cities, towns and villages or "Shi-Cho-Son") in the TMA. The figure offers a perspective of the contrast in regional demographic patterns between the central TMA and the metropolitan fringe. While the population in and around the central TMA shows a slight increase, that in the metropolitan fringe between 50-70km from the central TMA has tended to decline. The metropolitan fringe includes 58 municipalities, among which 44 municipalities had decreased in population, which show us the legend less than 0 % on the figure 1. The number of municipalities that decreased in population (44 municipalities) was 3.1 times larger than that of municipalities with populations that increased 0 % or more (14 municipalities). In contrast, the population in and around the central part of TMA shows a slight increase. Out of 179 municipalities all of which were located within a 50km radius of the central TMA, which we can consider as the area in and around central TMA, 149 municipalities had populations that increased 0% or more, which was 5.0 times larger than the number of municipalities with populations that decreased less than 0 % (30 municipalities). In addition, the population living between 50-70km from the central TMA in 2010 had dwindled by -0.1% compared to 2005; in contrast, the population within a 50km radius from the central TMA grew by 3.8%.

Figure 1 also indicates that the population decreased slightly from 2005 to 2010 in both sample municipalities. The total population of the three municipalities in 2010 had dropped by -1.22%; meanwhile, that of the Saitama Prefecture as a whole increased by 1.99% (Saitama Prefecture 2012). Specifically, the population in Kumagaya fell by -0.73%, in Fukaya by -1.35 % and in Yorii by -3.47% between 2005 and 2010. These municipalities, therefore, were characterized by overall population decrease compared to other areas of the Saitama Prefecture.

These population decreases were related not only to the greater number of out-migrants than in-migrants into these municipalities during the period, but also to the natural population decline caused by a higher number of deaths than births in an aging population. The data in Table 1 allowed us to determine population decline due to the greater number of out-migrants than in-migrants into each municipality. According to the rate of increase per mil (1,000 persons) using migration data between 2005 and 2010, the population level grew by less than 0 per mil in every city except Kumagaya in 2007. It is also reasonable to conclude from the data that the population decline was partly due to a higher death rate than birth rate, according to the crude natural rate of increase per mil. This crude natural rate kept population increase levels to less than 0 per mil every year since 2005 in Kumagaya and Yorii, and since 2007, they have fallen to less than 0 per mil in Fukaya as well. Additionally, looking at women's total fertility rate, we see a trend toward fewer children per family. The total fertility rate of Yorii and Kumagaya has been less than that of Saitama Prefecture and Japan since 2006.

Table 1　Demographic trends in the sample municipalities, 2000-2010

City/ Region	Demographic movement		Year										
			2000	'01	'02	'03	'04	'05	'06	'07	'08	'09	'10
Kumagaya	Total fertility rate		N.D.	N.D.	N.D.	N.D.	1.20	1.29	1.15	1.25	1.21	1.22	1.32
	Rate of natural increase	per mil	2.7	2.7	1.6	1.7	0.9	0.6	−0.3	0.0	−1.1	−0.9	−1.6
	Rate of social increase	per mil	−12.2	−0.5	−3.3	−4.5	1.4	−3.8	−1.5	0.3	−2.6	−0.9	−1.8
Fukaya	Total fertility rate		N.D.	N.D.	N.D.	N.D.	1.34	1.46	1.36	1.29	1.26	1.32	1.43
	Rate of natural increase	per mil	3.6	2.2	2.8	1.9	1.9	1.4	1.0	−0.3	−0.3	−0.2	−1.0
	Rate of social increase	per mil	2.2	0.0	−3.9	−3.0	−3.2	−1.8	−1.4	−1.6	−0.7	−0.6	−8.8
Yorii	Total fertility rate		N.D.	N.D.	N.D.	N.D.	1.01	1.12	1.17	1.02	1.22	1.07	1.2
	Rate of natural increase	per mil	0.0	0.3	−1.1	−2.0	−2.2	−2.5	−2.1	−3.6	−2.7	−3.4	−3.4
	Rate of social increase	per mil	−1.7	−0.5	1.3	−2.5	−1.4	−8.5	−3.5	−3.3	−2.6	−3.8	−8.8
Saitama Prefecture	Total fertility rate		1.30	1.24	1.23	1.21	1.20	1.22	1.24	1.26	1.28	1.28	1.32
	Rate of natural increase	per mil	3.9	3.6	3.3	2.8	2.6	1.8	1.9	1.6	1.4	1.1	0.7
	Rate of social increase	per mil	−2.0	2.0	0.8	1.5	1.0	−3.1	1.6	2.2	3.2	3.1	2.6
Japan	Total fertility rate		1.36	1.33	1.32	1.29	1.29	1.26	1.32	1.34	1.37	1.37	1.39
	Rate of natural increase	per mil	1.8	1.6	1.4	0.9	0.7	−0.2	0.1	−0.1	−0.4	−0.6	−1.0

Sources: Database created by Saitama Prefecture
Note: "N.D." means no data.

7.2.2　Areal pattern of population change

We then analyzed areal patterns of population change through a case study of the three municipalities on a small scale using census data. Figure 2 presents population distribution patterns and increases by small residential districts (Chocho) in each municipality between 2000 and 2010. The figure indicates contrasting population changes for areal conditions even in the same municipality. While the population has basically declined in a large part of this area, the population was maintained or increased slightly in small parts of the urbanized area along main roads mainly due to in-migrants from other residential districts within the same municipality. The number of districts with less than 100% population change that means population decrease reached 286 districts, which corresponded to 67.9% of the 421 districts (excluding 50 districts with "No Data") in the three municipalities. This means that population has basically declined in a large part of this area. In particular, population declined in suburban areas 2km or more from each JR station (beyond the 2km radius from the center) and in a large part of the central area of each municipality. On the other hand, mainly due to in-migrants from other residential districts within the same municipality, the population was maintained or increased slightly in small parts of the urbanized area along main roads connecting the north Kanto region with central Tokyo. Several residential estates were developed in these areas, as well as in a few districts of the central city, where there are several large newly built apartments. It is noteworthy that the population has just begun to decline around the urban centers, which contain not only economic facilities such as retail shops or offices, but also cultural and service facilities including schools and city halls.

The observed population decrease was caused by several factors. As already noted, the birth rate and social population change has been declining, while there has been a concurrent

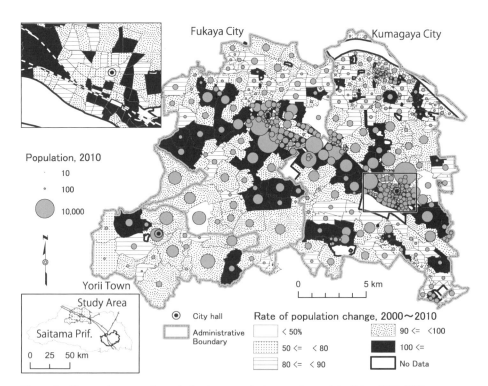

Figure 2 The areal pattern of population increases in the sample municipalities, 2000-2010
Source: Population census 2000 and 2010

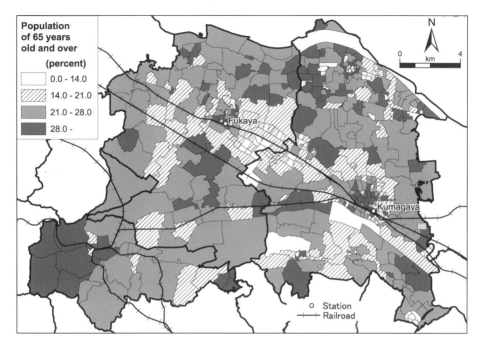

Figure 3 The distribution pattern of aging people of 65 years old and over, 2010
Source: Population census 2010

increase in the number of deaths associated with a rapidly aging population. The census data show that the population is definitely aging in these municipalities. In 2005, the population of those 65 years and over in the three municipalities was already higher than that in Saitama Prefecture (16.4 percent): Kumagaya 18.3%; Fukaya 18.0%; and Yorii 20.3%. Kumagaya and Fukaya were, however, slightly lower than the national average (20.2 percent). In 2010, the percentage of elderly in Kumagaya had increased by 3.5 points (to 21.8%), in Fukaya by 3.4 points (21.4%), and in Yorii by 3.9 points (24.2%). These increases were larger than the national average of 2.8 points (23.0%).

Figure 3 illustrates the distribution pattern of those 65 years of age and over in 2010. The figure shows that a large part of the study area was classified as having an elderly population of more than 14%, which generally represents an index of demographic aging in Japan (Jinkogaku Kenkyukai ed. 2010). Districts with more than 21% also represented concentrated areas of aging population. Districts with rates higher than 21% were mainly concentrated in the suburban rural area beyond the 2km radius and in the urban center around the JR Kumagaya Station and Fukaya Station. Thirty-five districts were classified as having more than 21% of the population 65 years and over within the 2km radius from the JR Kumagaya Station, which contains 55 districts; 16 out of 29 districts within a 2km radius of the JR Fukaya Station were designated as having the highest percentage population of elderly (28%+). As mentioned earlier, these districts have also lost population gradually. It is reasonable to conclude that the

114

aging population has had a large influence on population decline in the urban centers.

7.3 Areal characteristics of citizens' daily life activities

Based on the questionnaire responses in the sample areas in August 2011, we attempted to clarify the areal characteristics of daily life from a socio-economic point of view. We selected two sample areas located in the urban center of Kumagaya (Hongoku) and Fukaya (Higashi-Ohnuma). Both have faced the problems of the population aging. Additionally, the questionnaire survey was administered in suburban residential areas of Kumaga (Tamai) and Fukaya (Arai & Akedo-Higashi) so that results could be compared between the urban center and suburban areas in each city. The questionnaire asked about: 1) family configuration; 2) consumption behavior; and 3) relationship with families and local communities. Interviewers circulated the questionnaire to all residents of the four districts (2,148 households). They received responses from 564 households for a response rate of 26.3% (Table 2).

According to the results, 81.7% of household heads were male and 17.6% were female; 51.1% of respondents (288 households) were classified into a group labeled "aging households" in which the head of the household was age 65 or older. Among aging households, 77.4% of household heads were male. Concerning the urban center, the rate of the aging households was as high as 56.9% in Kumagaya and 48.7% in Fukaya. In contrast, 39.5% of households in suburban Kumagaya were classified as "younger", meaning that household heads were age 50 or younger.

With regard to family configuration, the rate of single households was more than 30% in the urban center of Kumagaya, the highest value in the sample areas. In the other three districts, the rate of households with more than three people was over 50%. When we looked at aging households, the same tendency could be seen. In the urban center of Kumagaya, 32.8% of the elderly were single, but many elderly tended to live with their families in the other areas.

7.3.1 The areal patterns of shopping behaviors, with a focus on the elderly

The deterioration of the life environment of the elderly has been a serious problem in Japan. Therefore, we focused our research on elder residents' life environments. In particular, we paid attention to shopping environments. The research indicated that the elderly have not yet faced problems relating to low accessibility of retail stores in neighborhoods in the urban center. We assume, however, that many will face such problems in the near future, mainly due to the aging of the population.

As can be seen in Table 2, 77.4% of elderly residents were able to shop for daily foods at supermarkets in their neighborhood. Only 2.4% used small family shops. Even in the urban center of Kumagaya, which is located in the central shopping street area, only 4.2% of residents used family shops; 87.4% of the elderly population used the neighborhood supermarket. In suburban Kumagaya and the urban center of Fukaya, we found similar shopping behaviors.

Table 2   Shopping behavior of those 65 years and older in the sample areas, 2011 (percentage)

	Total	Kumagaya city		Fukaya city	
		Urban center	Suburban area	Urban center	Suburban area
Total number of respondents (households)	(564)	(209)	(172)	(76)	(107)
The number of households headed by individuals 65 or older (aging households)	51.1 (288)	56.9 (119)	47.7 (82)	48.7 (37)	46.7 (50)
Daily food purchased in					
Family stores	2.4	4.2	1.2	• 2.7	0.0
Super market of same district	77.4	87.4	84.1	81.1	40.0
Super market in same city	11.8	2.5	6.1	10.8	44.0
Super market in different city	2.8	1.7	2.4	0.0	8.0
Other	2.8	2.5	4.9	0.0	2.0
No data	2.8	1.7	1.2	5.4	6.0
Travel time from house to grocery store					
Within 10 minutes	64.6	78.2	53.7	78.4	40.0
11 - 30 minutes	25.7	16.0	34.1	10.8	46.0
31 - 60 minutes	3.1	2.5	2.4	5.4	4.0
More than 61 minutes	0.7	0.8	1.2	0.0	0.0
No data	5.9	2.5	8.5	5.4	10.0
Frequency of shopping					
Every day	24.0	35.3	15.9	21.6	12.0
3 - 5 times per week	37.2	38.7	46.3	35.1	20.0
1 -2 times per week	33.3	21.8	35.4	37.8	54.0
1 -3 times per month	2.4	1.7	0.0	2.7	8.0
No data	3.1	2.5	2.4	2.7	6.0
Means of transportation					
On foot	25.3	55.5	0.0	16.2	2.0
By bicycle	23.3	31.1	18.3	37.8	2.0
By private car	46.6	10.9	76.9	40.6	86.0
Other	1.7	0	2.4	2.7	4.0
No data	3.1	2.5	2.4	2.7	6.0
Food delivery services					
Now using	12.5	7.6	19.5	13.5	12.0
Under consideration	11.8	10.9	12.2	10.8	14.0
No use	71.9	79.0	62.2	73.0	70.0
No data	3.8	2.5	6.1	2.7	4.0

Source: Questionnaire by the authors in August 2011.

In suburban Fukaya, however, where there are few food stores, more than 50% of the elderly population used suburban supermarkets located far from their houses. As to the frequency of daily shopping, 35.3% of the respondents reported shopping "almost every day" in the urban center of Kumagaya. In contrast, in suburban Fukaya, many people reported shopping only "once or twice per week".

In terms of traveling time from house to food stores, 78.2% of elderly residents in central Kumagaya and 78.4% of those in central Fukaya said that stores were "within 10 minutes" of their homes. Conversely in the case of suburban Fukaya, the percentage of respondents choosing the option "from 11 to 30 minutes" was 46.0%. In terms of transportation, many elderly residents in both urban centers reported traveling "on foot" or "by bicycle." However, many people answered "by car" in the other two districts. Especially in case of suburban Fukaya, 86.0% said they traveled "by car." Moreover, food delivery services, which have recently gotten popular in Japan, accounted for only 12.5% of residents in the four districts.

These results indicate that elderly residents in the urban centers of both cities have not yet faced problems of low accessibility to retail stores in their neighborhoods. But we can assume from the fact that many of the elderly went shopping on foot or by bicycle that those problems will arise in the near future, together with the aging of the population in the urban centers.

7.3.2 Social relationships within local communities

The findings discussed above reveal prospective social problems related to low accessibility of retail stores as the population aging. In Japan, urban social problems such as so-called "food deserts" have been caused not only by special factors, such as the distance between houses and grocery stores, but also by social factors like the isolation of individuals from social communities and families, which can be understood as social capital (Iwama ed. 2011). Geriatric gerontologists and nutritional scientists have pointed out that isolation from society often causes a decline in elderly people's intellectual activities, such as critical thinking and communication abilities. The drop in intellectual activity makes it difficult for the elderly to purchase and cook food, or communicate with neighbors (Kumagai et al. 2003). Therefore, in this study, we surveyed elderly individuals' social relationships with their families and local communities (Table 3). Factors investigated included: address of nearest family or relatives; brief contacts with neighbors where we asked, "Do you give a greeting to the neighbors when you meet them or not?; and information on family configuration where we asked, "Do you know the neighbor's family configuration or not?" These are frequently used items in the social sciences (Asakawa and Tamano 2010).

With regard to "address of nearest family or relatives," 40.5% of elderly residents in the urban center of Fukaya and 31.1% of those in central Kumagaya answered "same block." In suburban Kumagaya and Fukaya, around 30% also answered "same block." The questions about whether residents were "brief contacts with neighbors," and knew "information on fam-

Table 3 Relationships with family and local communities of those 65 years and older in the sample areas, 2011 (parcentage)

	Total	Kumagaya		Fukaya	
		Urban center	Suburban area	Urban center	Suburban area
The number of households headed by individuals 65 or older (aging households)	(288)	(119)	(82)	(37)	(50)
Address of nearest family member					
Same block	29.9	31.1	24.4	40.5	28.0
Same city	34.0	32.8	34.1	24.3	44.0
Same prefecture	21.2	19.3	28.0	18.9	16.0
Different prefecture	9.4	10.9	8.5	10.8	6.0
Other	2.1	2.5	2.4	2.7	0.0
No data	3.5	3.4	2.4	2.7	6.0
Brief contacts with neighbors					
Yes	93.7	95.8	92.7	91.9	92.0
No	2.8	2.5	2.4	5.4	2.0
No data	3.5	1.7	4.9	2.7	6.0
Information on family configuration					
Known	89.9	86.6	92.7	94.6	90.0
Unknown	5.9	10.9	1.2	2.7	4.0
No data	4.2	2.5	6.1	2.7	6.0

Source: Questionnaire by the authors in August 2011

ily configuration," also had high scores. Many inhabitants seemed to maintain good relationships within local communities. However, in the urban center of Kumagaya, 15.3% of the elderly did not know even the family configuration of their neighbors. This suggests that a proportion of the elderly are experiencing a weakening of connections, and that they may become isolated from their local communities. As already mentioned, not only low accessibility of retail stores but also decreased social capital like isolation often create the so-called food deserts issues in urban settings in Japan. This tendency is clear among single isolated elderly people. These findings suggest a high likelihood that serious urban social problems will occur, especially in urban centers, in the near future.

7.4 Need for urban policies for an aging society

As has been shown, several data trends have indicated that large urban centers face the aging of their populations due to both an increasing number of elderly and a decreasing number of births. Social problems caused by the population aging include not only low accessibility to retail stores that sell daily necessities such as fresh food, but also fewer chances of relationships with neighbors. In response to the population aging, citizens themselves have tried to organize volunteer groups to help the elderly with their daily lives. Members of a shopping association in Kumagaya, for instance, have organized a group named "Otasuketai," which means the group provides support services in order to maintain the daily life activities of the elderly living in their neighborhood. Additionally, municipalities have implemented several urban policies. It is extremely important for Japanese society, which shall soon face serious problems in terms of population aging, to introduce new types of urban policies for the aging, including both direct and indirect public subsidies.

This section therefore targets urban political challenges for an aging society from the viewpoint of the citizens' demand, according to the findings of our questionnaire survey. The survey was administered in August 2011, and respondents included 285 males and females. We selected two sample areas within the urban centers of Kumagaya and Fukaya, both of which have faced the problems of populating aging. The questionnaire survey allowed respondents to choose what they believed were the five most important issues from a list of 29 urban political challenges in either the "present" or the "near future" when we are likely to face more serious problems with population aging.

Table 4 shows the respondents' choices and ranking of these challenges in each sample area. Respondents chose a total of 999 issues in the "present" and 981 in the "near future" as the most important political subjects for the urban center of Kumagaya; these numbers were 374 in the "present" and 375 in the "near future" for the urban center of Fukaya. We define the total number of answers in each time period by the sample area as 100%, and calculate the percentage of the number of answer for each topic. An higher percentage, therefore, indicates political topics that inhabitants selected as more important. In the table, we highlight numbers with over 5% in italic-bold.

As can be seen in Table 4, fewer citizens attached a high value to measures having to do with public facilities (e.g., 6: Main roads' repair or development, or 18: Parking facilities development), or to measures to stimulate social systems or practices (e.g., 23: Promote measures of international exchange, or 27: Citizen' participation in the information society). This suggested that inhabitants felt a sufficient number of public facilities that had already been constructed in their urban center. It also indicated that many people didn't realize the importance of measures for social systems that tend to be less connected with their daily activities.

The table also reveals that inhabitants rated three types of topics as most important when it came to urban policy challenges. The first, concerning the aging population, had to do with increasing problems mainly in the urban center. The second focused on worsening economic decline in the central part of urbanized areas. Finally, the third was related to countermeasures regarding the falling birth rate that could result in a very serious situation in the near future.

Table 4 Need for urban policies to meet political challenges in sample areas, 2011 (percentage)

Urban political challenges	Kumagaya Urban center		Fukaya Urban center	
	Present	Near future	Present	Near future
1: Water quality improvement of rivers or lakes	2.1	0.8	0.5	0.8
2: Construction of parks or improvement of green space	4.3	3.3	4.8	4.5
3: Green zone preservation	3.4	2.1	2.1	1.1
4: Protection of public health from air pollution	*5.7*	1.9	1.9	2.4
5: Improvement of sewerage system	2.3	1.3	4.3	1.6
6: Main roads' repair or development	1.9	2.7	2.7	2.1
7. Improvement of bus line	*5.5*	*5.2*	2.9	4.3
8: Redevelopment in the urban center	*9.5*	*8.1*	*12.8*	*9.3*
9: Construction of municipal houses or housing estates	1.9	4.9	1.1	4.3
10: Promotion of cultural and artistic activities	1.9	1.6	2.1	1.6
11: Improvement of lifelong learning for the citizens	1.5	1.5	1.6	2.1
12: Improvement of nursery schools and kindergartens	3.2	*10.7*	3.5	*10.1*
13: Reformation of the public education system	2.9	4.4	3.7	2.9
14: Attract university and research facilities	1.3	4.2	2.7	*5.1*
15: Contract sports and leisure facilities	2.7	2.9	2.4	2.1
16: Improvement of health-care institutions	*12.2*	*10.1*	*13.6*	*12.0*
17: Welfare reform for the elderly and handicapped persons	*10.8*	*5.5*	*9.4*	4.8
18: Parking facilities development	0.9	1.0	1.3	0.5
19: Agriculture promotion	0.5	0.7	0.8	2.1
20: Industry promotion	2.2	4.2	3.7	*6.1*
21: Retail business promotion	*7.3*	*6.9*	*11.0*	*9.3*
22: Development of resort destinations or attractions for tourists	2.1	3.6	2.1	2.1
23: Promotion of measures for international exchange	0.2	0.5	0.3	0.5
24: Promotion of measures to increase participation of women in society	1.9	3.8	1.6	2.1
25: Promotion of re-employment of the elderly	*6.1*	3.4	4.5	3.5
26: Promotion of measures of NPO and volunteer activities	1.7	1.1	0.8	0.8
27: Citizen's participation in the information society	1.2	1.2	0.5	0.5
28: Citizen's participation in municipal government	2.1	1.4	0.3	0.3
29: Other	0.6	1.0	0.8	0.8
Total	100	100	100	100
(the number)	(999)	(981)	(374)	(375)

Source: Questionnaire by the authors in August 2011

Note: Numbers higher than 5% are emphasized with *italic-bold style*.

Concerning the aging population, more than 10% of respondents selected topic 16: Improvement of health-care institutions, in both the "present" and "near future", together with topic 17: Welfare reform for the elderly and handicapped persons in the "present". These results indicated that many citizens realized the increasing necessity of well-developed health care services and welfare programs in step with the population aging in each city. In terms of the economic decline in the central part of urbanized areas, more than 8% selected topic 8: Redevelopment in the urban center" for both periods of time in both cities, and topic 21: Retail business promotion" was rated above 7%. This showed that citizens widely recognized the urgent need for retail business promotion including urban redevelopment projects in the urban center. Finally, regarding countermeasures to the falling birth rate, over 10% of citizens selected topic 12: Improvement of nursery schools and kindergartens in the "near future". Rating of this last item in the "present" was only 4%, but in the "near future" time frame, the number increased significantly. It is reasonable to say that many inhabitants are interested in measures to counteract the falling birth rate that could be the source of serious social problems in the near future.

7.5 Conclusion

This study examined the socio-economic reconfiguration of urbanized areas experiencing population decreases through a case study of the northwestern part of the TMA, and discussed the urban policy challenges facing Japan's aging society. We focused on demographic changes by municipalities and small areas using statistical analysis, and on socio-economic changes through analysis of daily activity data gathered by a survey questionnaire. The urban policy challenges were discussed based on the results of the questionnaire.

Our findings showed that the population has slightly increased in and around the central part of TMA, but has tended to decline beyond 50 kilometers from the central TMA. Analysis of the study area on the fringe of the TMA illustrated that the population has just begun to decline around urban centers containing important social and economic facilities, together with natural and social population decline. In particular, the aging of the population has exerted a strong influence over population decline in the urban centers. The results of the questionnaire survey indicated that the elderly in urban centers have not yet faced the problem of low accessibility to retail stores in their neighborhoods. But we can also assume from the fact that many of the elderly went shopping primarily on foot or by bicycle that they will face those problems in the near future. Questionnaire results also revealed that the social connections of some elderly residents were getting weaker, and that they may soon become isolated from the local community in urban centers.

According to the results from the section of the questionnaire that asked about urban political challenges for an aging society from the viewpoint of citizens' demand, fewer inhabitants would emphasize measures to promote facilities development, because a certain number of public facilities have already been constructed in the urban centers. Also, many people didn't realize the importance of measures having to do with social systems that are less connected with their daily activities. In contrast, the inhabitants rated three types of issues as the most important urban policy challenges: countermeasures to the population aging, urban policies to counteract economic decline in the urban center, and countermeasures to the falling birth rate.

This study mainly targeted the metropolitan fringe areas that had grown due to in-migrants from other parts of Japan. The results indicated that the recent reduction of in-migrants has caused a population decline in these fringe areas and an increase in the rate of elderly residents in the urban center. Population decline in step with population aging may be an important factor in the socio-economic deterioration of urban centers. Inhabitants there lose the opportunity for communication in their communities. Population decline in urban centers is likely to be connected with economic decline in the local shopping areas of the old urban centers, due to a decline in customers, sales and profit margins. These socio-economic problems caused by population decline in the urban center are common traits in cities located in the TMA fringe area, and should be urgent targets for urban policies in each municipality. Local governments have introduced several urban policies, such as renewal projects in the central shopping districts and implementation of subsidies, but it is difficult for them to become fully effective as a measure against the aging of society.

References

Asakawa, T. and Tamano, K. 2010. *Urban city and community.* Tokyo: Foundation for the promotion of the Open University of Japan. (J)

Esaki, Y. 2006. *Population geography of the city center and suburbs —the future of metropolitan area population.* Senshu University Publication Bureau. (J)

Ito, T., Iwama, N., and Hirai, M. 2012. Socio-economic reconfiguration through population decline in a fringe of the Metropolitan Area —A case of Northern Tokyo Metropolitan Area—. *Bulletin of Geo-Environmental Science (Rissho University)* 14: 7-22. (J)

Iwama, N. ed. 2011. *Food deserts issues.* Tokyo: Association of Agriculture and Forestry Statistics. (J)

Jinko-gaku Kenkyukai ed. 2010. *Dictionary of Contemporary Demography.* Tokyo: Hara Shobo. (J)

Kumagai, S. et al. 2003. Effects of dietary variety on declines in high-level functional capacity in elderly people living in a community. *Japanese journal of public health* 50 (2): 1117-1124. (J)

Saitama Prefecture ed. 2012. Basic official count of the 2010 population census of Japan. (J) (http://www.pref.saitama.lg.jp/soshiki/c08/) (last accessed 27 January 2012)

The National Institute of Population and Social Security Research ed. 2002. *Population Pro-*

jections by Prefecture: 2000-2030. Tokyo: Health and Welfare Statistics Association (Ko- sei- Tokei- Kyokai). (J)

(J) means "written in Japanese" (with an English summary, in some cases).

8. Aging Suburbs and Increasing Vacant Houses in Japan

Tomoko KUBO, Yoshimichi YUI and Hiroaki SAKAUE

Abstract

This study dealt with (1) why the number of vacant houses has increased in Japanese suburbs, (2) the geography of aging suburban neighborhoods in Tokyo, and (3) how local governments in Tokyo suburbs have reacted to the problems related to increasing vacant houses. The Japanese suburban neighborhoods that were developed in the 1960s to 1970s are standing at a crossroads; one path leads to sustainable communities to which young people move in, while the other leads to "ghost towns" in which both young and old people leave vacant houses in unpleasant condition. Regarding the demographic characteristics and housing conditions of Tokyo suburbs, a large number of housing estates are at risk of heading towards the second road. Aging and the following increase in vacant houses are some of the most serious and urgent topics to be surveyed by scholars in a variety of academic backgrounds.

Keywords

aging, suburban neighborhoods, vacant houses, the Tokyo metropolitan area, Japan

8.1 Introduction

8.1.1 Purpose of this study

Since the 1960s, suburban housing estates have developed because high housing prices caused a lack of affordable housing in city centers. Detached houses in the suburbs have welcomed the increasingly large middle-class. Householders who did not own real properties in metropolitan areas and who moved from the countryside rushed to the suburbs, and suburbanization spread rapidly in Japan (Tani 1997; Kawaguchi 1997). Soaring land prices in the 1980s strengthened the preference for detached houses in suburbs. Since the late 1990s onwards, however, housing market has drastically changed in Tokyo.

Suburban housing estates have rapidly lost their appeal; whereas, potential homeowners are showing preferences for condominiums in city centers (Hirayama 2005). Suburbanization was gone, and the city started to decline due to changes in socioeconomic conditions, the housing market, and lifestyles. Now, suburban neighborhoods have become less popular as residential areas and are facing serious social problems, such as the aging of residents. The aging population phenomenon has also highlighted unique characteristics of the housing market in Japan. In Japan, people had strong preferences for newly-built houses. The secondhand-housing market is weak in Japan as a whole. Therefore, once people have had purchased their houses, they tended to remain in the same house for decades. After a few decades, as the existing residents' age, the aging rate of a housing district naturally increases (Yui 1991, 1999).

This study aims to examine how suburban neighborhoods have changed in the Japanese metropolitan regions, and deal with conditions of vacant houses in suburbs.

8.1.2 Methodology

To achieve the above mentioned purposes, we first overview the history of Japanese housing market from the Second World War, which leads the ageing problems in suburban housing estates. Secondly, we examine the outcomes of our field survey in a suburban neighborhood in Hiroshima pref. in order to clarify why vacancies increases in suburbs, and how they cause problems in neighborhoods. The case clearly explains how suburban neighborhoods turn into aged communities; we selected Hiroshima cases because basic process to be ageing suburbs is found in the case neighborhoods.

Thirdly, relationship between ageing population and increasing vacancies in Tokyo is examined by the GIS analysis. Regarding these outcomes, we focus on problems caused by aging population and increased vacancies in Tokyo. Reactions of local governments to these problems are examined. Here, we conducted interview surveys to several local governments in Tokyo suburbs who have established regulations on the maintenance of vacancies. Tokorozawa and Ushiku cities, our case governments, are pioneers that established regulations on vacant houses in suburbs. Finally, we discuss how suburban neighborhoods in Tokyo have changed over half century in terms of demography, housing condition, and residential environment.

8.2 Geography of aging problems in Japan

In this chapter, the history of Japanese housing market from the 19th century is examined in order to clarify why rapid aging problems in suburban housing estates have occurred there. GIS maps illustrate relationship between aging population and increasing vacancies in Tokyo.

8.2.1 Japanese housing custom and aging suburbs

8.2.1.1 Family and housing system before the 1950s

Family and housing systems are closely connected with each other, and these traditional systems can determine how we live, work, get marriage or have babies, or communicate with family members. One example would be that young couples have notion that they'll have to live together with their aged parents in order to take care of them. We'll show overview of traditional family and housing systems in Japan in the following part.

The Japanese civil law passed in the 1870s was based on "*ie-seido*" (family institutions), which categorized people by the unit of family or parentage, and allowed them to maintain real property such as houses and land. "*Ie-seido*" was a legal, economic, social, and cultural mechanism that even now has provided the roots for the modern Japanese social structure (Iwakami 2003). It was devised based on the housing custom of the *samurai*, the stem family system. The patriarchs succeed the real properties and transferred them to their eldest sons, and the other sons and daughters left the head family and formed collateral families. The younger sons (i.e., the collateral families) needed to find jobs in the other areas, and this led to the residential mobility from rural areas to densely populated areas. Based on the housing custom of the family institution, the ideology of home-ownership was intensified in Japan (Ronald 2004).

Although this institution was abolished in 1947, in many rural areas, patriarchal housing customs remained until recent days. According to Kato's doctoral dissertation on the Japanese family system (2003), more than 30% of couples who have been married for more than 10 years moved to live together with their parents.

8.2.1.2   The influence of postwar housing legislations on the promotion of home ownership

In the 1950s, as dwellings became scarce owing to the lack of building materials after the Second World War, legislation was implemented to improve the quality of housing. In 1950, the Japanese Housing Finance Agency began financing home ownership for high-income households. The Japan Housing Corporation (now the Urban Renaissance Agency) was established in 1955 to develop collective housing estates for middle-class households. Rented houses and public housing were provided for low-income households (Japan Federation of Housing Organizations 2002; Kageyama 2004).

The ideology of homeownership has achieved increasingly greater currency (Hirayama and Ronald 2007), with the rate of home-ownership reaching 60% at the beginning of the 1960s and until recent years, although the rate of homeownership was 22% in major cities in 1941 (Ronald 2008). Since the 1960s, suburban housing estates have developed because of the high housing prices caused lack of affordable housing in city centers (Hasegawa 1997; Matsubara 1982). Detached houses in the suburbs have welcomed the increasingly large middle-class. Commuters to city centers have tended to move when life events occurred (e.g., marriage) and ended up in the suburbs when they purchased housing (Kawaguchi 1997). Householders who did not own real properties in metropolitan areas and who moved from the countryside rushed to the suburbs, and suburbanization spread rapidly in Japan (Tani 1997).

Soaring land prices in the 1980s, so-called "myth of real property", that pushed many people to homeownership because land price was believed to be higher and higher and most people were afraid not to be homeowners, strengthened the preference for detached houses in suburbs (Japan Federation of Housing Organizations 2002; Van Vliet and Hirayama 1994), while condominiums were thought of as temporary residences before the purchase of detached houses[1]. A large part of Japanese prefers newly built detached houses in suburbs, and they tend to stay in one house they purchased for decades (see next part for more detailed information). At that time most Japanese shared similar "dreams" and climbed up similar "housing ladder" during suburbanization; getting marriage to live in rental apartments, having babies to move to condominiums in near suburbs, and child raring to buy suburban detached houses. Housing ladder ended at the purchase of suburban detached houses, but now new stories await suburban residents; sons and daughters leaving parents' home and parents remain in houses getting old, most residents being elderly, gradually vacancies increase, and shopping centers and bus services start to be closed. Increasing vacancies may increase risks of crimes in neighborhoods. What we are to illustrate in this paper is these new stories await suburban residents after climbing up the traditional housing ladder.

8.2.1.3 Housing condition in Japan

Japan has a long history of providing housing for families. Non-nuclear households were marginalized in the owner-occupied market in Japan (Kubo and Yui 2011). The number of housing construction increased rapidly from 1970 to 1995; suburbanization and bubble economy period (Statistics Bureau of Japan 2008). In this period, supply of detached houses was dominant, followed by rented apartments. During 1980s, there were remarkable numbers of moves of young people from rural area to metropolitan areas. They tended to move into rented apartments first. As they got marriage or had children, they moved to suburban detached houses (Kawaguchi 1997). These uniformed and passive movement trends were supported by government policies. When it comes to housing types of whole housing stock in Japan, owned detached houses have kept high percentages for decades. However, as many people have experienced the lives in apartment houses from 1960s, the percentages of owned apartments (condominiums) have increased steadily.

"Housing and Land Survey" (Statistics Bureau of Japan 2008) also shows that more than 50% of home owners obtained their residences by building new houses or purchasing newly built houses. It is often said that the Japanese housing stock is increased by demolishing old houses and building new ones. Therefore, the second-hand housing market in Japan as a whole is fragile and limited to highly populated areas such as Tokyo and Osaka. As the survey indicates, the first peak of home ownership occurs when people are in between 30 and 50 years of age. This is the age at which a large number of middle-class people get married and become parents and are thereby prompted to purchase their own houses. In addition, the households that purchase housing using mortgages have to make decisions to purchase housing before they are 40 years old, because a large majority of them have to pay for the mortgage for more than 20 years until their retirement.

The second peak is seen in people between 50 and 60 years of age. It should be mentioned that these individuals' previous residences are typically owner-occupations; however, this is the age at which they need to rebuild their houses in order to live together with their children and their families. It should be noted that this group includes people who obtained new houses to reflect the decrease in family size owing to their children's independence. The value of real property tends to decrease gradually in the Japanese housing market. Therefore, the mobility of middle-aged people and the elderly is not as much as that of their counterparts in Western countries (Tahara et al. 2003).

8.2.2 Increasing vacancies in Japanese suburbs

According to the Housing and Land Survey (Statistics Bureau of Japan 2008), vacancies are defined as non-resident houses, and they are divided into five categories: (1) secondary housing such as vacation homes, (2) houses kept vacant to be rented out, (3) houses kept vacant to be sold, (4) houses that are vacant because residents are in the hospital or elsewhere, and (5) houses under construction. Figure 1 demonstrates increases in vacant houses in Japan, the number of which has doubled in just 20 years, from 1978 to 1998. The distribution of vacant houses shows unique characteristics (Figure 2). The vacant house rate is higher in metropolitan suburbs and rural areas than in the countryside; most vacancies are left to be sold in metropolitan regions (Fig. 2-b), whereas houses are kept vacant without residents in rural areas because of depopulation (Fig. 2-a).

Reflecting such conditions, local governments in rural areas have worked on making better use of vacant houses and attracting younger generations to their region.[2] Several local governments have established measures for vacancies in order to make better use of them in rural areas and to encourage the appropriate maintenance of vacancies to be sold or rented out in metropolitan suburbs. The latter will be examined in the proceeding chapter. First, we will clarify how vacancies have increased in suburbs and what problems they can cause in communities through the case of Hiroshima prefecture.

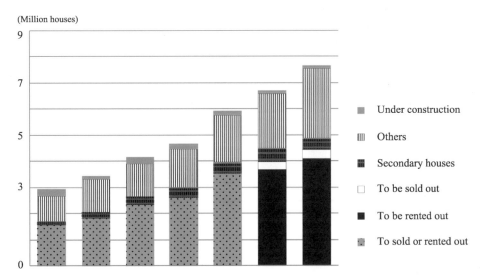

Figure 1 The number of vacant housing by their conditions in Japan (2008)
Source: Statistics Bureau of Japan, "Housing and Land Survey, 2008"

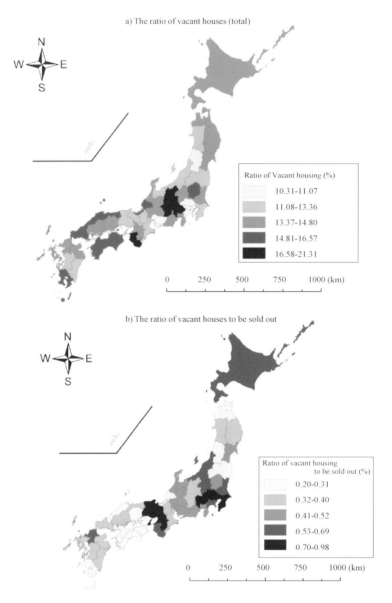

Figure 2 The ratio of vacant housing among whole houses in Japan (2008)
Source: Statistics Bureau of Japan, "Housing and Land Survey, 2008"
a) The ratio of vacant houses (total)
b) The ratio of vacant houses to be sold out

8.3 Why vacancies increase in suburbs: The case of a suburban neighborhood in Hiroshima

8.3.1 Geographic and demographic characteristics of the neighborhood

8.3.1.1 Geography of Showa district, a Hiroshima suburb

We conducted fieldwork in a neighborhood of Hiroshima suburbs in order to address the above-mentioned questions. This neighborhood, Showa district in Kure City, has developed as a bedroom community for commuters to Hiroshima City and coastal industrial zones in the region.

Kure City first developed the Sakuragaoka-Danchi housing estate in 1964, followed by private housing developments until 1998. The largest housing estate, which was developed by a prefectural housing institute, includes 1000 lots and 30.9 ha of land. From 1964 to 1973, a total of nine mid-size and two large-size (more than 1,000 lots) housing estates were developed in Showa district. Its population reached 25,000 in 1975, up from 5,000 in 1965. After that, five more housing estates were developed within the district; the population peaked at 36,000 in 2005. We conducted a field survey in 12 of the 17 housing estates in the district.

8.3.1.2 Residential environment of the district

It is a common measure to make mountainous or hillside areas into flat land for housing developments in Japan. Both Tama New Town in Tokyo and Senri New Town in Osaka were built on hilly land in the 1960s to 1970s and were regarded as frontiers, and later models, of post-war Japanese housing developments.

Showa district is also characterized by precipitous slopes and steep stairs leading up to

Figure 3 Steep stairs in the Showa district, Hiroshima prefecture
Source: Yui photographed (2012)

Figure 4 The location of steep slopes and houses with entrance-stairs of five or more steps in neighborhood B in the Showa district, Hiroshima prefecture
Source: Authors' field surveys

Figure 5 Houses with entrance-stairs in the Showa district, Hiroshima prefecture
Source: Yui photographed (2012)

building entrances (Figure 3). The location of precipitous slopes and houses with stairs between the roads to their entrances in Showa district is demonstrated in Figure 4. Indeed, residents have to walk up slopes and stairs anytime they go out or come home (Figure 5). Of course, there is no trouble if residents are young and healthy. The troubles arise when people get older and have difficulty walking, bicycling, and driving.

8.3.1.3 Demographic characteristics of residents

Figure 6 clearly explains how the demographic characteristics of residents changed in a 25-year period. In 1980, the balance among age groups was well proportioned; parents in their 30s and 40s, their children, and grandparents or elderly couples lived there. Yet, the elderly population rate rose to 30% in 2005, by which point, members of the young generation rarely lived with their parents and most had left their parents' homes, while elderly people remained in the neighborhood. Therefore, the elderly population rate increased over time (Fig. 6).

In most neighborhoods in the Showa district, detached houses are the dominant housing

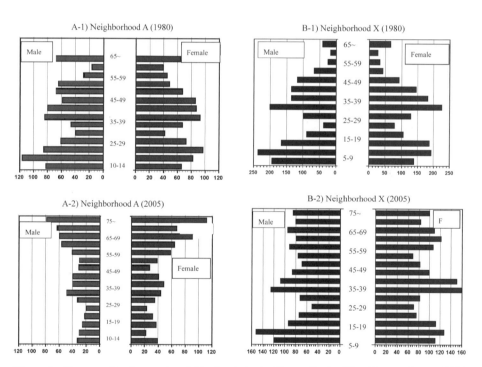

Figure 6 Demographic changes in neighborhoods in the Showa district, Hiroshima prefecture (1980 and 2005)
Source: Statistics Bureau of Japan, "Population Census, 1980 and 2005"
A-1) Neighborhood A (1980)
A-2) Neighborhood A (2005)
B-1) Neighborhood X (1980)
B-2) Neighborhood X (2005)

Table 1 Attributes of neighborhoods in Showa district, Hiroshima prefecture (2012)

ID	Developed year	Vacant-house ratio
A	1964	7
B	1971	7.7
C	1971	15.2
D	1977	5.3
E	1971	4.1

Note: Vacant housing ratio denotes the percentage of vacant housing among whole households

Source: Authors' interview surveys

Table 2 Condition of vacant houses in Showa district, Hiroshima prefecture (2012)

ID	Well-mainteined	Negative condition	Others	Total
A	6	15	1	22
B	13	7	0	20
C	24	9	1	34
D	29	5	4	38
E	6	5	2	13
F	5	11	0	16
Total (%)	83(58.0)	52(36.4)	8(5.6)	143(100)

Source: Authors' interview surveys

type. Company housing, rental apartments, and public housing were only built in few neighborhoods. In such neighborhoods, the proportion of age groups was maintained for more than 20 years (Figure 6). As Kubo et al. (2010) noted, mixed development can weaken the process of aging in Japanese suburban neighborhoods, while detached-house neighborhoods with white-collar residents are the most dangerous in terms of social sustainability. Indeed, a large number of the neighborhoods in the Showa district are detached-house neighborhoods with white-collar residents. More than half of the residents live alone or with one person (usually elderly couples) in a large number of neighborhoods in the district.

8.3.2 Condition of vacant houses in the district

8.3.2.1 Vacant housing rate

Supported by local residents' associations and authors' field surveys, we made several maps

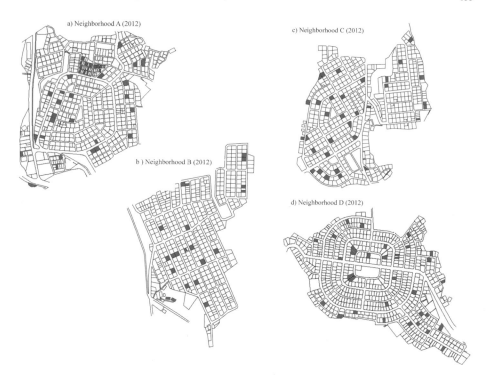

Figure 7 The location of vacant houses in neighborhoods in the Showa district, Hiroshima prefecture
Source: Authors' field surveys

of vacancies in the neighborhoods of the Showa district (Figure 7). The attributes of each neighborhood are listed in Table 1. The ratio of vacant houses to all houses in a neighborhood ranges from 4.1% to 15.2%; both neighborhoods were developed in 1971. What made the difference was the area planning: one consists of several housing types due to mixed-development area planning, while the other is composed of owned detached houses. In addition, the road conditions, slopes, and stairs in front of houses' entrances affect the ratio of vacancies.

8.3.2.2 Condition of vacancies

Table 2 explains the condition of vacant houses. The 58% of vacancies were maintained in good condition; trees and grass in their gardens were kept in good shape, windows were closed, and mail was removed from their home mailboxes. The 36% of them were judged as being in negative condition, having not been looked after for a long time or devastated. Five percent of the vacancies were under construction, used as offices, or turned into vacant lots to be sold. Houses in good condition were regularly maintained by the original residents, their relatives, or maintenance companies. The 36% of vacant houses that undergo no maintenance cause other residents to fear the potential for fire and accidents and risk becoming refuges for the homeless and delinquents.

Table 3 Period houses turned into vacant (2012)

ID	~One year	~Three years	~Five years	~Ten years	Ten years and more	Secondary use	Unknown	Others	Total
A	7	4	1	1	3	0	5	1	22
B	4	2	1	0	0	4	9	0	20
C	11	2	4	6	1	0	10	0	34
D	10	10	2	4	3	4	2	3	38
E	0	3	1	2	0	0	7	0	13
F	2	4	2	3	1	0	4	0	16
Total (%)	34(23.8)	25(17.5)	11(7.7)	16(11.2)	8(5.6)	8(5.6)	37(25.9)	4(2.8)	143(100)

Source: Authors' interview surveys

Table 4 Household types when houses turned into vacant (2012)

ID	Elderly & relatives	Elderly singles	Elderly couples	Young couples	Young families	Others	Unknown	Total
A	1	14	1	0	0	0	6	22
B	1	6	1	1	1	0	10	20
C	2	13	3	1	3	2	10	34
D	0	13	7	2	7	3	6	38
E	1	4	0	0	0	1	7	13
F	0	3	6	2	0	1	4	16
Total (%)	5(3.5)	53(37.1)	18(12.6)	6(4.2)	11(7.7)	7(4.9)	43(30.1)	143(100)

Source: Authors' interview surveys

8.3.3 Reasons why houses become vacant

8.3.3.1 Periods of vacancy

The time period in which houses become vacant is listed in Table 3. Among 143 vacant houses, 24% became vacant less than one year before our survey in 2012, and 25% in five years, while about half of the houses became vacant in less than five years. On the other hand, some houses were left vacant or unused from the beginning, while some were used as vacation homes or secondary housing.

Table 4 provides the age and household types of the main owners of houses before they were vacated. Among the 143 vacancies in the district, we collected 100 cases of houses whose original residents have communicated with local residents' associations or nearby residents. Fifty-three (38%) of original residents were elderly and single, while 12.6% were elderly couples. It is clear that suburban houses whose residents are elderly are at high risk to be vacancies in subsequent decades. Aging is a strong factor in the increase in vacancies in Japanese

Aging Suburbs and Increasing Vacant Houses in Japan

Table 5 Main reasons why houses turned into vacant (2012)

ID	Temporary moving by job transfer	Moving to hospitals or nursery home	Purchased new houses	Death of main owners	Live together with relatives	To be sold or rented out	Un-known	Other	Total
A	0	1	1	12	0	1	4	3	22
B	0	4	5	1	1	1	8	0	20
C	2	5	3	9	1	5	8	1	34
D	1	3	13	8	6	1	3	3	38
E	1	4	0	1	0	0	7	0	13
F	0	3	4	2	3	0	4	0	16
Total (%)	4(2.8)	20(14.0)	26(18.2)	33(23.1)	11(7.7)	8(5.6)	34(23.8)	7(4.9)	143(100)

Source: Authors' interview surveys

suburban neighborhoods. As we mentioned before, weak second-hand housing market in Japan strongly affects the increasing vacant houses and subsequent decline in suburban neighborhoods.

8.3.3.2 Reasons to be vacant houses

Table 5 indicates the reasons why houses became vacant. These reasons are divided into eight categories; (a) death of residents (33 of the 143 vacancies); (b) purchasing new residences (26); (c) moving to hospitals or elderly nursing-care facilities (20), (d) moving to relatives' houses (11), (e) waiting to be sold or rented out (8), (f) temporarily vacant due to residents transferring offices (4), (g) unknown (34), and (h) other reasons (7). Among these categories, (a), (c) and (d) are closely connected with the aging of residents; category (d) included cases in which residents moved to their relatives' homes in order to get nursing care from them. In total, 45% of the houses studied became vacant due to the aging of their residents.

Suburban neighborhoods developed during the 1960s to 1970s are at high risk to become vacant communities due to the ageing of residents. Steep slopes and entrance stairs create barriers to elderly residents' houses, which may decrease satisfaction in their daily lives and activities. Now, the younger generations prefer living in condominiums in central areas or near suburbs, and they also prefer new housing; children do not tend to return to their parents' houses when their parents get older or die. Old, detached houses in suburban neighborhoods tend to be less popular in the second-hand housing market as well. Therefore, these houses are often kept vacant when the original residents leave them.

8.4 Aging and increasing vacancies in Tokyo suburbs

In order to avoid vacant suburban communities, local governments in suburban regions have begun to establish regulations on vacant houses. In this chapter, we first examine aging and vacant house problems in Tokyo suburbs. Then we discuss the reaction of local governments to these problems.

8.4.1 Aging and increasing vacancies

In this section, we analyze the distribution of aging problems in Tokyo using the 2010 Population Census of Japan (Statistics Bureau of Japan 2010) with the Arc-GIS platform. Before beginning our analysis of the aging population, we will briefly explain the residential and family structure of Tokyo.

Figure 8 indicates the ratio of the elderly population among general households in Tokyo. It is clear that the ratio is higher in peripheral regions and in suburbs in the 30- 60km belt around Tokyo. The peripheral regions are the rural/fishery areas in Chiba, Kanagawa, and Tokyo Tama region, while the Tokyo suburbs are largely composed of housing estates developed during Japanese suburbanization.

When it comes to elderly singles (Figure 9), single men are found primarily in central Tokyo, near the suburbs of Kanagawa and China prefectures, and in peripheral regions; single women shows similar patterns to single men, but their distribution shows a clear contrast compared to single men.

Figure 10 illustrates the ratio of elderly couples among general households in Tokyo, and shows that they tend to live in the Tokyo suburban belt and in peripheral regions. We can easily imagine that many old suburban neighborhoods are rapidly becoming elderly communities. Housing conditions and the aging population are also closely connected. Figure 11 indicates 1) the ratio of detached houses (Fig.11-a) and apartments (Fig. 11-b) to whole houses and 2) the high aging ratio region. Detached houses are dominant in peripheral regions, which are characterized as having a high aging ratio, as well as apartments in central Tokyo and its suburbs. The suburban belt contains a mixture of apartments and detached houses, with apartments dominating.

As the findings in this section show, elderly couples in old suburbs will gradually become single persons due to death of their partners, which results in some high-ratio areas of elderly singles in suburban belt areas. Suburban belts are characterized as a mixture of apartments and detached houses, and our prediction is that the latter compose the bulk of increasing vacancies. We examine this estimation in the next section.

8.4.2 Reaction of local governments in Japan

In order to avoid social problems and to make better residential environments, a large number of local governments in Japan have established their own regulations on the maintenance

Aging Suburbs and Increasing Vacant Houses in Japan 137

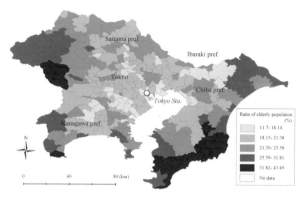

Figure 8 The ratio of elderly population in the Tokyo metropolitan area (2010)
Source: Statistics Bureau of Japan, "Population Census of Japan, 2010"

a) The ratio of single women over 65 years old

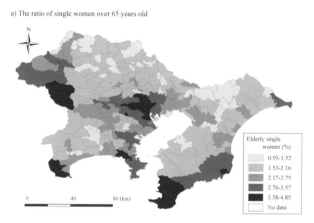

b) The ratio of single men over 65 years old

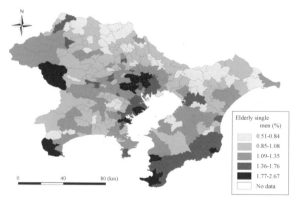

Figure 9 The ratio of elderly single-person households among whole general households in the Tokyo metropolitan area (2010)
Source: Statistics Bureau of Japan, "Population Census of Japan, 2010"
a) The ratio of single women over 65 years old
b) The ratio of single men over 65 years old

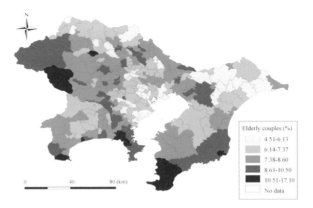

Figure 10 The ratio of elderly couple households among whole general households in the Tokyo metropolitan area (2010)
Source: Statistics Bureau of Japan, "Population Census of Japan, 2010"

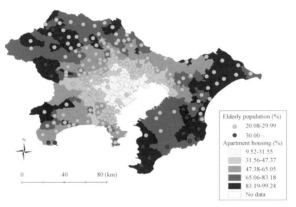

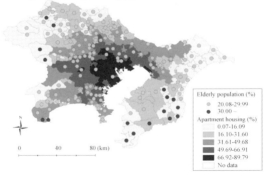

Figure 11 The ratio of elderly population and each housing type in the Tokyo metropolitan area (2010)
Source: Statistics Bureau of Japan, "Population Census of Japan, 2010"
a) Ratio of detached houses and elderly population
b) Ratio of Apartment housing and elderly population

or better use of vacant houses in their cities, towns, and villages (Yoneyama 2013).[3] As the Japanese government does not have national standards on the maintenance of vacancies, local governments work on the establishment of regulations on vacant houses using their own measures. There are two reasons for this: 1) there is an unwritten rule that all the Japanese people should have equal access to government services and support (Igarashi 1996) and 2) most vacant houses and their land are private property whose owners should solve the problems on their own, without the help of governmental organizations.

The increase in vacant houses, however, is threatening people's safety and comfort in their neighborhoods. The risks of incendiary fires and burglaries increase, and vacant houses may be hotbeds of several types of crime. Crime prevention departments in local governments usually take responsibility for regulations on vacancies based on these perspectives. Really, however, the maintenance of vacancies is beyond the abilities of a single department because it requires measures based on a combination of community support, family relations, legislation matters, and architecture or town planning. In the following sections, we describe how local governments in Tokyo suburbs have established their own regulations and how they have taken care of problems related to increasing vacancies.

8.4.3 The case of Tokorozawa city in Saitama prefecture

Tokorozawa City in Saitama prefecture established a regulation on the proper maintenance of vacant houses in October 2010. In the regulation, owners of vacant houses are under an obligation to maintain their property, vacant houses, and land. The city accepts the statements of residents when they find vacant houses in negative condition. City officials conduct surveys on such houses in order to advise owners to maintain their property. When the houses' bad condition continues despite governmental advice, the city can officially publicize the names of the owners (interview to Ms. Maeda, a city Official working on vacant-house problems of Tokorozawa City). So far, there have been no cases in which the city has publicized the names of vacant house owners. The Tokorozawa regulation is regarded as a standard for regulations on vacant houses in suburbs, and other local governments refer to it when they make their own regulations on vacant houses. As of March 2013, there had been 514 inquiries from local governments and 155 on-site inspections by local governments and council members from all over Japan to Tokorozawa City.

From the late 1950s to 1960s, housing developments focusing on small detached houses (the average size of total land area was about 100 square meters), beginning in Tokorozawa City. At that time, young families with small children purchased detached houses there, and after several decades, the children left their parents' homes. Gradually, residents began to tell the city government that their residential environment was getting worse due to vacant houses in bad condition. When there was no specific department that dealt with problems of vacant houses; residents had to talk to the Town Planning Department when the physical condition of a vacancy was at issue, to the Fire Department when people were afraid of incendiary fires at vacant houses, and so on. Thanks to the regulation on vacant housing, residents can easily find the right department to talk to.

8.4.3.1　The regulation on vacant houses

Around the year 2007, the problems related to vacant houses were discussed in city council meetings. The residents asked the city to unify various departments related to vacant house problems and create one way of dealing with them. The city started to survey other authorities' regulations on vacant house problems, such as those of Shibuya Ward in Tokyo, in order to deal with the problems.

In March 2009, the Crime Provision Department was designated to work on problems of vacant houses in Tokorozawa, and the officials of the department have dealt with the maintenance of vacant houses with a focus on maintaining a pleasant residential environment and increasing security in neighborhoods. At a city council meeting held in June 2010, the regulation on the maintenance of vacant houses was discussed, and on July 5 the regulation was formally publicized. It was finally enforced on October 1, 2010. The Crime Provision Department accepted 262 resident complaints from April 2009 to March 2013, and the Fire Department accepted about 300 resident complaints on vacant houses during that same period. In addition, the Department of the Environment and Resident Life and the Town Planning have worked together on the problems of vacant houses when it has been necessary.

Among the 262 residents who complained to the Crime Provision Department, there were three main reasons why the houses in question were vacant: (1) elderly residents moved out in order to live with their children; (2) the children of house owners cannot decide whether vacant houses should be demolished or sold; and (3) if a vacant house is demolished and the land becomes empty, the land tax can increase to six times what it was when the house remained because land for housing is exempted from taxation. The Japanese government has promoted homeownership, especially single-detached houses in suburbs, for more then 60 years to activate economy. The tax reduction on housing land is a part of such housing policies.

8.4.3.2　City survey on vacant houses

The city conducts surveys on vacant buildings that local residents have asked the city to look at. City officers usually visit vacant houses, take photos, and conduct interviews with residents nearby. When conditions are negative, officers give advice to owners on how to properly maintain their property; when officials cannot contact the owners, they sometimes have to work together with the police to confirm whether someone is staying in a vacant house or to increase patrols around vacant houses. The city also works together with local residents; residents' associations select several members of the security countermeasure committee, and the designated members patrol their neighborhoods in order to understand the conditions of vacant houses. When the members find suspicious conditions, they talk to the city's Crime Provision Department. Residents' associations may gather information about vacant houses in their neighborhoods and bring it to the city.

In most cases, the owners of vacant houses quickly respond to governmental advice and repair or take care of their vacant houses, but there have been about 15 cases in which the city could not find the owners of vacant houses. In those cases, the city refers to information about land registration, but sometimes the registered information is not useful. The city then refers to updated information about land registration and visits the vacant houses to confirm their condition. Depending on the residential characteristics of housing estates in the city, the extent of problems with vacant houses differ; some housing estates were developed as vacation homes, while others were a mixture of small housing developments in which five to ten houses were generally sold at the same time.

Vacant houses can cause unexpected social problems. One example is *Kodoku-shi*, which means that a resident who passed away alone in his/her house and whom no one noticed for a while and gathered great interest in Japan. This happened in a house regarded as vacant in Tokorozawa City. When residents nearby asked the city to survey the vacant house, the city first took care of the trees around the house, cooperating with the Fire Department, then conducted surveys on land registration to find the owner, and finally sent letters to the owner and his relatives to provide governmental advice. Finally, the police entered the house to find the resident, who was by that time only a skeleton. The house was demolished and the land is now empty. This shows that vacant houses can sometimes cause serious accidents.

Tokorozawa City now tries to avoid problems with vacant houses by increasing residents' consciousness of those problems, restructuring local communities, and studying the approach other governments. There were 73 local authorities that established their own regulations on vacant house problems in March 2012 and the number is increasing at a rapid pace. Vacant house problems are now becoming one of the most important urban housing issues in Japan.

8.4.4 The case of Ushiku city in Ibaraki prefecture

Ushiku City, which is located in the southern part of Ibaraki prefecture, is 50-60km away from central Tokyo and is connected by the JR Joban line. The city established a regulation on the maintenance and better use of vacant houses in July of 2012. The Crime Prevention and City Planning departments worked together to create the regulation in Ushiku City, where housing developments began being built in the 1970s. About 100 housing estates were developed, mainly by a small housing developer, and it has already collapsed. In the northern part of the city, new developments around railroad stations continued until recent days. Vacant house problems are mainly found in old suburbs, usually far from train stations, and small housing estates; vacant houses there are difficult to sell when residents leave them, and they tend to remain vacant in bad condition.

8.4.4.1   The regulation on vacant houses

In 2010, Ushiku city first tried to establish a regulation on the maintenance of vacant houses. Reflecting the public opinion that better use of vacant houses is an important issue, the city created a project to facilitate the better use of vacant houses. In the project, the Crime Provision Department took initiatives and the Department of General Affairs considered related laws, while the Department of the Environment examined the proper maintenance of houses and trees in gardens. The Department of Information took care of personal data protection; the Department of Architecture and City Planning examined problems related to the better use of vacant houses (e.g. conversion of houses into community centers); and the Department of Social Affairs worked on making plans to use vacant houses in community-based activities (e.g., child-care gardens and elderly care houses). In April 2011, the city council decided to establish the regulation on the maintenance and better use of vacant houses, and the regulation took effect in July 2012. However, there have been no cases so far in which the city has changed a vacant house into another-purpose building, such as a child-care garden.

According to data provided by the city, the city had given governmental advice in 88 cases as of March 11, 2013. Among these 88 cases, 25 have been solved, 33 are in the process of resolving (in 20 of these cases, the owners promised that they would solve the problems), 16 have received no answers from owners, three cases are waiting for owners' response, one house will be contributed to the government by its owner, three cases are under other provisions of the city, and there were seven cases in which the city could not find the owners. These final cases have given the local government trouble.

8.4.4.2   Reaction of communities

City officials have mentioned different reactions by various communities in the city. Some residents take care of the trees or gardens of vacant houses in their communities, while others work on a project to recover old communities through the regulation of better use of vacant houses. The latter group is trying to make new community centers using vacant houses in their community. The problem here is that local residents do not need 10 or more community centers, so it is difficult to choose the best vacant house to be modified into a new community center, and usually the needs of residents and the condition of vacant houses are difficult to meet. The city now tries to communicate with local communities because each community has its own ideas, needs, and resources.

8.5   Conclusion

This study dealt with (1) why the number of vacant houses has increased in suburban, neighborhoods (2) the geography of aging suburban neighborhoods in Tokyo, and (3) how local governments in Tokyo suburbs have reacted to the problems related to increasing vacant houses. The Japanese suburban neighborhoods that were developed in the 1960s to 1970s are standing at a crossroads; one path leads to sustainable communities to which young people move, while the other leads to declining communities in which both young and old people leave vacant houses in unpleasant condition. Regarding the demographic characteristics and housing conditions of Tokyo suburbs, a large number of housing estates are at risk of heading towards the second road. Aging and the following increase in vacant houses are some of the most serious and urgent topics to be surveyed by scholars in a variety of academic backgrounds.

Many scholars have dealt with such problems from the following perspectives: deficiency and problems of laws and regulations, systematic problems in the Japanese housing market, reactions of local governments in Japan, and introduction of cases of foreign countries such as the U.S. and Germany (Yoneyama 2013). In addition, community recovery in old suburban neighborhoods has been discussed in sociology and architecture, but these studies do not deal with the relationship between the social and physical condition of suburban housing estates (e.g., Fukuhara 2005). Problems related to an increase in vacant houses, however, are comprehensive, complicated, and usually geographical; the conditions of settlements are always different and they greatly affect how the problems occur over time. Geography, with a comprehensive perspective, should contribute to solving these problems, with which we continue to cope.

Notes

1) The relationship between life stages and housing purchase was analyzed by Morrow-Jones (1988). Independence from parents' houses leads young people to move into condominiums or apartments, while after marriage young people proceed to home ownership. Divorce is the life event that most often leads to movement from owner-occupation to rental apartments.

2) Such famous cases are the training programs of agriculture or traditional crafts that remain in rural communities. In O-nan town in Shimane pref., which have serious depopulation problems in their regions, the town accept young women who wish to take training of herb rearing, for one or two years. The town also distribute vacant-house information via the Internet in the town and accept young people. Saku city in Nagano pref. give special treatments to people who decide to live in vacant houses in the city; the city provides free lunch service for their children going to public elementary schools. Some local governments established vacancy-banks in order to make better use of vacant houses and to stimulate in-migration to such depopulated areas.

3) For example, Nagasaki city, whose roads are mostly steep slopes, designated several vacant houses as small community parks; the city entrust their management to local residents' as-

sociations, and local residents make better use of these parks.

References

Fukuhara, M. 2005. *Revival of the New Town through community networkings.* Tokyo: Kokon Shoin. (J)

Hirayama, Y. 2005. Running hot and cold in the urban home-ownership market: The experience of Japan's major cities. *Journal of Housing and the Built Environment* 20: 1-20. (J)

Hirayama, Y. and Ronald, R. 2007. *Housing and social transition in Japan.* New York: Routledge.

Igarashi, T. 1996. The Great Hanshin Earthquake and the new rule. *City Planning review* 200 (1): 121-129. (J)

Iwakami, M. 2003. *The Sociology of the Family: Gender and Life-course Perspectives.* Tokyo: Yuhikaku. (J)

Japan Federation of Housing Organizations. 2002. *Seikatsusya to tomoni tsukuru asu no juutaku heno bijonn.* Japan Federation of Housing Organizations. (J)

Kageyama, H. 2004. *Urban Space and Gender.* Tokyo: Kokon-shoin. (J)

Kawaguchi, T. 1997. Analysis of the household relocation process in a suburban setting: Case study in Kawaguchi City, Saitama, Japan. *Geographical Review of Japan* 70A: 108-118. (J)

Kato, A. 2003. *Has the Japanese Family Changed from the Stem Family System to the Conjugal Family System during the Past Half Century?* Doctoral Dissertation of Meiji University. (J)

Kubo, T., Onozawa, Y., Hashimoto, M., Hishinuma, Y., and Matsui, K. 2010. Mixed development in sustainability of suburban neighborhoods: The case of Narita New Town. *Geographical Review of Japan* SeriesB 83: 47-63.

Kubo, T. and Yui, Y. 2011. Transformation of the Housing Market in Tokyo since the Late 1990s: Housing Purchases by Single-person Households. *Asian and African Studies* 15 (3): 3-20.

Hasegawa, T. 1997. Residential developments by private railroad enterprises: A case study of Nankai Electric Railway. *Japanese Journal of Human Geography* 49: 465-480 (J).

Matsubara, H. 1982. The development of large-scale residential estates by private developers in Japan. *Annals of the Japan Association of Economic Geographers* 28: 279-295 (J).

Morrow- Jones, H. A. 1988. The housing life-cycle and the transition from renting to owning a home in the United States: a multistate analysis. *Environment and Planning A* 20: 1165-1184.

Ronald, R. 2004. Home ownership, ideology and diversity: Re-evaluating concepts of housing ideology in the case of Japan. *Housing, Theory and Society* 21: 49-64.

Ronald, R. 2008. *The ideology of home ownership.* New York: Palgrave Macmilan.

Statistics Bureau of Japan. 2008. *Housing and Land Survey.* Statistics Bureau of Japan.

Statistics Bureau of Japan. 2010. *Population Census of Japan*. Statistics Bureau of Japan.

Tahara, Y., Hirai, M., Inada, N., Iwadare, M., Naganuma, S., Nishi, R., and Wada, Y. 2003. Towards a gerontological geography: Contributions and perspectives. *Japanese Journal of Human Geography* 55: 451-473. (J)

Tani, K. 1997. An analysis of residential careers of metropolitan suburbanities: A case study of Kozoji New Town in the Nagoya Metropolitan suburbs. *Geographical Review of Japan* 70A: 263-286. (J)

Van Vliet, W. and Hirayama, Y. 1994. Housing conditions and affordability in Japan. *Housing Studies* 9: 351-368.

Yoneyama, H. 2013. Reactions of local government on increasing vacant houses and foreign cases. *Fujitsu Research Institute Research Report* 403: 1-30. (J)

Yui, Y. 1991. Differentiation of residents according to housing supply type: A case study of Fukuoka City. *Geographical Sciences* 46: 242-256 (J).

Yui, Y. 1999. *Housing studies in geography: Changing characteristics of residents*. Tokyo: Taimeido. (J)

(J) means "written in Japanese" (with an English summary, in some cases).

9. Gentrification in a Post-Growth Society: The Case of Fukushima Ward, Osaka

Yoshihiro FUJITSUKA

Abstract

In a post-growth society, extended urban forms must be considered with the goals of protecting the global environment, accommodating an aging society, and revitalizing the central areas of cities. In Japan, the government published a report on its vision for urban regeneration in 2003 in which it was noted that an adequate urban structure is needed for a sustainable city. In this vision of urban regeneration, sites that had been displaced during the economic bubble period should be merged to heighten intensity of land use. Additionally, to accommodate an aging society, life spaces should be supplied for the elderly near public transportation stations, and walkable distances from these stations to various amenities are also important. Traditional houses and high-quality modern buildings should be preserved and rehabilitated. This paper surveys gentrification in Osaka in terms of urban regeneration, sustaining society, and the urban landscape, with three specific objectives: to clarify contemporary gentrification and the urban regeneration policy; to scrutinize urban housing for aging people and the community; and to examine whether contemporary gentrification matches the urban landscape.

Keywords

gentrification, urban regeneration, post-growth society, sustainable city, urban landscape

9.1 Introduction

In a post-growth society, extended urban forms must be considered with the goals of protecting the global environment, accommodating an aging society, and revitalizing the central areas of cities. Advanced countries aim to intensify population density in central areas of cities. Major cities of advanced countries plan new uses for brownfield sites. In London, for example, 'the Blue Ribbon Network' was formulated to revitalize brownfield areas along rivers and canals (Mayor of London, 2004).

In Japan, the government published a report on its vision for urban regeneration (Ministry of Land, Infrastructure, and Transport, 2003:3) in which it was noted that an adequate urban structure is needed for a sustainable city:

> In the 21st century, cities have reached a turning point in history.
>
> In Japan, cities possess a negative legacy in terms of urban landscape, housing, and social capital, and are entering a new phase of 'shrinking cities' that lose

population and become hollow. The population is aging and the birth rate is declining extremely rapidly; the percentage of old people in the population will be over thirty percent in the 2030s.

Eighty percent of the total population was born, grow up, study, work, gather together, spend their leisure time, and end their lives in cities. Urban regeneration is urgently needed in order for a community to sustain life, activity, and exchange.

Urban regeneration attracts people from all over the world to Japan, which then boosts competitiveness on an international scale and revitalizes the economy and society. Both major cities and provincial cities should vie with their own knowledge and characteristics based on economic and cultural accumulation.

The vision of urban regeneration in the report focuses on three points. The first point concerns sites that had been displaced during the economic bubble period, and that should be merged to heighten intensity of land use. Since land prices were increasing sharply in the 1980s and early 1990s, speculators bought properties near central business districts as investments, and then sold them on to other speculators. Many sites were merged to form parking lots, which could be easily redeveloped later for other purposes. However, in many cases, the parking lots were retained due to very low land prices in the second half of the 1990s after the bubble burst (Fujitsuka, 2005). The government designed to stimulate private development in under-utilized sites by incentives.

The second point has to do with an aging society, and how to provide life spaces for the elderly near public transportation stations, with walkable distances from those stations to various amenities.

The third point addresses the preservation and rehabilitation of traditional houses and high-quality modern buildings. The vision criticized "a freedom of construction that drastically altered the urban landscape" (Toshi Saisei Bijon Kenkyukai, 2004).

Tokyo and Osaka are important cities that attract people from all over the world (Ministry of Land, Infrastructure, and Transport, 2003:25). In Tokyo, new-build gentrification was reported by Lützeler (2008). Gentrification is cascading down the urban hierarchy (Lees et al., 2008:169). In Osaka, Nanba (2000) points out that a shopping street has been losing local customers due to gentrification.

This paper surveys gentrification in Osaka in terms of urban regeneration, sustaining society, and the urban landscape, with three specific objectives: to clarify contemporary gentrification and the urban regeneration policy; to scrutinize urban housing for the elderly and the community; and to examine whether contemporary gentrification matches the urban landscape.

9.2 Gentrification and the urban regeneration policy in the 2000s

In the 1980s, the population in the central areas of major cities in Japan declined because of the development of office buildings. In the 1990s, housing linkage programs were introduced in Tokyo (Kishino, 1990; Yoshida, 1990) and Osaka. One feature of these programs was the addition of a floor area ratio bonus in the construction of office buildings and housing units. In Chuo Ward of Tokyo, housing linkage programs had a major impact of population recovery. In the late 1990s, massive population recovery occurred in the central area of Tokyo. In 2004, Chuo Ward government abolished the linkage program because the population had recovered to over 100,000.

In Osaka City, the housing linkage program was enacted in 1994 (Osaka City, 2013.4.1a), an applicable case has not occurred. One reason is that developers have avoided constructing mixed-use buildings because of the high cost of construction. Furthermore, demand for offices was low after the collapse of the bubble economy.

Since 2001, the government has promoted a deregulation policy for the construction of high-rise condominiums. It should be noted that the municipal government applies the deregulation of height and floor area ratio bonuses to buildings with designated open spaces in the environs for public use.

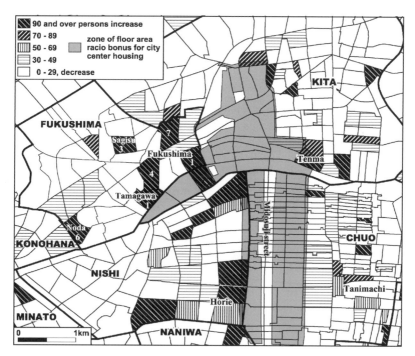

Figure 1 Change of professional, technical workers, managers and officials in central Osaka (2005-2010)
Source: population census of Japan and Osaka City (2013.4.1b)

In 2004, the urban regeneration policy was enacted. The Urban Regeneration Policy involved the designation of Emergency Urban Development Areas in the central areas of Japan's major cities. In Osaka, the urban regeneration district is shown as zones of floor area ratio bonus for city center housing in Figure 1. The government offered incentives for private-sector urban development: building height controls were exempted from the height district, and zoning limitations on the floor area ratio were deregulated in these areas. Super high-rise condominiums have been constructed under this deregulation (Sorensen et al., 2010; Sorensen, 2011; Yamaguchi, 2012).

The paper investigates a case in second half of the 2000s, by using changes in professional, technical workers, managers and officials as an index of gentrification in central Osaka (Figure 1). There are a few agglomerations of increases in these workers, particularly in the districts of Horie, Tanimachi, Tenma, and Fukushima.

In Nishi Ward, urban changes were initiated through the construction of condominiums in the 1980s (Kagawa, 1988). Horie is a wholesale district of furniture and interiors. In the 2000s, Horie attracted the attention of young people as a commercially regenerated area (Tatemi, 2008). Some warehouses were converted to clothing shops along Tachibana Street (Kawaguchi, 2008).

A district around Tanimachi 6 is called as Karahori. The Karahori district escaped damage from a major air raid during World War II. There are many wooden detached and terraced houses in the district. In 2001, the Karahori Club was established to preserve urban landscape of wooden terraced houses along small arrays (Rokuhara, 2008). In 2004, Osaka City established the HOPE zone to preserve and rehabilitate traditional houses (Yoshino, 2006). Since many terraced houses had been converted to shops, cafes, bars, and restaurants, the district has attracted artists and visitors in recent years.

In Tenma, there is a convenient shopping street and an elementary school that is in great demand. Because of these factors, the construction of condominiums has attracted families (Tokuda et al., 2009).

In Fukushima Ward, many industries house their bases of operation, such as factories for automobile parts, knitting mills, print shops, and distribution centers. There was a large freight depot in Umeda. Accessibility to the Umeda freight depot was important before the rise of motorization. Since the shift in the preferred means of transportation from railways to trucks, Fukushima has been losing locational predominance for industries. Since the 2000s, the freight depot yard has been developed for commercial use. In the late 2000s, the social upward movement in districts occurred because of the supply of high-rise condominiums. These sites were formerly industrial in nature and included a distribution center, a warehouse, and a hospital. The number of blue-collar workers decreased in Fukushima. It implies social change by gentrification there.

The paper makes Fukushima ward as a case study. Urban regeneration district was designated in the city center (Figure 1). A part of the district was the southeastern part of Fukushima 1, which was the site of a government-owned hospital. Office buildings, a shopping center, and a super high-rise condominium are located in the block. The ground floor of the condominium has a commercial facility, bustling with people. By providing this facility, extra floor area bonus was added. The condominium was constructed to be 50 stories high.

6.3 Gentrification and the surrounding community

The vision of urban regeneration (Ministry of Land, Infrastructure, and Transport, 2003) clearly indicates the importance of housing the elderly near public transportation stations. The chapter examines community surrounding high-rise condominiums.

Figure 2 is a map of high-rise condominiums constructed in Fukushima Ward in the late 2000s. The condominiums are located near the JR, Hanshin train stations and subway stations. The number of floors and number of housing units in the complex are shown in the figure. The rate of dwelling households and vacancies is also shown in the figure. The difference between the number of housing units and the number of dwelling households is shown as a vacancy in the population census. It might indicate that some housing units are owned as second homes

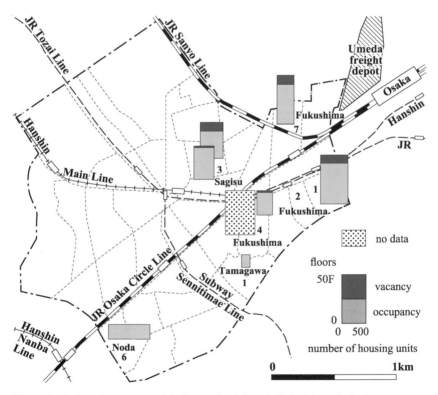

Figure 2 Scale and vacancy of high-rise condominiums in Fukushima Ward (2010)
Source: population census of Japan

Figure 3 High-rise condominium constructed in an industrial district in Fukushima 4
Source: Fujitsuka photographed (2013)

Figure 4 A large banner of criticism in the neighborhood of the high-rise condominium in Fukushima 4
Source: Fujitsuka photographed (2013)

Gentrification in a Post-Growth Society: The Case of Fukushima Ward, Osaka

Table 1 Cohort change of five year groups in small areas of Fukushima Ward (2005-2010)

2005 2010	Fukushima			Tamagawa	Noda	Sagisu
	1	4	7	1	6	3
→ 0- 4	67	89	73	176	372	264
0- 4 → 5- 9	16	−8	4	−18	209	−2
5- 9 → 10-14	17	7	10	−23	52	12
10-14 → 15-19	22	81	108	1	48	33
15-19 → 20-24	48	13	94	24	59	94
20-24 → 25-29	77	52	138	86	101	186
25-29 → 30-34	103	82	151	94	303	233
30-34 → 35-39	100	52	121	18	399	177
35-39 → 40-44	79	30	61	−26	173	91
40-44 → 45-49	74	1	48	10	101	95
45-49 → 50-54	66	6	23	25	67	53
50-54 → 55-59	50	14	43	−6	70	30
55-59 → 60-64	68	−3	13	−8	63	25
60-64 → 65-69	31	−12	15	−2	11	0
65-69 → 70-74	30	−9	3	−18	23	9
70-74 → 75-79	10	−7	5	−5	26	0
75- → 80-	0	−38	−22	−34	35	−42
population change	899	374	876	302	2,120	1,285

Source: population census of Japan

and that some households object population census survey.

The height of condominium structures is higher near Osaka Station. Each condominium in Fukushima 1 and 7 has 50 floors. The condominium in Noda 6 has 15 floors and its vacancy rate is only 1%, and The condomnium in Tamagawa 1 has 13 floors and it has no vacancy. The rate of vacancy is higher near Osaka Station. The findings show a surplus of available dwellings. Therefore, the developer had better build lower condominiums.

Figure 3 shows a super high-rise condominium constructed in an industrial district. There is a building for a commerce and industry association in Fukushima 4. A large banner severely criticizes future buyers of the condominium (Figure 4) with a message that reads "If you bought a home in this condominium, you might be sued for wind damage from the high-rise building." Super high-rise condominiums have caused construction disputes in the community.

Table 1 shows cohort change of five year groups in small areas in which high-rise condominiums have been constructed. The number of residents over 65 years of age increased in Fukushima 1 and Noda 6, as did the number of younger people from 25 to 44 years of age. The number of children under 4 also increased. These changes imply an influx of families in

Fukushima Ward. Most housing units in high-rise condominiums are not inhabited by the elderly, who may not be able to afford them if they are living on their pensions. Thus, these condominiums do not help the elderly to live near public transportation stations.

9.4 Urban landscape of gentrification

In the vision of urban regeneration, life spaces are insufficient in both beauty and abundance. Freedom of construction after World War II focused on efficiency and function, with a negative impact on the urban landscape (Ministry of Land, Infrastructure, and Transport, 2003:15).

Gentrification was reported by Glass (1964) in London, and 50 years have passed since then. A classic form of gentrification is that old houses are rehabilitated as residences for newcomers, and the urban landscape is preserved in the district.

Since the mid 1990s, the physical structure of gentrification has been changing in cities. In London, new-build gentrification has occurred at the site of old industries along the River Thames (Davidson and Lees, 2005, 2010).

Smith (1996:39) mentioned the following in his book:

> Gentrification is no longer about a narrow and quixotic oddity in the housing market but has become the leading residential edge of a much larger endeavor: the class remake of the central urban landscape.

Figure 5 Super high-rise condominium constructed near a traditional terraced house in Fukushima 1
Source: Fujitsuka photographed (2013)

Figure 6 Conversion of terraced houses into restaurants and bars in Fukushima 2
Source: Fujitsuka photographed (2013)

He paid attention to the change in the urban landscape. This paper also examines it.

Figure 5 shows a super high-rise condominium constructed near a traditional terraced house. There is a parking lot in front of the terraced house. The parking lot was the site of the former terraced houses. Stone pavement has been used among terraced houses. When land prices soared in the late 1980s, residents in terraced houses were displaced and the houses were demolished. Since the 1990s, land prices have decreased severely, and the site has been used as a parking lot.

The government pointed out that the use of historical and cultural resources was important in making Tokyo and Osaka attractive world cities (Ministry of Land, Infrastructure, and Transport, 2003). Nevertheless, the loss of traditional houses such as terraced houses is a serious issue.

Most houses in Fukushima Ward avoided war damage. Production and related workers have lived in terraced houses (Osaka Toshi Jutakushi Henshu Iinkai, 1989; Tani and Takehara, 2013). However, there is no sufficient policy to preserve such terraced houses in Osaka City. One problem is lose of traditional houses such as terraced houses. Terraced houses have been seen as a target for conversion by young people in recent years (Toshi Osaka Sosei Kenkyu-kai, 2009). Some terraced houses have been converted into restaurants or bars (Figure 6).

The construction of super high-rise condominiums has brought and a mismatch in the urban landscape. In Fukushima 7, for example, there is a church that has been registered as an important historical resource of the urban landscape (Osaka City, 2012.12.21). It stands near a

Figure 7 A resource of urban landscape and a super high-rise condominium in Fukushima 7
Source: Fujitsuka photographed (2013)

super high-rise condominium. In terms of the urban landscape, the condominium does not chime in with the surrounding architecture (Figure 7).

9.5 Conclusion

The paper clarifies that deregulation caused construction of high-rise condominiums. Judging from the vacancy rate of high-rise condominiums, there is a surplus of housing units. Although most of these units are located near public transportation stations and might therefore be expected to be attractive to the elderly, most condominium occupants are young people; the elderly are few.

In terms of preservation of the urban landscape, the government criticised the freedom of construction. Osaka City designated historical buildings as resources of the urban landscape, however, super high-rise condominiums nearby destroyed low height landscape of historical buildings. Super high-rise condominiums have also caused construction disputes.

Given that gentrification has a significant impact on urban change in a post-growth society, it should be controlled so that it does not damage the community.

References

Davidson, M. and L. Lees. 2005. New-build 'gentrification' and London's riverside renaissance. *Environment and Planning A* 37 (7): 1165-1190.

Davidson, M. and L. Lees. 2010. New-build gentrification: its histories, trajectories, and critical geographies. *Population, Space and Place* 16 (5): 395-411.

Fujitsuka, Y. 2005. Gentrification and neighbourhood dynamics in Japan: the case of Kyoto. In *Gentrification in a global context: the new urban colonialism*, ed. R. Atkinson and G. Bridge. 137-150. London and New York: Routledge.

Glass, R. 1964. Aspects of change. In *London: aspects of change*, ed. the Centre for Urban Studies, xiii-xlii. London: MacGibbon & Kee.

Kagawa, T. 1988. Changes with the surrounding area of CBD as affected by the construction of condominiums: a case study of Osaka City. *Geographical Review of Japan* 61A: 350-368. (J)

Kawaguchi, N. 2008. How street fashion is shaped in Horie, a commercially regenerated area. *Japanese Journal of Human Geography* 60 (5): 443-461. (J)

Kishino, I. 1990. Juutaku Fuchi Gimu Yoko: Tokyo-to Shinjuku-ku. *Chiiki Kaihatsu*, 311: 41-44. (J)

Lees, L., Slater , T., and Wyly, E. 2008. *Gentrification*. New York and London: Routledge.

Lützeler, R. 2008. Population increase and "new-build gentrification" in central Tokyo. *Erdkunde*, 62 (4): 287-299.

Mayor of London. 2004. *London Plan: spatial development strategy for Greater London.* London: City of London.

Ministry of Land, Infrastructure, and Transport. 2003. *Toshi saisei bijon.* (J) (http://www.mlit.go.jp/kisha/kisha03/04/041224/01.pdf).

Nanba, T. 2000. Gentrification of pre-war inner city housing in Japan. *Bulletin of Nagoya College* 38: 109-123. (J)

Osaka City. 2012. 12.21. *Toshi keikan shigen list.* (J) (http://www.city.osaka.lg.jp/toshikeikaku/cmsfiles/contents/0000017/17850/list.pdf).

Osaka City. 2013. 4.1a. *Jutaku Fuchi Yudo Seido.* (J) (http://www.city.osaka.lg.jp/toshikeikaku/page/0000004899.html).

Osaka City. 2013 4.1b. Osaka-shi sogo sekkei kyoka toriatsukai yoko jisshi kijun. (J) (http://www.city.osaka.lg.jp/toshikeikaku/cmsfiles/contents/0000012/12322/soukei-kijyun-1.pdf).

Osaka Toshi Jutakushi Henshu Iinkai ed. 1989. *Machini sumau: Osaka toshi jutakushi.* Tokyo: Heibonsha. (J)

Rokuhara, M. 2008. Nagaya fuzei wo mamori seicho saseru manejimento sisutemu: Karahori kara. In *Osaka shigaichi saikaihatsu sokushin kyogikai*, ed. Toshi saisei machidukuri gaku, 112-121. Osaka: Sogensha. (J)

Smith, N. 1996. *The new urban frontier: gentrification and the revanchist city.* London and New York: Routledge.

Sorensen, A., Okata, J., and Fujii, S. 2010. Urban renaissance as intensification: building regulation and the rescaling of place governance in Tokyo's high-rise manshon boom. *Urban Studies* 47 (3): 556-583.

Sorensen, A. 2011. Uneven processes of institutional change: path dependence, scale and the contested regulation of urban development in Japan. *International Journal of Urban and Regional Research*, 35 (4): 712-734.

Tani, N. and Takehara, Y. ed. 2013. *Ikiteiru nagaya: Osaka shidai moderu no kochiku*. Sakai: Osaka Municipal Universities Press. (J)

Tatemi, J. 2008. Cultural industries, knowledge creation and industrial agglomeration. In *Regional problems of Japan in the 21st century*, ed. Y. Ito and Y. Fujitsuka, 12-13. Tokyo: Kokon Shoin. (J)

Tokuda, T., Tsumaki, S., and Ajisaka, M. 2009. The reurbanization of Osaka after 1980. *Social Science Review* 88: 1-43. (J)

Toshi Osaka Sosei Kenkyukai, ed. 2009. *The book of Noda + Fukushima: rojiura kara "Hotarumachi" made*. Osaka: Sogensha. (J)

Toshi Saisei Bijon Kenkyukai. 2004. *Shigaichi shukusho jidai no machidukuri: toshi saisei bijon wo yomu*. Tokyo: Gyosei. (J)

Yamaguchi, S. 2012. Development of tower condominiums in Japan: 'exclusivism' or 'popularization' of high-rise residence? *The Kwansei Gakuin Historical Review 38: 67-105.* (J)

Yoshida, U. 1990. Juutaku fuchi to juutaku seisaku: Tokyo-to Chuo-ku. *Chiiki Kaihatsu* 311: 37-40. (J)

Yoshino, K. 2006. Karahori: HOPE keikaku jigyo niyori saisei wo mezasu. In *Roji karano Machidukuri*, ed. Y. Nishimura, 128-140. Kyoto: Gakugei Shuppansha. (J)

(J) means "written in Japanese" (with an English summary, in some cases).

10. Spatial Characteristics of Land Evaluation in the Tokyo Metropolitan Area after the Great East Japan Earthquake

Hirohisa YAMADA

Abstract

Following the Great East Japan Earthquake in March 2011, security and safety have been taken into account more than ever before. The high interest in risk management in daily life appears to have created a new standard for individuals seeking their properties. This study focuses on the fluctuation of residential land prices in the Tokyo Metropolitan Area, and it clarifies the spatial characteristics of land evaluation by the damage situation and its continuity. Residential land prices are largely determined by distance from the inner city and are influenced by commercial land prices. However, the damage of the earthquake in 2011 caused specific fluctuations in residential land prices. Although a tsunami did not occur in practice, its threat induced broad changes in land evaluation. On the other hand, liquefaction damages that occurred actually induced local changes in the short term. The most noticeable phenomenon is that the presence of hot spots indicating extremely high radiation locally caused discontinuous declines in land evaluation. It was not until inhabitants themselves measured radiation level that they evaluated the land.

Keywords

Land price, Land evaluation, Financial crisis, Great East Japan Earthquake, Tokyo Metropolitan Area

10.1 Introduction

Most Japanese cities based on the pre-modern castle-town still maintain their spatial structure centered on a castle, and the urbanization centers have been taken over. For example, in the Meiji era (approx. 1868 to 1912), the city hall, courthouse, and police station of a city were typically constructed in a district adjacent to the castle. Since the deterioration of Japanese architecture was relatively mild compared to those of cities in Europe and the United States, people in Japan tend to live in the inner city even today (Narita 1987). As the Nomura Research Institute (1988) pointed out, in Japan, a country in which a taxation evaluation method to divide the land and the buildings on it is used, even if productivity were to be evaluated at zero as a result of building deterioration, the land would still be taxable. Landowners therefore find it difficult to leave land unattended or unimproved. This is one of the factors underlying the continued high land prices in a Japanese city's downtown area. Another significant factor is the destruction of the majority of urban areas in many large Japanese cities by air raids during World War II. New urban facilities have been established on the previous frame by reconstruction projects after the war. Additionally, loose restrictions on suburban development gave rise to the 'land myth' that land prices in Japan do not fall in both urban areas and suburban areas (Morinobu 2006).

The land myth begot the bubble economy in the late 1980s, and land prices soared led by land transactions for speculative purposes. Given that the land price is the comprehensive index of land evaluations, it can be said that rising land prices during the bubble period greatly affected the commercial district in the metropolis and its suburbs. On the other hand, commercial districts are more likely to be speculative targets compared to residential lands, and residential land prices mostly increase in response to commercial land prices. However, the land myth disappeared in the early 1990s with the collapse of the bubble economy, and commercial land was then evaluated by an assessment of individual attributes (Yamada 2004). As a result, in the process of the significant long-term decline in land prices in the 1990s, the projection of land price distribution in the suburbs was leveled in the Tokyo Metropolitan Area. The decline in land prices accelerated condominium construction in central Tokyo (Yamada 2008). These constructions housed many people who would have previously moved out to suburban areas for residential home purchases. Although residential land prices in the suburbs also fell, regional characteristics were widely observed, unlike commercial land prices. Since the ground rent of residential land cannot be determined clearly, the land evaluation of consumers changes by the 'regional reputation.'

In the early 2000s, the long-term decline in land prices subsided. However, the financial crisis occurred in 2008 and the Great East Japan Earthquake occurred in 2011, and Japan was in a situation that made it difficult to predict future land price fluctuation. Especially, since residential land prices depend on spatial factors that vary with the 'regional reputation' — unlike commercial land prices that reflect the ground rent sensitively — it is assumed that evaluations of residential areas diversified by different types of decline factors that occurred in the late 2000s.

This study focuses on residential land prices in the Tokyo Metropolitan Area and investigates the effects of the Great East Japan Earthquake on land evaluations in order to clarify their spatial characteristics after the disaster. Although safety was a significant consideration, more than ever in land evaluation we find that the impacts of the earthquake hazard have distinct characteristics caused by continuity and the status of the damages, which are tsunami, liquefaction, and radiation. Although we cannot say that the earthquake did not affect the evaluation of commercial land at all, this paper clarifies the relationship between residential land evaluation and changes in awareness of the living environment. In terms of commercial land, we must mainly investigate its direct productivity or short-term ground rent, and think about user awareness on a secondary basis. These themes need to be discussed in other papers.

The remainder of this paper is organized as follows. In Sections 2 and 3, I review land price fluctuations in the Tokyo Metropolitan Area and clarify their changes over time by drawing distribution maps of land prices. In Section 4, I consider the impact of the Great East Japan Earthquake on residential land evaluation from the differences in variation rates, and Section 5 provides conclusions.

10.2 Overview of land price fluctuations in the Tokyo metropolitan area

The Land Market Value Publication (LMVP) was used as the land price data in this study. The LMVP is called Chika-Koji in Japanese and has been published as the index for real estate transactions every year since 1 January 1970 by the Land Appraisal Committee under the Ministry of Land, Infrastructure, Transport, and Tourism (MLIT). Land price in the LMVP is assessed at the appraisal site, called the 'standard site.' It is the probable land value that would be formed in an assumed transaction without any extraordinary incentives that induce participants to sell off or initiate buying, as assessed using the appraisal approach published based on ordinances of the Ministry regarding the appraisal of standard sites, Real Property Appraisal Standards, etc. (MLIT 2013). Altogether, 26,000 standard sites across Japan were valued in 2013.

The LMVP value is the appraised value, but not the present price of the real estate transac-

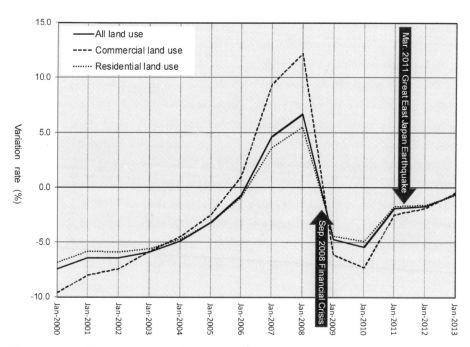

Figure 1 Transition of average variation rate in the Tokyo Region
Source: Land Market Value Publication

tion. This should be taken note of in a study considering land price as the result of economic activities, and deriving its exact formation model from an economic viewpoint. However, the present study considers land price as a result of land evaluation and attempts to clarify its regional differences. The LMVP provides the optimum data, which assists in obtaining a quantified land evaluation for a fixed point at the national scale.

In the LMVP, the 'Tokyo Region' is comprised of municipalities including the Existing Urban Areas and the Urban Development Zone of the National Capital Region Development Act. Looking at the transition of the average variation rate of land prices in the Tokyo Region, the long-term decline in land prices during the 1990s subsided in the first half of the 2000s (Figure 1). The variation rate of commercial land price reached 12.2% in 2008 (i.e., from Jan. 2007 to Jan.2008). However, land prices began to decline again under the effect of the financial crisis in September that same year. Although the degree of decline weakened in 2011, changes in the later years were almost flat. It is assumed that this is because the Great East Japan Earthquake in March 2011 lessened the recovery tone from the financial crisis. In addition, the difference in the variation rate between residential and commercial land prices has almost disappeared since the earthquake. The tendency for the fluctuation of commercial land prices to provoke that of residential land prices is no longer seen.

Land price fluctuations in Japan after World War II can be divided into three periods (Yamada 1999). In the first period, before the early 1960s, industrial land prices in large cities mainly grew following the reconstruction of the industrial zone after the War. The second period, from the late 1960s to the early 1980s, included the period of rapid economic growth in Japan when the surge in residential land prices led to a rise in land prices for other uses due to the enormous population inflow into urban areas. As the third period, since the late 1980s the fluctuation of commercial land prices has come to lead fluctuations in land prices for other uses. Although it is unclear whether the earthquake is related to the crossing of the variation rate curves of commercial and residential land prices in recent years, varied land evaluations might change the dynamism of the land price fluctuation mechanism.

I studied an area with a 60-km radius centered on Tokyo Station, which is located essentially in the center of downtown Tokyo, and analyzed the land prices of the standard sites that have been continuously valued from 2008 to 2013[1]. In total, there are 6,328 such sites: 4,685 residential land sites, 1,423 commercial land sites, 188 industrial land sites, and 32 other sites. Most of the Tokyo Region in the LMVP is included within this radius (Figure 2). In the following analysis, this radius is called the Tokyo Metropolitan Area (TMA).

Notice: Figure 2 in P.163 is replaced by the below figure.

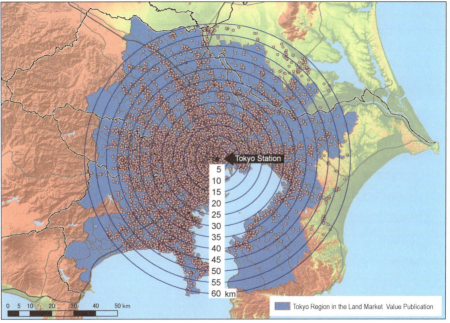

Figure 2 Standard sites in Tokyo Metropolitan Area
Source: Land Market Value Publication, National Land Numerical Information

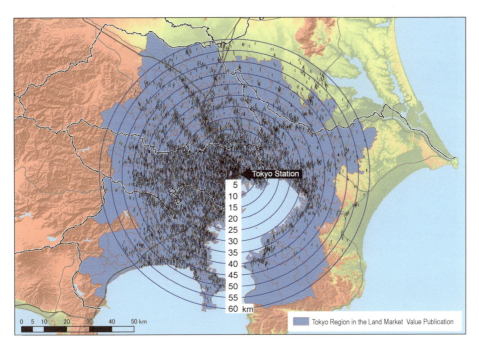

Figure 2 Standard sites in Tokyo Metropolitan Area
Source: Land Market Value Publication, National Land Numerical Information

10.3 Land price distribution and its changes

In this study, several raster maps interpolated by the GIS (Geographic Information System) were used to observe regional characteristics. Figure 3 presents the land price distribution in 2008 in the TMA, when land prices reached a peak in the 2000s. We can find the following features in the raster map. First, the area representing high land prices (i.e., Japanese yen [JPY] 1 million/m^2 or more) is concentrated within the inner 10-km radius (Figure 3). As symbolized by this shift, land prices in the TMA demonstrate a trend of higher land prices in the west compared to the east as a whole for historical reasons of land development. Second, in suburban areas, protrusions in the land price distribution appear along the main railways that extend radially from Tokyo Station. In 2008, the highest commercial and residential land prices were JPY 39 million/m^2 and JPY 3.3 million/m^2, respectively, at the ratio of approx. 12:1. Incidentally, the highest commercial land price in 1991, when land prices reached a peak during the bubble period, was JPY 38.5 million/m^2. In terms of the peak of commercial land prices, the land prices in the TMA can be said to have almost reached the level of the bubble period.

Looking at the land price distribution shape for each type of land use, it can be seen in Figure 4 that a high-level area (JPY 1 million/m^2 or more) of commercial land prices spreads across the 15-km radius, and nearly the entire TMA shows prices at JPY 100,000/m^2 or more (Figure 4). In addition, it can be seen that the protrusion observed in the suburban area is due

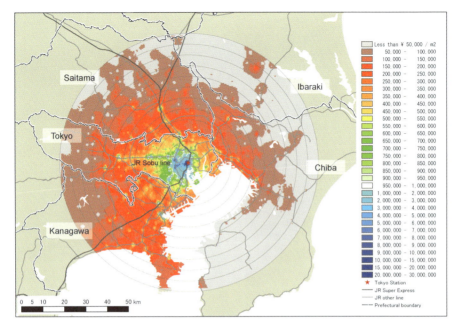

Figure 3 Land price distribution in 2008 (all land use)
Source: Land Market Value Publication

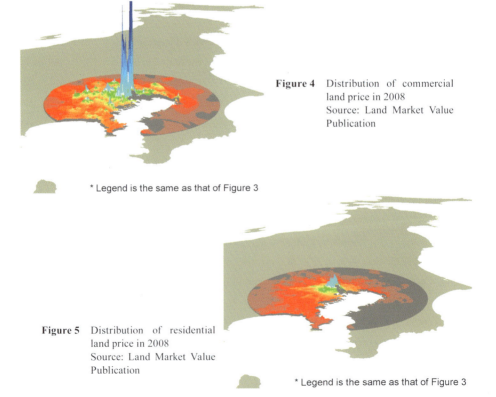

Figure 4 Distribution of commercial land price in 2008
Source: Land Market Value Publication

* Legend is the same as that of Figure 3

Figure 5 Distribution of residential land price in 2008
Source: Land Market Value Publication

* Legend is the same as that of Figure 3

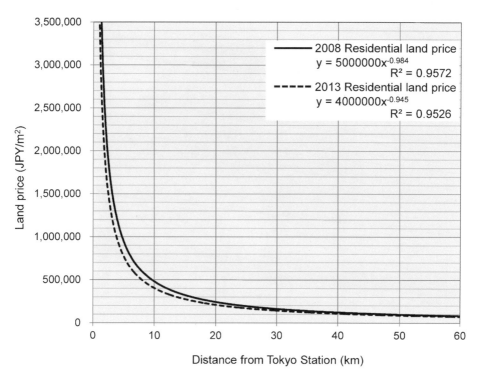

Figure 6 Approximation formulas between land price and distance from Tokyo Station
Source: Land Market Value Publication

to commercial land prices. On the other hand, residential land prices gradually decrease as the distance from the Tokyo Station increases (Figure 5). Therefore, by calculating the average residential land price in each distance band, I set up an approximation formula showing the relationship between the distance from the inner city and the residential land price (Figure 6). The formula can be represented by a power function of the distance, which has a shape similar to the bid rent curve of the mononuclear city model introduced by Alonso (1964). The coefficient of determination (R^2) was 0.96 and 0.95 in 2008 and 2013, respectively. As apparent from these coefficients, land prices are largely determined by the distance from the inner city. A comparison of the two curves reveals that land price decline over the past five years was remarkable in the 3–15-km zone from Tokyo Station. Since few residential standard sites exist in the 3-km zone, it can be said that the decline in residential land prices during this period occurred in the inner city and the adjacent district.

As Figure 3, Figure 4 and Figure 5 show, it is easier for commercial land — which is often appraised higher compared to land for other uses due to its productivity (or ground rent) — to induce fluctuation in other land prices. This has played a proactive role in the formation of land price distribution in the TMA. However, large economic changes have not occurred in Japan since the financial crisis. It is therefore assumed that commercial land prices, which are

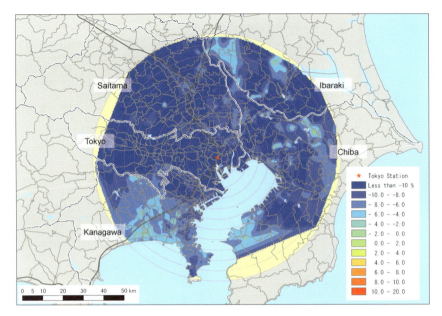

Figure 7 Distribution of variation rates from 2008 to 2011 in residential sites
Source: Land Market Value Publication

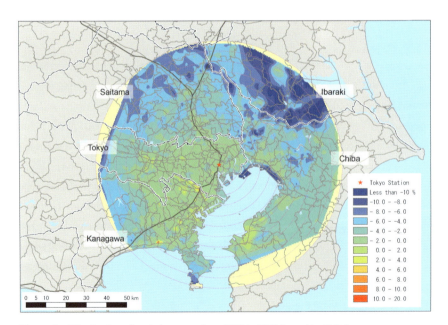

Figure 8 Distribution of variation rates from 2011 to 2013 in residential sites
Source: Land Market Value Publication

sensitive to changes in ground rent, have largely not influenced other land price formations. Residential land prices could have fluctuated by their own evaluation. [2]

Figure 7 shows the variation rate distribution of residential land prices from 2008 to 2011. With the exception of some parts of the suburban areas, land price decline more than 10% occurred throughout the TMA during that period. After the Great East Japan Earthquake, fluctuations in a range of ± 2% have been observed over a wide area for the two years from 2011 to 2013 (Figure 8). However, a decline in land prices is still in progress in the northeastern part of the TMA, especially in Chiba Prefecture, where the decline is continuing in the residential districts located within a 30-km radius centered on Tokyo Station and with high population density (i.e., Chiba City, Urayasu, and Kashiwa).

In the following section, I examine the changes in land evaluation after the Great East Japan Earthquake in light of weak fluctuations in the residential land prices.

10.4   Impact of the Great East Japan Earthquake on land evaluation

10.4.1   Evaluation trend index

In the process of the decline in land prices, a higher decline was observed throughout the northeastern part of the TMA since the Great East Japan Earthquake. In addition, regional differences were observed in the urban area of Chiba Prefecture in particular. However, the year-on-year variation rates of residential land prices for the entire TMA for 2012 and 2013 were −1.6% and −0.7%, respectively. Therefore, it is not possible to clarify the more detailed changes following the Earthquake by merely drawing the distribution of variation rates.

This study examines the weaker changes during this period by determining the difference between the variation rates of individual standard sites, in order to extract those standard sites showing a higher rate compared to others. Hereinafter, that difference is called the Evaluation Trend Index (ETI). For example, in 2012, the ETI of each site was obtained by subtracting the variation rate in 2011 from that in 2012. Using the average (Avg) 0.15 and the standard deviation (SD) 1.22, the sites that show an ETI in the range of 0.15 ± 1.22 were judged as showing little changes in land evaluation [3]. On the basis of this judgment, changes in land evaluation in the standard sites were divided into six categories as follows:

large increase	: (Avg + 2SD)	≤	ETI	
increase	: (Avg + SD)	≤	ETI	< (Avg + 2SD)
small increase	: Avg	≤	ETI	< (Avg + SD)
small decrease	: (Avg − SD)	≤	ETI	< Avg
decrease	: (Avg − 2SD)	≤	ETI	< (Avg − SD)
large decrease	:		ETI	< (Avg − 2SD)

Since the ETI also increases by merely shrinking the decrease in the range of land prices, its increase does not reflect an absolute rise in land price. The ETI refers to a relative rise or fall in land evaluation. Therefore, the ETI is suitable for finding the salient points in cases of minute fluctuations in the short term. In that sense, the target phenomena of this analysis might be small enough to be ignored compared with the land price fluctuations that Japan has experienced so far. However, looking back, there must be a transition period when the land price fluctuation began moderating gradually before a new dimension of fluctuation was observed in Japan (Yamada 2002). In order to identify the new trend, it is necessary to conduct research and analyses of the recent phenomena in the TMA, because the Great East Japan Earthquake can be considered a factor that would influence land evaluations and transform the land price formation mechanism dynamically.

10.4.2 Awareness of tsunami damage

To clarify the relationship between earthquake hazards and land evaluation, I used the ETI to analyze the relationship from the points of altitude, land liquefaction, and radiation damage. The death toll from the earthquake was at 15,883 people[4], most of whom were victims of the tsunami. Although the TMA did not suffer from tsunami damage, the threat of damage is assumed to have varied the residential land evaluations of the inhabitants and influenced their housing preferences. A particular district in Toyo is approximate 120 square kilometers below sea level. It is clear that this district is the most vulnerable to the tsunami. Residents should have been keenly aware of the need to live at high altitudes to avoid tsunami danger. However, a perfectly safe altitude cannot be determined in advance. For example, if the area less than 10 m above sea level were not safe, most of the wards in Tokyo would have been exposed to danger. The residents who had recognised the fear of the tsunami by the Earthquake behaved on the basis of individual thought and information. The change in land demand as a result of their behavior is thought to eventually be reflected in land prices.

As shown in Figure 9, on overlaying the ETI distribution in 2012 on an altitude map, although there were no changes in the district below sea level, an increase in land evaluation was found on the outer edge of that district. The phenomenon of an increase in land evaluation in the part adjacent to a vulnerable district was observed in the coastal area of Tohoku Region, which suffered greatly from the tsunami (Yamada 2012). Although many residents of that region tried to move out to higher land to escape damage from any future tsunami, some of them disliked living far away from familiar locales. As a result, the demand for land in safe neighborhoods increased, and land evaluation witnessed relative growth around the vulnerable district. In the case of the TMA, however, the lands that qualify as safe neighborhoods are only two to three meters above sea level, and thus are not absolutely safe. The ETIs in the district below sea level did not change because the residents did not move. Although their interest in obtaining safe residences was increased by the Earthquake, they also knew that it was impossible to acquire perfect safety within a short distance.

Spatial Characteristics of Land Evaluation in the Tokyo Metropolitan Area after the Great East Japan Earthquake   169

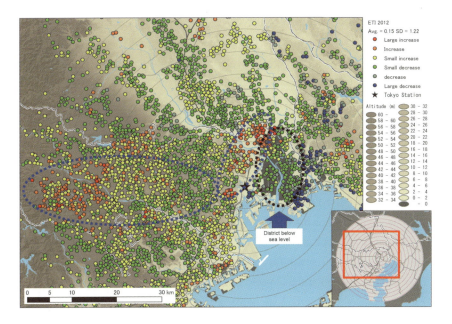

Figure 9 Relationship between altitude and Evaluation Trend Index in 2012
Note: Blue dotted circles are explained in the text.
Source: Land Market Value Publication

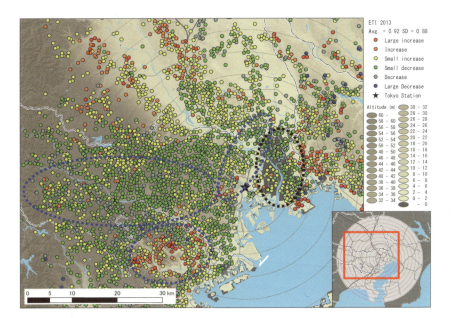

Figure 10 Relationship between altitude and Evaluation Trend Index in 2013
Note: Blue dotted circles are explained in the text.
Source: Land Market Value Publication

In addition, in the western part of the TMA, the regional characteristic was underlined within the 5–50-km radius, where the ETI showed a 'small decrease,' a 'small increase,' and an 'increase' successively for the suburbs. Since both a 'small decrease' and a 'small increase' are in the extent of Avg ± SD, they cannot be said to have fluctuated significantly. However, from that continuous distribution, land evaluation was judged to have risen as it headed inland. That distribution spreads along the main railway extending linearly from the inner city of Tokyo to the west (JR Sobu Line in Figure 3), which many people easily recognize. Although high ETIs in the neighboring land of the district below sea level are in the interest of the community's residents, those in the wide western part are thought to reflect the general picture of residents across the entire TMA.

Real estate appraisers had not apparently taken into account the risk of the earthquake disaster on land evaluation (Yamada et al. 2011). Since it is difficult to appraise an unaffected land site by quantifying the possibility that it might potentially suffer from disaster damage in the future, land evaluation at the moment had no choice but to resort to the changes in the supply and demand of land on the basis of the 'regional reputation,' which was created by the imagination of the residents and was not supported by any clear evidence. Given this feature of the appraisal method, the earthquake can be said to have instilled a fear of the tsunami in the residents and regions of the TMA at various scales in the short term.

In 2013, the ETIs in the above two districts were leveled (Figure 10). This implies that the land evaluation change in 2012 has continued, assumed to be caused by the 'regional reputation.' On the other hand, in the southwestern part of the TMA, a prime residential district where land prices easily grew, the ETI increased in 2013. This case is interpreted as a result that the 'regional reputation' in the entire TMA led the re-evaluation for that district. That is, it took a certain amount of time, about two years, for the threat of tsunami to become an evidence for land evaluation in the TMA. It does not seem that the fear of a tsunami, which did not occur in practice, is maintained for a long period in the same form. Awareness of a disaster hazard would be reflected in land evaluations while changing its form.

10.4.3 Liquefaction damage at the waterfront

The TMA suffered from liquefaction damage due to the Great East Japan Earthquake. Figure 11 shows the ETI distribution in 2012 on the liquefaction damage map, which was published by the Kanto Regional Development Bureau under the MLIT. According to the survey by the Development Bureau, liquefaction was observed in northern coastal areas of Tokyo Bay and areas along the Arakawa and Tonegawa Rivers. The land evaluation fell greatly in the coastal areas in Chiba Prefecture because liquefaction occurred in housing estates, unlike what occurred in the two riverbeds. Liquefaction distorts the foundation of a house and greatly reduces its function, and owners must pay the costs of the necessary repairs. Because they are directly reflected in the ground rent, land prices of the affected areas rapidly decreased. In

Spatial Characteristics of Land Evaluation in the Tokyo Metropolitan Area after the Great East Japan Earthquake

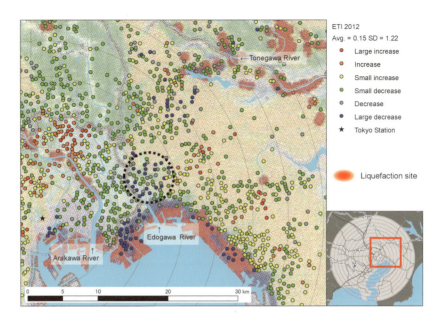

Figure 11 Relationship between liquefaction and Evaluation Trend Index in 2012
Note: Black dotted circle is explained in the text.
Source: Land Market Value Publication, Kanto Regional Development Bureau (2011)

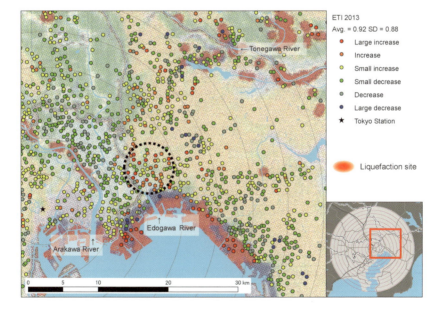

Figure 12 Relationship between liquefaction and Evaluation Trend Index in 2013
Note: Black dotted circle is explained in the text.
Source: Land Market Value Publication

contrast, residential land evaluation in the areas along the Arakawa River relatively increased. The liquefaction that occurred in the riverbeds caused no direct damage to the residential areas. In addition, the factor related to the altitude of the land led to rising land evaluations in those areas, as was pointed out above.

In the case of liquefaction damage, the situation can be confirmed on the spot, and land prices in an area that suffered from actual liquefaction damage decrease rapidly. However, for the same reason, there is little possibility that the land price decline that was once appraised would accelerate in the next year. This is also recognized by a comparison with the map that shows the ETI distribution in 2013 (Figure 12). The ETI in the coastal area indicated a 'large increase,' because the decreasing rate of land prices in 2012 was very high. The land price decline is ongoing.

In the area east of the Edogawa River, a 'large decrease' and a 'large increase' were observed in 2012 and 2013, respectively. Although these standard sites were not included in the affected area of liquefaction, the fluctuation pattern of the ETI resembled those in the coastal areas of Tokyo Bay, and it is thought that the same change occurred in the evaluation. That area is included in the district with a possibility of liquefaction, which is predicted in the liquefaction hazard map produced by Chiba Prefecture (2012). The future risk in that area might have been the subject of land evaluation. However, the area west of the Edogawa River, which does not show large changes in the ETI, is also included in the vulnerable district of the liquefaction hazard map produced by Tokyo Metropolis (2012). Land appraisal methods are not different according to municipalities. Since the liquefaction damage in residential areas is concentrated in Chiba Prefecture, land evaluations are assumed to have responded sensitively to hazard information in that prefecture.

Although the fear of tsunami damage that did not occur in practice continued to impact land evaluations gradually, the recovery from liquefaction decreased the land evaluations rapidly before calming down. The area affected by liquefaction was the waterfront, which is a popular residential area always in excess demand. Even if residents affected by liquefaction move to other places, since the next consumer is going to want to occupy the land immediately, the land market would not show a long-term change according to the market principle; the decline in land valuation would not continue. When the negative evaluation caused by a disaster risk is wiped out by the positive evaluation of popular places, land prices would begin to rise. Landowners would find it difficult to meet the costs of disaster prevention or mitigation, and they would not conduct land use modifications such as ground improvement and earthquake-resistant construction. As a result, the seismic strength of the entire region would not be enhanced forever. This study advances the analysis based on the notion that land evaluations should be reflected in land prices. However, for disaster prevention and mitigation, a land price policy such as obliging seismic reinforcement by suppressing the rise in land prices might be required.

10.4.4 Radiation damage in the long term

The accident at the Fukushima Daiichi nuclear power plant that followed the Great East Japan Earthquake caused a variety of problems across the country. The health hazards posed by radioactive materials scattered by the explosion of the reactor building are a major concern. People are highly interested in the amount of residual radiation in the residential area. Land prices have dropped significantly over the entire region in Fukushima Prefecture, where the nuclear power plant is located (Yamada 2012). The land cannot even be appraised in the off-limit area in the prefecture[5]. Since the accident occurred in the early spring when the northeast and north winds dominate, the residual radiation drifted into the Kanto Region and has been increasing the anxiety level of those residents (Asahi Shinbun 2012).

When the ETIs in 2012 are put on the distribution map of the radiation (Hayakawa 2013)[6], it is found that the decrease in land evaluation, which was observed in the inland of Chiba Prefecture, is related to the drop of radioactive materials (Figure 13). According to Hayakawa's map, a band of 0.125 μSv/h or more is hanging over toward the center of the TMA from Kasumigaura Lake in Ibaraki Prefecture. The contours of radiation that were drawn in the TMA indicate higher radiation (0.500–1.000 μSv/h) near Kashiwa in Chiba Prefecture. Although that city is located about 200 km away from the nuclear power plant, the same amount of radiation was measured in Iwaki in Fukushima Prefecture, located only 50 km away. Radioactive materials were not necessarily scattered in concentric circles centered on the nuclear power plant, but were spread amoeba-like all over eastern Japan under the influence of the wind and terrain. As a result, a higher contour is drawn over an unanticipated area. Since radiation damage is immediately invisible, residents will not be able to notice it until such information is published. The most disturbing issue of radiation damage is that it is invisible.

Therefore, the land evaluation decline due to radiation is characterized by the standard points which indicate a significant decrease of land evaluation, dotted in a wide area centered on Kashiwa. This decline is distinctly different from those caused by tsunami fears and liquefaction damage, the former of which shows spatial continuity; the latter appears to be concentrated on the affected place. As Hayakawa annotates, he drew contours interpolated using GIS, but did not express the amount of radiation measured at individual sites. In order to obtain more exact information, inhabitants must measure their housing estates themselves or with help from experts. Because of the shapes of buildings and the conditions of the ground surface, there are cases in which the deposition of radioactive materials progresses. When the presence of a hot spot indicating extremely high radiation locally becomes apparent, land evaluation rapidly decreases. As a result, residential lands were discontinuously evaluated with a time lag. This is a factor that caused a unique ETI distribution. Such features of radiation damage resulted in reputational damage over a wide area in terms of housing acquisition and agricultural production. The impact will continue for many years.

Looking at the ETI distribution in 2013, although land evaluation continued to decrease

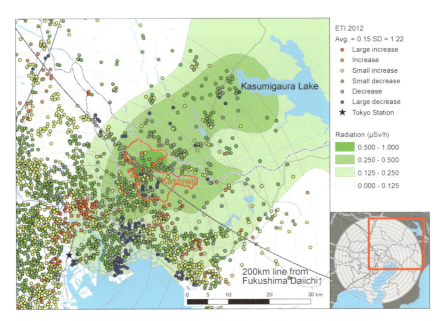

Figure 13 Relationship between radiation and Evaluation Trend Index in 2012
Source: Land Market Value Publication

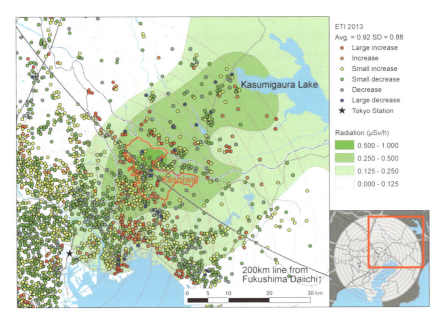

Figure 14 Relationship between radiation and Evaluation Trend Index in 2013
Source: Land Market Value Publication

significantly in a few standard sites in the 0.250–1.000 µSv/h zone, some new sites were observed to indicate a 'large decrease' (Figure 14). As mentioned above, radiation damage tends to rapidly decrease land evaluations locally. Since there is possibility that a new hot spot is confirmed, the negative image would spread over that zone gradually. Accordingly, land evaluations in the area affected by radiation damage may continue to decline as a whole.

After the Great East Japan Earthquake, safety has come to occupy an unprecedented position in land evaluations in the TMA. In this study, direct factors of disaster damage were covered. In the future, a discussion of the relationship between land evaluation and indirect factors such as house aging and residential density is necessary.

10.5 Conclusion

Since the Great East Japan Earthquake, security and safety have been taken into account more than ever in the Tokyo Metropolitan Area. High interest in risk management in daily life is thought to have created a new standard for selecting a house and its location. This paper focused on residential land price fluctuations in the TMA following this earthquake. I organized the disaster impacts on land evaluation and clarified the spatial characteristics of residential land evaluation by the damage situation and its continuity. The results of this study have critical significance in generating a new point of view for discussing the spatial constitution of the TMA in the future and the price formation mechanism of residential land in Japan. The result of this study can be summarized as follows.

In the TMA, the land price decline that occurred in the 1990s after the bubble subsided in the early 2000s, and the variation rate of land prices in all forms of land use turned positive in 2007. However, following the collapse of Lehman Brothers in September 2008, land prices fell again, and this fall continues in 2013. The Great East Japan Earthquake occurred in March 2011, at a time when the land price reduction caused by the financial crisis had begun to stabilize. The comparison of the land price fluctuations in 2011–2013 with those in 2008–2011 revealed that the land price fall in the former period was milder than that in the latter period. Although residential land prices in the TMA are largely determined by distance from the inner city, the decline continued in the northeastern part of the area, and as such a directional bias was observed.

In order to clarify the regional differences in weak land price fluctuations, I used the Evaluation Trend Index (ETI) in this study. Using the ETI shows the regional differences by subtracting the variation rate in the previous year from that in the current year. When land prices in the entire area have fallen, a positive ETI means that the degree of decline is weakened and that land evaluations rise relatively. On the other hand, a negative ETI implies that the degree of decline has strengthened and that land evaluations fall relatively. By using the ETI, I examined the relationship between land evaluation and fears of tsunami, liquefaction damage, and residual radiation, and the characteristic of each in 2012–2013 was clarified.

In the TMA, which did not suffer from the tsunami, since large population movements did not occur, the supply and demand balance of land did not change significantly. However, the fear of the tsunami, which left thousands dead or injured after the earthquake, impacted residential land evaluations. A high ETI appeared in the outer edge of the district below sea level because the inhabitants in that district were keener on moving to a safe area. Regarding the ETI distribution spreading in the western suburbs of Tokyo, a vague image of safe places for the general inhabitants of the TMA corresponded to the comprehensible terrain. Risk perceptions of the residents who did not suffer from tsunami damage are varied. These differences are thought to have caused the diversified pattern of ETI distribution.

Since liquefaction was the disaster damage that actually arose in the TMA, unlike the tsunami, it is easy to point out the relationship between the damage and land evaluation. Liquefaction occurred in the waterfront properties. In general, the land evaluations restrictively decreased in the area where liquefaction damaged houses. The coastal area of Tokyo Bay, where significant damage was observed, needs seismic strengthening of the entire area. However, an increase in land evaluations might precede the strengthening, because it is a popular residential area.

On the other hand, the radiation damage caused by the nuclear power plant accident is problematic since the radiation damage, though significant, is invisible. Therefore, to determine the safety of individual land, measurement by suitable instruments must be carried out. As a result of this process, land evaluations rapidly fell wherever a hot spot was observed. The land evaluation decline due to radiation damage has progressed sporadically over a wide area, with a time lag. This decline is predicted to influence the spatial structure of the TMA in the long term.

It is clear that after the Great East Japan Earthquake, safety must be made a higher priority than ever. However, there are various risks to land depending on its position, geology, and the surrounding situation. Locality is also a relevant factor for risk management of the residents and land consumers. Moreover, for future research in economics, analyses from a geographical perspective are more effective for residential land evaluations than quantitative analyses.

Notes

1) This does not mean that the standard sites are fixed eternally. Some sites disappear or are put up newly as the situation demands. Thus, the sites appraised on an ongoing basis were selected in this paper.

2) Konagaya (2003) stated that residential land is dependent on its position and is easily simplified. In his study, the commuting cost was used as a value representing the 'position' of the residential land.

3) The ETI Avg and SD in 2013 were 0.92 and 0.88, respectively.

4) Fatality figures are based on the data released by the National Police Agency on 10 Decem-

ber 2013 (National Police Agency, 2013).

5) There are 17 standard sites where the LMVP was not appraised in 2013.

6) The first edition of Hayakawa's map was published on 21 April 2011.

References

Asahi Shinbun. 2012. Hotto supotto no 'Meian'. Asahi Shinbun Weekly AERA 30 Apr – 7 May 2012: 30-34. (J)

Alonso, W. 1964. Location and land use. Cambridge, Mass: Harvard University Press.

Chiba Prefecture. 2012. Liquefaction Hazard Map. (J) (http://www.bousai.pref.chiba.lg.jp/portal/05_sonae/58_hazard/ejk/) (last accessed 1 December 2013)

Hayakawa, Y. 2013. Radiation counter map of the Fukushima Daiichi accident, 8th edition. (J) (http://kipuka.blog70.fc2.com/) (last ccessed 1 December 2013)

Kanto Regional Development Bureau. 2011. Tohoku chiho taiheiyo oki jishin niyoru kanto chiho no jiban ekijoka gensyo no jittai chosa. (J) (http://www.ktr.mlit.go.jp/ktr_content/content/000043569.pdf/) (last accessed 1 December 2013)

Konagaya, K. 2003. Generalized formulation for the spatially-dependent utility model in urban economics. The Quarterly Journal of Economic Studies 26 (1): 19–36. (J)

Ministry of Land, Infrastructure, Transport, and Tourism. 2013. How to look at land market value publication. (J) (http://tochi.mlit.go.jp/english/land-prices/land-market-value-publication/) (last accessed 1 December 2013)

Morinobu, S. 2006. The rise and fall of the land myth in Japan: some implication to the Chinese land taxation. PRI Discussion Paper Series, No.06A-08, 1–14, Policy Research Institute, Ministry of Finance, Japan. (J)

Narita, K. 1987. Daitoshi suitai chiku no saisei: Jumin to kino no tayoka to fukugoka wo mezashite. Tokyo: Taimeido. (J)

National Police Agency. 2013. Damage Situation and Police Countermeasures on 10 December 2013. (J)

 (http://www.npa.go.jp/archive/keibi/biki/index_e.htm/) (last accessed 15 December 2013)

Nomura Research Institute. 1988. Chika to tochi sisutemu. Nomura Research Institute, Japan. (J)

Tokyo Metropolis. 2012. Liquefaction hazard map. (J) (http://www.metro.tokyo.jp/INET/OS-HIRASE/2013/03/DATA/20n3ra00.pdf/) (last sccessed 1 December 2013)

Yamada, H. 1999. Dynamism of land price fluctuation. Tokyo: Taimeido. (J)

Yamada, H. 2002. Interaction between land price increase and spatial changes in the metropolitan area. Quarterly Journal of Geography 54 (4): 236–246. (J)

Yamada, H. 2004. GIS analysis on land price fluctuations in Tokyo metropolitan area. Journal of History, Geography and Cultural Anthropology, Yamagata University 5: 1–13. (J)

Yamada, H. 2008. Relationship between condominium location and land price fluctuation in central city of Tokyo metropolitan area. Journal of History, Geography and Cultural Anthropology, Yamagata University 9: 1–12. (J)

Yamada, H. 2012. Regional differences of land price fluctuation in recent years. Proceedings of the 2012 annual meeting of the human geographical society of Japan: 80–81. (J)

Yamada, H., Kawabata, F., and Miyamoto, K. 2011. Impacts of natural disaster risk on land estimation. Quarterly Journal of Geography 63 (1): 43–44. (J)

(J) means "written in Japanese" (with an English summary, in some cases).

11. Image of the Post-Growth City: Recent Transformation of Japanese Regional Central Cities

Masateru HINO

Abstract

This paper proposes the concept of "post-growth city" through an examination of the recent transformation of Japanese regional central cities. As of 2010, Japan had already entered a stage of demographic transition in which the total population begins to decrease due to low birth rate and ageing. Regional central cities are no exception. Moreover, the agglomeration of branch offices, which functioned as an economic base in these regional central cities, started declining in the late 1990s. These phenomena are symptoms of the shrinking city. However, the period following the 1990s saw the rise of various activities carried out by citizens and local organizations. We believe that cities that have sustained their vitality through the expansion of actor-centered networks organized by citizens, civil society organizations, local companies, their industrial groups, local governments, and local cultural organizations should not be considered shrinking cities, but are more properly evaluated as post-growth cities.

Keywords

post-growth city, shrinking city, regional central city, intercity linkage, branch office, Japan

11.1 Introduction

The problem of city shrinkage has been one of the main themes in studies on urbanization worldwide. Although city shrinkage is not a new phenomenon[1], its present manifestation is, however, new in that the reasons for the shrinkage originate from structural changes in society and in that the number of shrinking cities is increasing. In advanced countries, many industrial cities have reduced their economic bases due to both a global shift of industries and structural changes in industry composition, followed by decreasing employment opportunities and population (Martinez-Fernandez et al., 2012; Pallagst et al., 2014). In developing and semi-advanced countries, we see many shrinking cities among small and medium-sized cities due to population outflow to larger cities, the family planning that suppresses the birth rate, and drastic social transformation with decreasing social welfare. In the field of urban planning, it is a challenge to seek ways to lead the shrinkage of cities systematically through planning (Pallagst, 2010).

In Japan, the demographic transition has reached the stage at which the birth rate has become smaller than the death rate. In 2005, the number of deaths exceeded the number of births; this may be the first time in its long history, excluding World War II, that the population of Japan has decreased, though this decrease was anticipated based on a remarkable decrease in fertility after the 1970s. A conversion from city planning for expansion to plans corresponding to a population decrease was therefore requested in the 1990s (Kaido, 2007). The concept of the compact city was proposed and accepted in the master plan of cities.

However, the specific manifestations of city shrinkage are various. In the present study, we explain the structural changes in the economic bases of Japanese regional central cities as a shrinking phenomenon since the late 1990s, and we examine other new phenomena that promote the vitality of cities. Based on our results, we propose the concept of "post-growth city" instead of "shrinking city" to refer to cities that maintain sustainable vitality even with a decrease in population and infrastructure.

11.2 Characteristics of Japanese regional central cities

11.2.1 Rapid growth since the 1950s

In Japan, the term "regional central city" has been generally applied to only four cities: Sapporo, Sendai, Hiroshima, and Fukuoka (Figure 1). These cities grew rapidly beginning in the 1950s in spite of a nation-wide tendency for the population to concentrate in three largest metropolitan areas, especially the Tokyo metropolitan area.

In Japan the municipality system was enacted in 1888. Under this institution, all municipalities were equally placed under the control of a prefectural government in spite of large differences in city size. Therefore, beginning in the early 20th century, the traditional six largest cities (Tokyo, Osaka, Nagoya, Yokohama, Kyoto and Kobe) demanded of the national government the enactment of a metropolitan system given their background of high-level administrative and fiscal ability (Kitamura, 2013). This demand was never met during the pre-war period, but Tokyo shifted to the metropolitan system in 1943 under the wartime regime. However, the designated city system was introduced as a substitute for the metropolitan

Figure 1 Locations of major cities in Japan

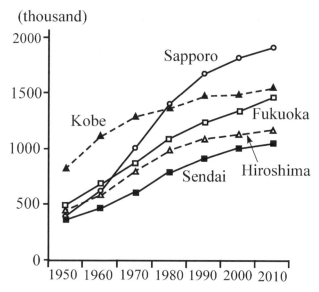

Figure 2 Rapid growth of the four regional central cities after the 1950s
Source: Japanese Population Census of 1950-2010

system in 1956. Under this system, designated cities took over a certain amount of administrative authority, such as urban planning, from the prefectural government. A designated city was necessarily a metropolis in Japan.

In 1956, only the five largest cities were recognized as designated cities: Osaka, Nagoya, Yokohama, Kyoto and Kobe. At that time, regional central cities were not examined to determine whether they met the requirements to become designated cities because of the large differences in population and economic power between the traditional six largest cities and the four regional cities. For example, while Kobe, the smallest of the traditional six largest cities, had 960,000 people in 1955, Fukuoka, the largest of the four regional cities, had only 550,000 (Figure 2).

Since the 1950s, however, regional central cities have grown rapidly. In the 1970s, Sapporo and Fukuoka each attained a population of 1 million and achieved designated city status. In the 1980s, Hiroshima and Sendai also became designated cities. The rapid growth of regional cities is a characteristic of the urbanization of the latter half of the 20th century in Japan.

11.2.2 Based on a branch office economy

The rapid growth of regional central cities was brought about not by industrialization but by the agglomeration of branch offices of nation-wide companies. Table 1 shows the fundamental statistics of the regional central cites. It is easy to see that white-collar jobs and the service sector, rather than blue-collar jobs, account for most employment.

Table 1 Fundamental characteristics of four regional central cities

City	Population in 2010	Area (km²)	Industry structure		Job structure	
			Tertiary industry	Secondary industry	White-collar	Blue-collar
Sapporo	1,913,545	1121	77%	14%	31%	23%
Sendai	1,045,986	786	81%	15%	33%	22%
Hiroshima	1,173,843	905	73%	21%	30%	27%
Fukuoka	1,463,743	342	78%	13%	32%	20%

Source: Japanese Population Census of 2010

Sapporo   Sendai

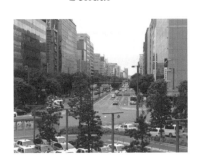

Hiroshima   Fukuoka

Figure 3 Central business districts of the four regional central cities
Source: Hino photographed in 2013.

The four regional central cities had from around 5,000 to 17,000 branch offices as of 2006: Fukuoka, 16,837; Sendai, 6,720; Sapporo, 5,940; Hiroshima, 5,041[2]. The number of employees of those offices reached from 80,000 to 160,000 individuals. These figures clearly indicate that branch offices provide a main supply source of white-collar jobs in these cities. In addition, a large number of branch offices were established in these cities during the post-war period of rapid economic growth, and likewise, a large number of offices buildings were constructed to accommodate these branch offices, along trunk streets in downtown areas. As a result, office districts emerged in the downtown areas of the regional central cities (Figure 3).

Moreover, many of the branch offices in regional central cities belonged to companies headquartered in Tokyo or Osaka, and were assigned the functions of controlling and coordinating marketing activities throughout their entire respective regions. Thus, the agglomeration of such branch offices in regional cities has increased the centrality of these cities (Abe, 1991; Hino,1996). For example, the share of Sendai in wholesale sales within the Tohoku Region increased from 31% in 1960 to 46% in 1991 (Hino, 1999). As a result, these cities are sometimes called *shiten-keizai no machi* (city based on branch office economy).

11.3 Background of social change and reduction in the agglomeration of branch offices

The agglomeration of branch offices in regional central cities which had continued to increase after the 1950s then entered a decline in the late 1990s. Figure 4 shows the transition of employment of branch offices in the four regional central cities. Although data before 1981 are not shown due to the lack of available statistics, the continuous increase in branch offices in regional central cities was confirmed by an intensive survey of Sendai (Hino, 1996). It can be seen in the figure that the agglomeration of branch offices stagnated when the bubble economy burst in 1991 and began to decrease for the first time in 1996.

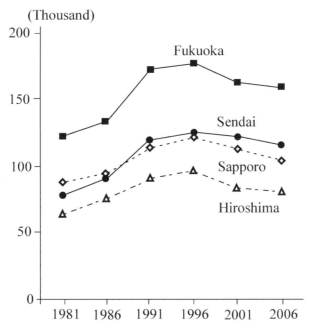

Figure 4 Changes in number of branch office employees in the four regional central cities
Source: Japanese Establishment and Enterprise Census of 1981-2006

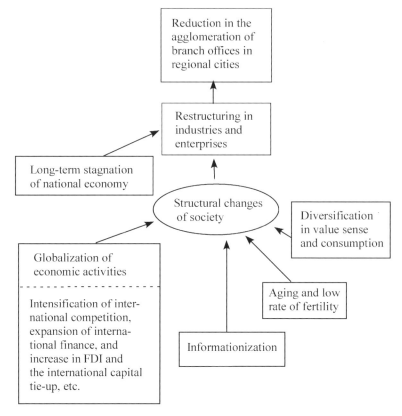

Figure 5 Background of the reduction in the agglomeration of branch offices in regional central cities
Source: Hino (2009)

The structural changes in society shown in Figure 5 can be cited as the background factors contributing to the reduction in agglomeration of branch offices. The five elements of social change in the figure were already noted by the fifth National Development Plan adopted by the Cabinet in 1998 (National Land Agency, 1998). Although the overseas expansion of Japanese companies has progressed further in response to the rapid appreciation of the yen due to the Plaza Accord of 1985, this influence did not appear in a significant manner until the burst of the bubble economy. However, after the bubble economy collapsed, corporate restructuring of large companies progressed, including not only the consolidation of branch offices but also a shift of production bases to abroad. Moreover, the rationalization of the distribution system based on the advancement of information and communication technology promoted the decrease in branch offices. On the social level, the declining birth rate and increase in the aging population became prominent in the 1990s.

These changes constitute an irreversible trend. Additionally, since the reduction of agglomeration of branch offices in regional central cities came about because of such changes, it is unlikely that the trend in agglomeration of branch offices would be reversed by a recovery of the Japanese economy. Moreover, although branch offices of companies providing producer services are increasing in regional central cities, they are not increasing in sufficient numbers to offset the reduction of agglomeration of branch offices in wholesaling, the construction industry and the financial insurance industry (Hino, 1996).

11.4 Symptoms of shrinkage in the landscape
11.4.1 Increase in the vacancy rate of office buildings

The reduction in agglomeration of branch offices brought about an increase in the vacancy rate of office buildings in the downtown areas of regional central cities. Figure 6 shows the transition of vacancy rates of office buildings in the regional central cities since 1996. Although these rates fell below 5% before 1997, they then began to increase, reaching approximately 10% in 2002, after which they continued at 10% or more with some fluctuation.

As the vacancy rate of office buildings increased, many of these buildings began to display advertisements for tenant recruitment on their windows or walls (Figure 7), and many office buildings were converted into retail shops and shops used in personal service industry. The vacancy rate in Sendai was approximately 20% in 2009-2010, largely due to the construction

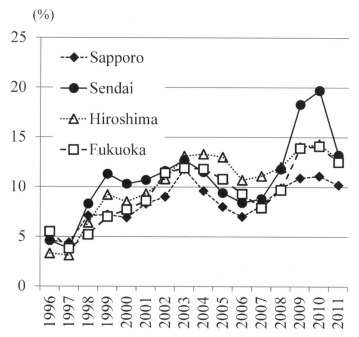

Figure 6 Transition of vacancy rates in the four regional central cities in and after 1996
Source: Ikoma Real Estate White Books of 2000-2007 and CBRE Real Estate White Books of 2009-2011

Figure 7 A former office building looking for tenants in Sendai
Source: Hino photographed in 2013.

Table 2 Characteristics of offices in new office buildings in Sendai

Location type of office	Number of office
Office moved from another building	28
Relocated office at the same site	7
Newly established office	3
Total	38

Source: Questionnaire survey in 2009

of new office buildings at a time of reduction of demand.

Table 2 shows the composition of offices in seven new office buildings constructed during 2007-2009 by location type in Sendai. The results of the questionnaire indicate that the majority of tenants in new office buildings had moved from other office buildings. Therefore, the construction of new office buildings does not accurately reflect the growth of the regional central cities.

11.4.2 Increase in the number of vacant lots in the suburbs of regional central cities

Many residential estates were developed in the suburbs of the regional central cities as well as in the three largest metropolitan areas during the post-war rapid economic growth period. These residential estates were characterized by the predominance of detached houses and nuclear families. In Sendai, housing estates of various sizes were developed in the hills surrounding the inner area of the city. An aging of population and a decrease in population pro-

Figure 8 Vacant plot in a suburban housing estate in Sendai
Source: Hino photographed in 2013.

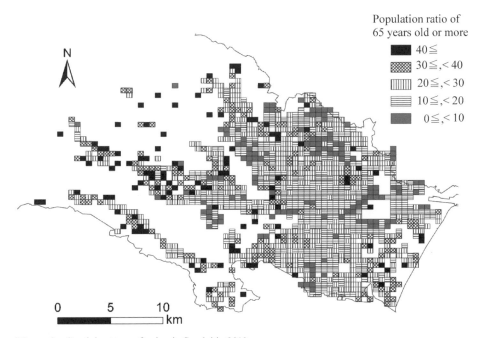

Figure 9 Spatial pattern of aging in Sendai in 2010
Source: Japanese Population Census of 2010.

gressed in housing estates developed early on. As a result, vacant plots appeared among these estates (Figure 8).

Figure 9 shows the spatial distribution of the percentage of the population aged 65 or more in Sendai in 2010. Until the 1990s, many nuclear families lived in the suburbs whose age structure was therefore young compared to that of the inner areas of the city. There was, therefore, a distinct contrast between inner city areas, which had an older population, and the suburbs, where comparatively younger generations lived. However, the second generation was independent from their parents and left their homes in the 2000s while the first generation continued to age. As a result, the earlier contrast in the age structure of the inner area and suburbs disappeared, and a mosaic pattern appeared in its place.

11.5 Vitalization of civil activities

While symptoms of shrinkage have appeared in the regional central cities, their citizenship has become more active. The Star Festival of Sendai, for example, is very famous throughout Japan. On August 6 – 8, the central shopping streets are decorated with beautiful Star Festival ornament (Figure 10)[3], and the area is visited by approximately two million people. This festival is a traditional one and is run primarily by merchants' organization of the main shopping streets.

Futhermore, in the 1990s, festivals organized by volunteer citizen groups became popular. The Jozenji Street Jazz Festival[4] is one such festival. It has been held in the second weekend

Star Festival of Sendai in 2010

Jozenji Street Jazz Festival in 2013

Michinoku Yosakoi Festival in 2013

Sendai Pageant of Starlight*

Figure 10   Festivals organized by civic volunteer groups in Sendai
*Downloaded from the following website:
http://ja.wikipedia.org/wiki/SENDAI%E5%85%89%E3%81%AE%E3%83%9A%E3%83%BC%E3%82%B8%E3%82%A7%E3%83%B3%E3%83%88
Source: Hino photographed in 2013.

of September since 1991(Figure 10), and attracted some 840,000 visitors in 2012. The number of participating bands reached 769 in 2012, including many amateur bands from other cities. The festival is supported financially by many local companies, the municipality and the citizens.

The Michinoku Yosakoi dance festival[5], which started in 1998, is held on a weekend in October. In 2012, it attracted 181 dancing teams from 85 cities around the country and approximately 780,000 visitors. A university student who experienced the original Yosakoi in Kochi City on Shikoku Island initiated this festival with fellow students in Sendai, and it was soon welcomed by the residents of the city. Although this festival is supported various local organizations at present, university students continue to play a central role in its management.

From the second week of December until New Year's Eve, the Sendai Pageant of Starligh[6] is held on Jozenji Street and Aoba Street which have a large zelkova trees. Since zelkova trees drop their leaves in November and the downtown atmosphere becomes rather desolate, several Jozenji Street merchants came together to enliven Sendai in the winter, creating the pageant of starlight, during which the zelkova trees are extensively decorated with miniature bulbs, as in the Christmas tree illumination in 1988[7]. The event is financed by donations from citizens, local businesses and Sendai City. Approximately 2.9 million people visited in 2012.

In addition to the above event, professional baseball, soccer, and basketball teams have been established in Sendai: Tohoku Rakuten Golden Eagles in 2004, Vegalta Sendai in 1994, and 89ers in 2004, respectively. The teams are widely supported. The Tohoku Rakuten Gold-

Figure 11   Tohoku Rakuten Eagles: The professional baseball team based in Sendai
Source: http://www.rakuteneagles.jp/news/detail/3551.html
©Rakuten Eagles

en Eagles won the baseball championship in 2013(Figure 11), when they also enjoyed a home stadium audience of 1.3 million. Vegalta Sendai also attracted 335,000 visitors to its home stadium in 2013.

These sport clubs supported by citizens and festivals run by citizen volunteer organizations have enriched the lives of the citizens. In addition, the Law to Promote Specified Nonprofit Activities was enacted in 1998 with the aim of bestowing corporate status on private volunteer groups that act for a public purpose in order to promote the activation of such activities (Nishide, 2009). The fact that a large number of volunteers took part in relief and recovery after the Kobe -Awaji Earthquake of 1997 was the impetus for this legislation.

Many Specified NPOs have emerged in response to the enactment of this law in Sendai with 400 being counted in 2013[8]. In addition, Sendai City and Miyagi Prefecture have both established support organizations to encourage the activities of the NPOs. Other volunteer organizations, such as the Executive Committees of the festivals mentioned above, are also active. This increasing involvement of the residents of the city is also occurring in the other regional central cities.

11.6 Implication of the coexistence of symptoms of both shrinkage and vitalization
11.6.1 Interpretation of contradictory phenomena based on the pattern of intercity linkages

The existing phenomena of shrinkage and vitality in the regional central cities seem to be contradictory, however, the situation can be interpreted focusing on patterns of intercity linkage.

Figure 12 shows four types of potential intercity linkages among regional central cities. Type A corresponds to intercity linkages in which a regional central city serves as an intermediary distribution center. Regional central cities are hierarchically connected to the national center, Tokyo, and play the role of a prominent center within the territory assigned by nation-wide organizations. Other main cities such as prefectural cities are likewise hierarchically linked to the regional central city within their region. This pattern has been strengthened by the increase in the agglomeration of branch offices in regional central cities after the 1950s. As stated above, the agglomeration of branch offices began to decrease in the late 1990s. Therefore, it is thought that this type of intercity linkage has stopped growing and its re-enlargement is not expected in the future.

Type B shows the pattern in which a regional central city serves as a gateway for other cities within the region. For example, when local companies establish their branch offices in the regional central city in order to extend their selling activities to the whole country, this type of linkage is formed. In Japan, since local companies tend to move their headquarters to Tokyo when they become large enterprises, this type of intercity linkage has not yet developed. However, in Kyushu, there are many local companies whose management bases have been

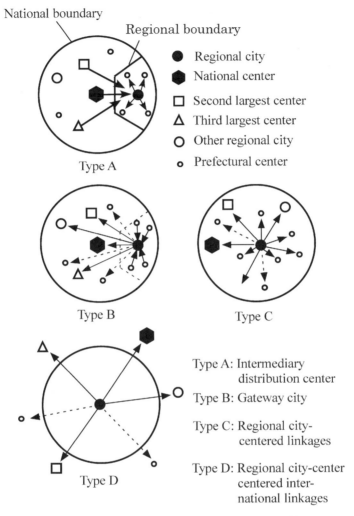

Figure 12 Types of intercity linkages among regional central cities
Source: Hino (2009)

located in Fukuoka for expansion purposes (Noma, 2000).

Type C is significantly different from Types A and B. In Type C, a regional central city occupies the center of intercity linkages. There are no boundaries that limit the activities of actors in the regional central city, which connects directly to other cities of various sizes throughout the country. Actors forming this type of linkage include citizens, various civil society organizations, local government, local companies of various sizes, and educational and cultural institutions such as universities. The development of this type of intercity linkages emerged later than that of Type A. However, with the upsurge in both festivals organized by civil volunteer groups and professional sports clubs supported by citizens, Type C intercity linkages are thought to have expanded remarkably since the 1990s. Since this type of intercity linkage is formed by a large number of actors, it is sustainable as a whole even although individual intercity linkage may be thin and fragile.

Type D is an expansion of Type C linkages to the international scale. Sister city relationships are typical of this type of intercity linkage. Sendai, for example, has nine sister cities throughout the world. In addition, Tohoku University, which is located in Sendai, had academic exchange agreements with 138 universities and research institutions in 38 countries in 2013.

11.6.2 Actors forming individual-city-centered networks

Figure 13 is a conceptual diagram of the network thought to be formed by a variety of actors of the city. Actors that participate in Types C and D of intercity linkages consist of citizens, civic groups, public organizations such as administrative bodies and educational institutions, trade associations, and cultural organizations that extend their activities outside the city. Trav-

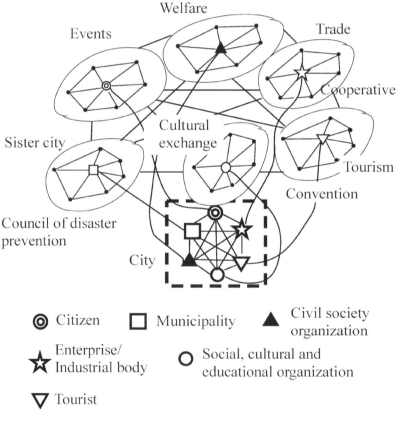

Figure 13 Image of actor-centered networks
Source: Hino (2013)

Image of the Post-Growth City: Recent Transformation of Japanese Regional Central Cities

elers also number among the actors forming these urban networks. All of these actors form intercity relationships with similar actors in other cities while also forming interrelationships with other types of actors within their own city.

In the case of the Michinoku Yosakoi festival mentioned above, the university student of Miyagi Prefecture native who went to Kochi and experienced original Yosakoi festival and then initiated the same festival in Sendai formed a linkage between Sendai and Kochi through the introduction of this festival. In addition, he initially demonstrated Yosakoi dancing through the cooperation of his dancing group with various actors in Sendai resulting in greater understanding and support among the citizens for the festival; that is, a Sendai-centered network was created and extended.

The sister city relation is often connected with a cultural and/or historical tie, and promotes friendship among the citizens of the involved cities. However, the managers of local businesses are also included among the citizens who participate in friendship activities and the possibility of the economic interchange is therefore also present. We can expect similar effects in the case of academic exchanges between universities as international students may return to the city and begin a business connecting the city to their home countries through the support of friends after graduation. Many different types of information, including information that contributes to sustaining and promoting the vitality of the city, are gained through the networks of a variety of actors as Type C and D intercity linkages extend.

Pred (1977) examined the relationship between the development of the city and transmission route of information. These transmission routes become channels of diffusion for the innovation that brings growth to the city. In that sense, it is thought that the probability that technical improvements spread early is high in cities that gather a lot of information from a large area through highly developed networks among various actors. The regional central cities discussed here show such conditions. Cities that maintains their vigor owing to the above networks and process are sustainable and should not be considered to be shrinking.

11.7 Conclusion

If the shrinking city is defined as a city whose population, employment and infrastructure are decreasing, the Japanese regional central cities might be thus defined in the near future. However, the persistent elevation of social vitality in these cities is also seen. It can be expected that these regional central cities will maintain their social and economic vitality through individual-city-centered networks even if the investment of large enterprises decreases together with a decrease in population and economic globalization.

In order for a city to maintain a sustainable vitality, it is necessary for it to develop human resources and to establish a socio-economic environment that enables linkages with various cities and regions worldwide. The Japanese regional central cities discussed here fit this description and should therefore be identified as post-growth cities" even if shrinking takes place.

With respect to branch agglomeration in regional central cities, the role that sustains their urban economy is still large despite its reduction. In other words, the importance of branch offices in regional central cities should be evaluated in the context of maintenance of the infrastructure of the city. Moreover, it is thought that attracting enterprises and talent from outside also increases the diversity of the city and expands the city's network. Therefore, the regional central city must promote the embedding of enterprises and talents from other regions and must take advantage of their potential to contribute to sustaining the vitalization of the city.

Acknowledgements

Some parts of this paper were first published in The Science Reports of the Tohoku University (Seventh Series) 56, 1-11 and 59, 1-12, 2013.

Note

1) In Japan, Takahashi (1971) published the book on declining cities for the reading public in the end of the 1960s when Japanese economy continued the rapid growth. He explained the declining of cities in the relation to structural transformation of basic industries of city.

2) These figure is based on the Japanese Establishment and Enterprise Census of 2006.

3) http://www.sendaitanabata.com/

4) http://www.j-streetjazz.com/

5) http://www.michinoku-yosakoi.net/yosakoi.html

6) http://www.sendaihikape.jp/0201about.html

7) http://flat.kahoku.co.jp/u/blog-seibun/EYgUF0KzeVL8Whjrpmi1/

8) https://www.city.sendai.jp/manabu/shimin/npo/1201564_2611.html

References

Abe, K. 1991. *Nihon no Toshitaikei Kenkyu*. Kyoto: Chijinshobo. (J)

Hino, M. 1994. Changes in the spatial system of wholesaling in Japan. *The Science Reports of the Tohoku University (Seventh Series)* 44: 77-97. (J)

Hino, M.1996. *Toshi-hatten to Shiten-ricchi*. Tokyo: Kokonshoin. (J)

Hino, M. 2009. An alternative direction for maintaining the vitality of Japanese regional cities in the transition stage, *The Science Reports of the Tohoku University (Seventh Series)* 56: 1-11.

Hino, M. 2013. Individual-city-centered networks for cities' self-sustainability: Lesson from the Great East Japan Earthquake. *The Science Reports of the Tohoku University (Seventh Series)* 59: 1-12.

Kaido, K. 2007. *Konpakutoshithi no Keikaku to Dezain*. Kyoto: Gakugeishuppansha. (J)

Kitamura, W. 2013. *Seireishitei Toshi*. Tokyo: Chuohkoronsha. (J)

Martinez-Fernandez, C., Audirac, I., Fol, S. and Cunningham-Sabot, E. 2012. Shrinking Cities: Urban Challenges of Globalization. *International Journal of Urban and Regional Research*, 36 (2): 213–225.

National Land Agency.1998. *Zenkoku- Sogo- Kaihatsu-Keikaku: 21seiki no Kokudo no Gurando-dezain*. Tokyo: Ministry of Finance Printing Bureau. (J)

Nishide. Y. 2009. *Social Capital and Civil Society in Japan*. Sendai: Tohoku University Press.

Noma, S. 2000. *Gurohbaru-jidai no Chiiki-senryaku*. Kyoto, Minervashobo. (J)

Pallagst, K., Wiechmann, T., and Martinez-Fernandez, C. 2014. *Shrinking Cities: International Perspectives and Policy Implications*. New York: Routledge.

Pallagst, K. 2010. The planning research agenda: shrinking cities-a challenge for planning cultures. *Town Planning Review* 81 (5): 1-6.

Pred, A. 1977. *City-Systems in Advanced Economies: Past Growth, Present Process and Future Development Options*. London: Hutchinson.

Takahashi, J. 1971. *Shayo Toshi*. Tokyo: Kobunsha. (J)

(J) means "written in Japanese" (with an English summary, in some cases).

196

12. The Characteristics of Office Location in Sapporo City, Japan

Jun TSUTSUMI

Abstract

The current study analyzes recent changes in the population and employment patterns of Sapporo from the census data and other governmental reports to determine whether the city is experiencing population concentration or decline. Recent growth indicators such as population, office vacancy rates, and land prices suggest that the regional economy in Sapporo has improved. However, the indicators do not necessarily reflect long-term changes to the Sapporo economy. Although the shift in employment from branch offices to information technology (IT)-related companies is significant, it is also unstable. The increase in IT-related workers has occurred as a result of an increase in the number of 'call centre operators' at customer service telephone operation centres, and many of these new IT-related jobs are temporary. For example, a large call centre office supporting a Tokyo company occupies several floors of the JR Tower. The relocation decision was driven by the availability of less expensive office space and lower labour costs relative to Tokyo. The lower labour costs are sustained by an influx of labour from rural communities throughout Hokkaido. Consequently, the present growth rate in Sapporo may not be sustainable in the long term because Sapporo's growth is occurring at the cost of declining economies in rural Hokkaido.

Keywords

Office location, branch office economy, IT-related workers, Hokkaido

12.1 Introduction

12.1.1 City development driven by the 'branch office economy'

Sapporo city had a population of about 1.9 million in the 2010 census, making it the 5th biggest city in Japan. However, unlike other Japanese major cities with long history, Sapporo has existed for only 140 years. Initially, a port was created in Otaru, which is 34km to the west of Sapporo. It played a pivotal role as a 'gateway' for development. Undoubtedly, Otaru was a naturally good port; however, it was located beside mountains that permitted very little room for city development. For this reason, the *Kaitakushi* government (development commission) was allocated to Sapporo, which permitted future growth on the wide Ishikari plain. The *Kaitakushi* government planned a green belt dividing the city into north and south. This belt became the present Odori Park. The city began to develop around the park in a grid pattern. Government buildings were centred around the *Kaitakushi* office in Sapporo's north, while its amusement and commercial quarters were located in the south.

Present development greatly depends on this original urban plan. The population of Sapporo City in 1945 was only about 200,000, which was less than those of other major cities in Hokkaido. The rapid rise of population started after the Hokkaido Comprehensive Development Plan, approved in 1950, which greatly encouraged leading business and manufacturers in Honshu (the main island of Japan) to open branch offices in Sapporo. This industrial expansion encouraged a huge increase in population. With more than one million residents (1970 census), Sapporo was designated as an ordinance-designated (autonomous) city on April 1, 1972. In the same year, Sapporo hosted the 11th Winter Olympic Games, which helped speed up improvements in its urban infrastructure, including the building of a subway system (Tsutsumi, 2004a).

The economic and population growth in Sapporo was supported by the government-mandated construction of branch offices by companies based in Tokyo. However, in his analysis of the accumulation process of urban office functions, Teraya (1993) found that approximately 60% of the major Japanese companies did not have branch offices in Sapporo. Despite this, branch offices still accounted for more than 40% of the establishments and employees in Sapporo and became an essential part of the local economy (Sapporo Chamber of Commerce and Industry 1988, 2003; Hirasawa and Kawanishi 2003). The current study analyzes recent changes in the population and employment patterns of Sapporo to determine whether the city is experiencing population concentration or decline.

12.1.2   Data

Data used were mainly taken from the Establishment and Enterprise Census (2006). Detailed data for each building in the central business district (CBD) (in Microsoft Excel-readable format) were also provided by the urban planning division of the Sapporo City Office. Aerial photographs, topographic maps, and residential atlases were interpreted to determine previous urban land-uses, and the results were translated into GIS attribute data. In addition, the Spatial Data Framework, distributed by the Ministry of Land, Infrastructure and Transport of Japan, was also used to acquire general vector data. A GIS package was used to assist in data processing, representation, and visualization (mapping).

12.2   The outline of Sapporo

The total population of Hokkaido grew from 5.34 million in 1975 to 5.51 million in 2010. Generally, the rate of population growth in Hokkaido stabilized after 1980. In contrast, Sapporo continued to grow and its dominance of the urban hierarchy in Hokkaido continued to expand during the past two decades. The rapid growth of Sapporo's population is in stark contrast to the constant population of the island's other major cities, such as Asahikawa, Hakodate, Kushiro, and Otaru.

Figure 1 shows the population flow into and out of Sapporo from 1972 to 2013. The dark bars indicate the number of people moving into and out of Sapporo from outside of Hokkaido,

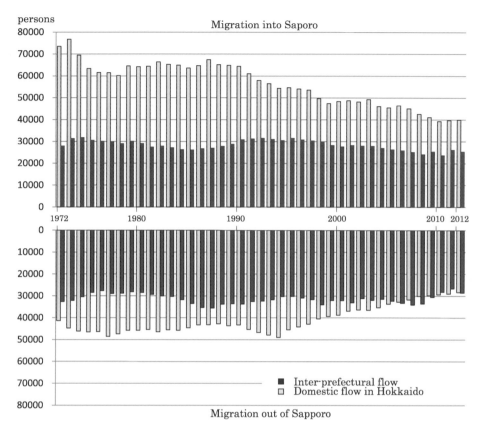

Figure 1 Social population flow of Sapporo (1972-2012)
Source: Data from Sapporo city office

and the light grey ones indicate movement into and out of Sapporo from within Hokkaido. The number of people leaving Hokkaido exceeded the number of people moving into Hokkaido during the period, indicating a net flow out of Hokkaido despite a net increase in the flow within Hokkaido.

The Hokkaido economy has stagnated several times in its history. The closure of coal mining sites during the 1970s and 1980s had the most significant impact on the Hokkaido economy, resulting in a major population shift from rural Hokkaido to the Sapporo metropolitan area. During the same period, many companies based in the Tokyo metropolitan area opened branch offices in Sapporo (Tsutsumi, 2004b). Although several reports have maintained that the growth experienced by Sapporo was brought about only by the branch office economy, these discussions do not reflect all aspects of the economy. Although the branch office economy has been one of the biggest factors in Sapporo's growth, the development of a service economy that created a substantial number of jobs in Sapporo has not been considered in previous studies.

12.3 The trend of office location in Sapporo

Historically, office buildings in Sapporo have been located mostly north of Odori Park. Therefore, the study area for the evaluation of office building supply was limited to the section of Sapporo north of the park. Two peaks in the supply of office buildings in Sapporo were identified (Figure 2). The first period occurred just before and after 1972, the year of the Sapporo Winter Olympics. The second occurred after 1985 when new high-rise buildings were built in the CBD, but were located farther away from the subway line because of higher land prices in those areas and a lack of available space along the subway line.

Figure 3 (above) shows the floors of each building in the CBD of Sapporo. High-rise buildings (i.e., more than 16 stories) are mostly located at the periphery of the study area, away from the subway line that serves as a major growth axis in the city. The lack of available land near the subway line and the low relative age of the existing buildings (approximately 30 years for buildings with a 50-year lifespan) were driving forces of the construction of the high-rise buildings farther away from the subway line. In contrast, relatively low buildings (i.e., under 10 stories) are found along the subway line.

The year of construction of each building in the CBD of Sapporo is identified in Figure 3 (below), along with a height profile. Many older and large-lot buildings are found along the

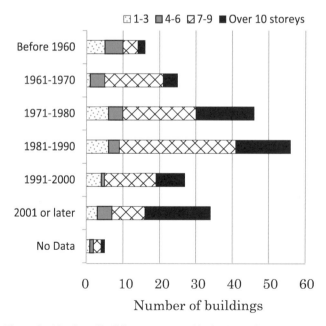

Figure 2 Number of buildings constructed in the CBD of Sapporo (2013)
Source: Data from the Urban planning division of Sapporo city office

a) 3D view of urban landscape

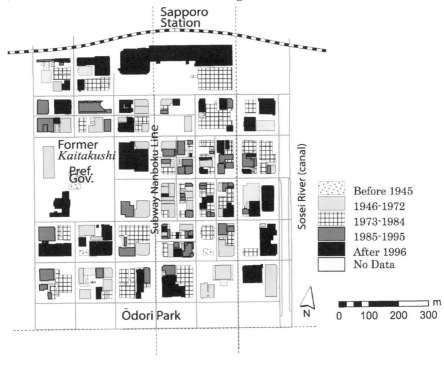

b) Year of construction of each building

Figure 3 Distribution of buildings by height and age in the CBD of Sapporo (2013)
Source: Data from the Urban planning division of Sapporo city office

subway line. Prior to 1972, major Japanese financial groups were the primary owners of these buildings. Height restrictions (31 m, roughly 9 storeys) in effect until 1971 limited the height of buildings in this high-demand area. Since the repeal of that restriction, many taller buildings have been built in the area.

Figure 4 shows the vacancy rate and the average rental cost of office buildings in the Sapporo CBD between 1996 and 2006. The average monthly office rental rate gradually decreased during the period to approximately 8,000 yen/m^2 in 2006. The office vacancy rate was lowest in the early part of this period and then rose to reach a peak of almost 12% in 2003 (resulting in the so-called 'office property crisis of 2003'). Rental rates declined in the office buildings built after 2000, including Sapporo's highest tower, the JR building (36 stories). By the end of 2007, numerous building renovations had begun to expand the amount of available high-rise office space in the CBD. The current redevelopment projects were driven by a chronic shortage in rental office space in the CBD and by the strong demand for space in renovated buildings built before 1972. The status of Sapporo office space has improved, and this desirability has changed the branch office management structure. Short-term changes in office distribution can already be observed, with the office vacancy rate improving to 6.8% by September 2006 (Ikoma CBRE, 2006). However, the proliferation of new building and renovation projects has raised the concern that another 'office property crisis' may occur.

The office relocation rate per building was investigated from September 2004 and January 2007. The author collected the company names listed on the tenant name boards displayed at

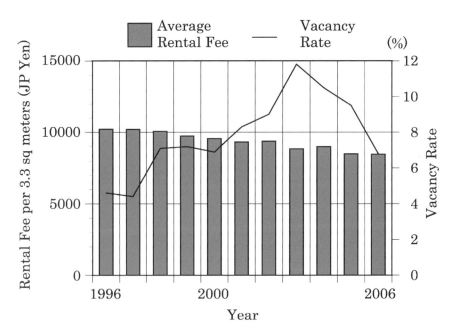

Figure 4 Office vacancy rate in the CBD of Sapporo (1996-2006)
Source: Ikoma CBRE 2006

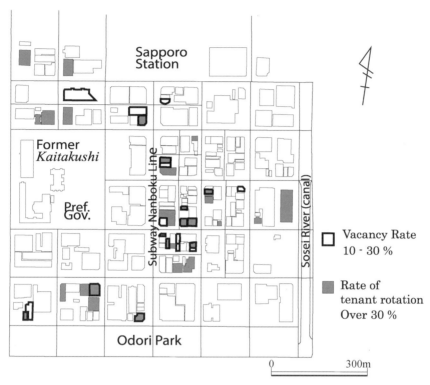

Figure 5 Tendency of tenant rotation in the CBD of Sapporo (2004-2007)
Source: Author's field survey

the main entrance of each building. All the data were compiled into a comprehensive database that included the following information: lot size, year of construction, number of tenants, number of employees and lease duration for each firm, and history of office remodeling. With this database, the relationships between the interval of tenant rotation (time elapsed between a new contract and notification of vacancy) and location could be analysed.

From 2004 to 2007, a high rate of tenant rotation (>30%) was identified in the eastern part of the CBD where relatively small-lot private buildings are located (Figure 5). Most of these buildings were built before 1985, during one of the major building periods in the Sapporo CBD. In the western part of the CBD, adjacent to the Hokkaido prefectural government buildings, even high-grade buildings (new construction above 20 storeys) had a high vacancy rate. In both areas, long-term vacancies on the ground floor of high-grade buildings along major streets were common.

12.4 Discussions: Is Sapporo really active?

Thus far, I have not spoken of the growth process of Sapporo. At first glance, the regional economy in Sapporo has been stable, since some indicators, such as the office vacancy rate, land prices, and population growth, have recently improved. However, I must pose the following important question: "Is Sapporo really active?"

Recent indicators of growth such as population, office vacancy rates, and land prices suggest that Sapporo's regional economy has been improving. However, the indicators do not necessarily reflect potential long-term changes to the Sapporo economy. Currently, a significant shift in employment from branch-offices to locally headquartered IT-related companies has been observed (Aoki, 2005). However, this shift has been unstable, and several small IT-related companies have established offices in the area north of the Sapporo train station where they have access to the student population at Hokkaido University (Figure 6). Despite the

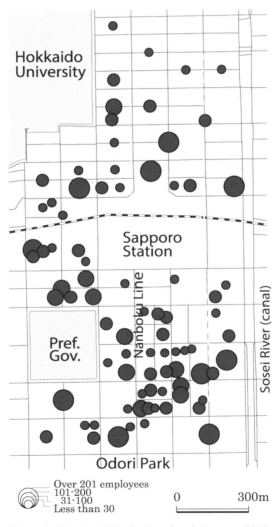

Figure 6 Number of IT-related workers in Sapporo (2006)
Source: Establishment and Enterprise Census

beneficial location, the number of IT-related workers and establishments is small relative to other industries in Sapporo. A continued stable increase in both sectors is not expected because the IT-related sector may be too weak to support further economic development in Sapporo.

In addition, based on standard industrial classification, the 'call centre operator' (telephone customer service operations) category is included in statistics related to the IT industry. The recent major increase in IT-related workers mostly reflects the increase in the number of call centre operators, which includes many temporary workers (Sapporo City Office, 2005). For example, a large call centre office supporting a Tokyo company occupies several floors of the JR Tower, which is the most prestigious building in the CBD and is located adjacent to the Sapporo train station. The relocation decision was driven by the availability of less expensive office space and lower labour costs relative to Tokyo. Office rental fees and labour costs in Sapporo were roughly 40–50% lower than in Tokyo (Ikoma CBRE, 2006). The lower labour costs are sustained by an influx of workers from rural communities throughout Hokkaido. Consequently, the present growth rate in Sapporo may not be sustainable in the long term because Sapporo's growth is occurring at the cost of declining economies in rural Hokkaido.

12.5   Concluding remarks

"Working in Sapporo" or "working in JR Tower, the most prestigious building in Sapporo" are very attractive phrases for young generation in rural Hokkaido. The types and permanency of their occupations are not, however, captured by these slogans. The recent improvement of major indices of growth in Hokkaido should be discussed from the viewpoint of its over-concentration in Sapporo. It is reported that the rate of the aged population will grow and that the total population will shrink faster in Hokkaido than in any other part of Japan. The present growth of Sapporo may be not sustainable, as long as it is just supported by a "winner takes all scenario" in Hokkaido.

Acknowledgements

Some parts of this article was first appeared in the *Annals of the Japan Association of Economic Geographers* 53, 478-489, 2008.

References

Aoki, Y. 2005. *Gyogan de nozoita Sapporo Valley.* Sapporo: Kyodo Bunkasha. (J)

Development Bank of Japan. 2002. *Hokkaido ni okeru call centre no genjo to kadai.* (J) (http://www.dbj.go.jp/hokkaido/report/0206callcenter.html) (last accessed 1 January 2009)

Hirasawa, K. and Kawanishi, K. 2003. *5th Report on the activity of Sapporo branch offices. Sapporo Gakuin Shoukei Ronshu* 20: 71-151. (J)

Ikoma CBRE. 2006. *Office Market Report 2006 Autumn*, vol.39. (J)

Hokkaido Prefectural Government. 2007. An economic white paper in Hokkaido. Sapporo: Hokkaido Prefectural Government. (J)

Sapporo chamber of commerce and industry. 1988. *Actual situation of branch offices in Sapporo under a soft society.* Sapporo: Sapporo chamber of commerce and industry. (J)

Sapporo chamber of commerce and industry. 2003. *5th Report on the activity of Sapporo branch offices –summary–* 14. Sapporo: Sapporo chamber of commerce and industry. (J)

Sapporo city office. 2005. *Heisei 16nen Jigyosho kigyo toukei chousa no gaiyou.* (J) (http://www.city.sapporo.jp/toukei/tokusyu/chosakekka/establishment/H16estabilishment.pdf) (last accessed 1 January 2009)

Teraya, R. 1993. Urban hierarchy in Hokkaido viewing from the processes of branch office placement of corporations. *Chiri Kagaku* 48: 175-183. (J)

Tsutsumi, J. 2004a. Regional characteristics of building supply in the CBD of Sapporo city focusing on the analysis of land-ownership change. *Journal of Geography* 113: 125-139. (J)

Tsutsumi, J. 2004b. Regional characteristics of building supply in a newly developed city in Japan. In *DELA 21 Cities in Transition*, ed. Pak Mirko, 495-504. Ljubljana :IGU Urban commission, Monitoring cities of Tomorrow, Department of Geography, University of Ljubljana.

(J) means "written in Japanese" (with an English summary, in some cases).

13. Spatial Government Systems of Newly Merged Municipalities and Population Changes within Municipalities Impacted by those Government Systems: Under a National Pro-merger Policy of Municipalities in Post-Growth Societies

Jun NISHIHARA

Abstract

Between 1999 and 2010, Japan's national government encouraged a pro-merger policy of municipalities to explore new shapes of municipal governance in her post-growth society. As a result, her municipalities decreased from 3,232 to 1,727 in all regions except the two largest metropolitan regions. In accordance with their new governance concepts and geographical conditions, these newly established municipalities chose their own systems from a traditional spatial government system (a centralized headquarters system), and two renovated systems (comprehensive branch and multi-locational headquarters systems). At the birth of these new municipalities, even though half adopted comprehensive branch systems, many changed to centralized headquarters systems after several years for more efficient operation at the detriment of the provision levels of public services for the peripheral areas. Impacted by the amalgamations, the spatial population patterns within municipalities drastically changed. Huge intra-differences emerged, due to the allocation of headquarters/branches and large/small branches related to the three government systems. This suggests that small branch areas, or the former municipal centers, might continue to decline more seriously.

Keywords

municipal amalgamation, intra-difference, headquarters/branch, spatial government system, population change

13.1 Pro-merger policy of municipalities and intra-area systems within newly merged municipalities

In any country, pro-merger action by the national government has changed the style of municipal politics and public services and geographically altered the intra-area systems within municipalities. The Japanese national government conducted a pro-merger policy of municipalities, called the Heisei pro-merger policy of municipalities, between April 1, 1999 and March 31, 2010 which was the third such nationwide attempt following the Meiji pro-merger policy in the 1880s and the Showa pro-merger policy in the 1950s[1]. This policy explored new shapes of municipal governance, responding to Japan's transformation into a post-growth society.

The purposes of this pro-merger policy included the following: 1) a decentralizing shift of some administrative authority from national to local (prefectural and municipal) governments; 2) actions to counteract aging and shrinking populations in the nation; 3) a corresponding change in the spatial expansion of people's daily activities; and 4) ameliorating the financial conditions of the national and local governments. During this 11-year period, the number of municipalities in Japan decreased from 3,232 to 1,727. In all, 66.3% of municipalities in Japan were involved in the amalgamations. Those municipal amalgamations happened in all of the regions except the two largest major metropolitan regions of Tokyo and Osaka[2] (Morikawa, H. 2011).

Seeking large-scale action of municipal mergers, Japan's national government proposed to prefectural and municipal governments two types of policies: generous and harsh. It established various generous policies, such as an additional transfer system of Local Allocation Tax to newly merged municipalities, a Special Merger Bond to develop new projects and special and temporary measures toward the merged municipal assemblies related to the number of seats and the terms of members. Moreover, the National Diet and the national government temporarily eased the requirements to become a Ordinance Designated City which has almost the same authorities as prefectural goverments, by the national government and a legally recognized city.

On the other hand, since 2003, under the strong leadership of Prime Minister Koizumi, the national government conducted a series of reformation policies called the Trinity Reforms to improve the financial conditions of the national government and to reorganize the local political systems by reducing subsidiaries and decentralizing political authority to local governments. The Trinity Reforms urged municipal governments to participate in this pro-merger action of municipalities (Volker, E. 2011). They were harsh policies.

The results of this Heisei pro-merger policy had quite different characteristics than those of the previous two pro-merger actions: 1) Extremely large municipalities emerged which transcended the boundaries of the people's daily activities. 22 new municipalities over 1,000 km^2 areas were established. 2) Based on the negative experiences of the two earlier national pro-mergers, as mentioned below, the national government proposed three spatial government systems of municipalities. The newly established municipalities were provided choices among a centralized headquarters system, a comprehensive branch system, or a multi-locational headquarters system. In Japan, especially in its peripheral regions, the allocation of the headquarters of municipal governments determines the lowest central places in the daily urban systems. In the previous two pro-merger actions of municipalities, the former central areas, which lost municipal headquarters, declined drastically, and the intra-area systems greatly changed after the mergers (Tsutsumi, M, 1971).

After the latest pro-merger policy, various problems were pointed out, not only by local residents but also by the mass media and researchers. Even in the 2010 formal report on it by the Ministry of Internal Affairs[3], the expanding intra-differences in various sectors between the central and peripheral areas within municipalities were considered the most serious. The peripheral areas suffered from declining populations and economies, reduced levels of public services, and lost opportunities for the political commitment of local citizens. The local residents had to accept fewer seats in the new municipal assembly and a smaller branch office, rather than their own previous assembly and municipal headquarters.

Taking these into consideration, I established three research questions that focused on the outcomes of Heisei pro-merger policy: 1) What spatial government system did the newly merged municipalities select at the start of their new governance? 2) How did the municipalities later reform their spatial government systems based to change their governance? 3) How largely did the adopted spatial government systems impact the emergence of intra-differences within municipalities?

To answer these three questions, I used the above three spatial government systems as my study's focus and adopted the changing population patterns of each former municipality as an index for intra-area differences. I selected all 557 newly merged municipalities between April 1, 1999 and March 31, 2006 in the first half step of the Heisei pro-merger policy of municipalities. These 557 municipalities occupied 94.7% of newly established municipalities during the Heisei pro-merger policy. Then I analyzed the adoption and reformation of the three spatial government systems and the changes of the intra-area systems from the viewpoint of municipal amalgamation to explore new shapes of municipal governance, especially in Japan's provincial regions in her post-growth society.

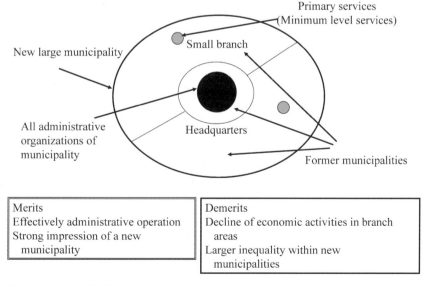

Figure 1 Centralized headquarters system

13.2 Three spatial government systems and their classification criteria

As mentioned above, in Japan's previous two periods that promoted municipal amalgamations, the former central areas, which lost municipal headquarters, declined drastically after the mergers[4]. Before the start of the Heisei pro-merger policy, the national government provided the following traditional spatial government system and two new styled systems to the merging municipalities. However, there are no well-established definitions. A temporary definition used by the Ministry of Internal Affairs is mentioned below.

13.2.1 Centralized headquarters system (1)

Basically, all of the administrative organizations of a municipality[5] (municipal assembly, mayoral departments, and administrative boards) are deployed in a single facility (Figure 1). All the mayoral departments are located in a headquarters (a central city office), and the small branches delivering primary services (or minimum-level services) to local residents are dispersed to each of the former municipalities. This system is expected to deliver relatively small government operating at a high level of efficiency. This enhanced a one-nuclear type of intra-area system[6].

13.2.2 Comprehensive branch system (2)

All the administrative organizations of a municipality are geographically allocated in a

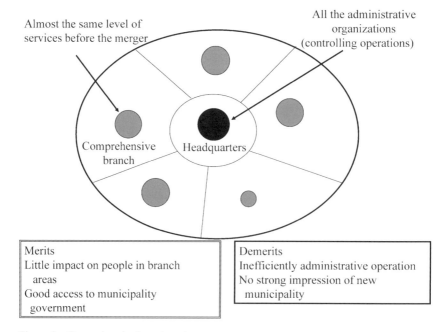

Figure 2 Comprehensive branch system

single facility, the same as in system (1). The functions of the headquarters are characterized as the controlling and coordinating operations of the entire municipality. The branches are functionally different from those in system (1) and have almost the same functions as before the merger and are called comprehensive branches. Originally, the branches located in the territory of each former municipality shared some decision-making powers with the headquarters. These branches have the right authority to make decisions about their own projects within their own territories within pre-planned budget limits. Such a system might encourage a multi-nuclei type of intra-area systems (Figure 2).

13.2.3 Multi-locational headquarter system (3)

The former municipalities share all of the municipal government's mayoral departments, as well as the municipal assembly and the administrative boards, within the new municipality. In this system two or more departments are allocated to some of the former municipal offices as sub-headquarters[7]. This unique multi-locational headquarters system might maintain a multi-nuclei type of an intra-area system (Figure 3).

Both the comprehensive branch and multi-locational headquarters systems are new and arose based on lessons harvested from the history of the Meiji and Show pro-merger policies of municipalities. According to my interviews with the merged municipalities that adopted these systems, although they much less efficiently, operate municipal governments and need

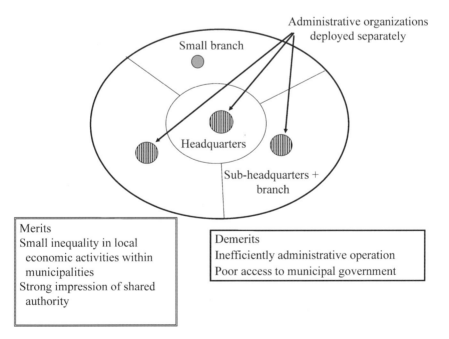

Figure 3 Multi-locational headquarters system

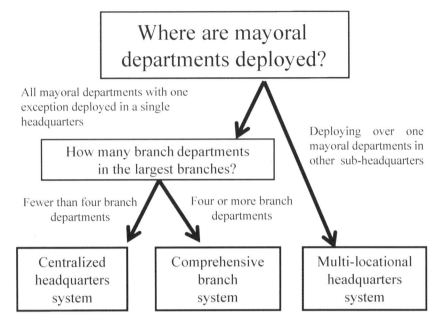

Figure 4 Classification criteria of three spatial government systems

more municipal budgets, both prevent the emergence of large inequalities within municipalities at the provision level of public services and encourage local involvement in municipal politics. Consequently, local citizens are likely to have good feelings about their new municipal governments (Nishihara, J. 2005 and 2007).

I established operational classification criteria for the three government systems, which are slightly different from the definitions of the Ministry of Internal Affairs (Figure 4). First, I examined only the allocation of mayoral departments and excluded municipal assemblies and administrative boards. Because they were independent from the mayors and basically operated independently regardless of their proximity to mayoral offices. Second, I identified the municipalities of the multi-locational headquarters system among all municipalities when over one mayoral departments were deployed at other facilities (sub-headquarters). Third, I classified all of the other municipalities into those of the centralized headquarters system with fewer than four branch divisions within the largest branches or those of the comprehensive branch systems with four or more branch divisions within the largest branches[8].

Based on my criteria, I classified 557 municipalities at both the start of the new municipalities and in 2009 into three spatial government systems, using the documents of the administrative organizations of their municipal governments. I got these documents through face-to-face interviews, postal and e-mail questionnaire research, by telephone, or municipality websites.

Spatial Government Systems of Newly Merged Municipalities and Population Changes within Municipalities Impacted by those Government Systems: Under a National Pro-merger Policy of Municipalities in Post-Growth Societies

13.3 Shares and reformations of the three spatial government systems between start of new municipalities and in 2009 and the geographical determinants of their government systems

13.3.1 Start of new municipalities

At the start of the 557 new municipalities, 150 (26.9%) adopted the centralized headquarters system, 259 (46.5%) selected the comprehensive branch system, and 148 (26.6%) chose the multi-locational headquarters system (Table 1). The share of the comprehensive branch system was the largest because the new municipalities most likely adopted policies that supported the people in the peripheral areas as before their mergers. Even though the multi-locational system was inefficient, it was adopted by one fourth of the municipalities. In this system, people can share the important administrative functions of the new municipality, regardless of where they live in their municipalities.

At the time of the mergers, the geographical background and the local political characteristics of the new municipalities are crucial in the selection of post-merger government systems. I selected six factors to examine the relationships among the three systems and those characteristics: 1) amalgamation type[9] (equal or absorbed), 2) region type (urban or rural), 3) population, 4) area, 5) number of former municipalities amalgamated into each new municipality, 6) and number of urbanized areas[10] within the new municipalities (Table 1 and Table 2).

Table 1 Municipalities of three spatial government systems and amalgamation characteristics

	Number of Municipalities	Amalgamation type		Region type	
		Equal amalgamation	Absorbed amalgamation	Urban region type	Rural region type
At start of new municipalities					
Centralized headquarters system	150	100	50	73	77
Comprehensive branch system	259	200	59	176	83
Multi-locational headquarters system	148	143	5	28	120
In 2009					
Centralized headquarters system	300	218	82	164	136
Comprehensive branch system	113	83	30	86	27
Multi-locational headquarters system	144	142	2	27	117
Total	557	443	114	277	280

Source: Author

Table 2 Averages of geographical data of newly merged municipalities by three spatial government systems

	Number of municipalities	Population	Area (km²)	Number of former municipalities	Number of urbanized areas*
At the start of new municipalities					
Centralized headquarters system	150	85,403	297	3.13	1.00
Comprehensive branch system	259	122,907	475	4.10	1.19
Multi-locational headquarters system	148	43,397	224	3.20	0.49
Total	557	91,680	361	3.60	0.95
In 2009					
Centralized headquarters system	300	75,703	351	3.37	0.89
Comprehensive branch system	113	190,556	540	4.61	1.72
Multi-locational headquarters system	144	44,699	241	3.29	0.49
Total	557	90,988	361	3.60	0.95

Note: Urbanized areas* are *Densely Inhabited Districts* from 2000 Population Census.

Source: 2000 Population Census

As the amalgamation type, 443 of the 557 municipalities selected equal amalgamation (Table 1). In comparison with absorbed amalgamations, discussions on making agreements for equal amalgamations are more likely to be completed successfully because equal amalgamation provides equality among the participants. Actually, at the start 343 of those 443 municipalities adopted the comprehensive branch and multi-locational headquarters systems. The reason why a large part of 443 municipalities adopted these two systems is that the concept of equal amalgamation is consistent with those of the two systems.

I classified the region type of the new municipalities, which include at least one central city as well as a number of towns and villages, as the urban region type. On the other hand, municipalities that include former towns and villages without former cities are the rural region type. The municipalities of the urban region type generally chose the comprehensive branch system. 176 of the 277 municipalities of the urban region type selected the comprehensive branch system. 120 of the 280 municipalities of the rural region type adopted the multi-locational headquarters system. In other words, 68% of the municipalities of the comprehensive branch system were the urban region type, and 81% of the multi-locational headquarters systems were the rural region type. The municipalities of the centralized headquarters system have almost the same rate of both urban and rural region types.

The averages of the population and the areas of the new municipalities by the three spatial government systems are also captured in Table 2. The centralized and multi-locational headquarters systems were more likely to have been adopted in new municipalities with smaller areas. Considering the regional type of new municipalities, municipalities adopting the cen-

Spatial Government Systems of Newly Merged Municipalities and Population Changes within
Municipalities Impacted by those Government Systems: Under a National Pro-merger Policy
of Municipalities in Post-Growth Societies

Table 3 Relationships among three spatial government systems and areas of municipalities

	Total	Under 50	50 -	100 -	300 -	500 -	700 -	1000 -
At the start of new municipalities								
Centralized headquarters system	150	3	19	73	32	12	11	0
Comprehensive branch system	259	2	8	92	58	46	33	20
Multi-locational headquarters system	148	12	27	72	22	9	5	1
In 2009								
Centralized headquarters system	300	5	28	137	63	33	26	8
Comprehensive branch system	113	1	3	28	28	24	19	10
Multi-locational headquarters system	144	11	23	72	21	10	4	3
Total	557	17	54	237	112	67	49	21

(km^2)

Source: Author, 2000 and 2010 Population Census

tralized headquarters system (population: 85,403, area: 297 km^2) generally had much larger populations than those adopting the multi-locational headquarters system (population: 43,397, area: 224 km^2), because they inherited central cities with large populations. New municipalities with larger populations and especially larger areas, however, tended to prefer the comprehensive branch system (population: 122,907, area: 475 km^2). From the viewpoint of spatially large municipalities, 53 of the 70 municipalities with areas of 700 km^2 or more adopted comprehensive branch systems (Table 3).

From the viewpoint of single nuclear or multi-nuclei of areal systems, the average number of the urbanized areas of the central headquarters system was almost one (1.00). Consequently, the municipalities in a single urbanized area were likely to choose centralized headquarters. The municipalities with a couple of urbanized areas were likely to select the comprehensive branch system because its average exceeds one (1.19). However, the multi-locational headquarters system was adopted by municipalities without urbanized areas (0.49) as well as by the rural region type.

Furthermore, I examined the geographical background factors of the adoptions of the three government systems using a kind of discriminant analysis, specifically Hayashi's discriminant analysis[11]. The dependent variable was the three spatial government systems, and the independent variables were the region type of the newly merged municipalities, the population class, the area class, the number of former municipalities, and the number of urbanized areas.

According to the results, the ratio of correct discriminations was 54.9%. The municipalities of the centralized headquarters, comprehensive branch, and multi-locational headquarters systems were identified by six geographical background factors at 10.7%, 69.5%, and 74.3% accuracy. In other words, discrimination of the municipalities of the centralized headquarters system among the three systems was very difficult. Such a traditional system is likely to be adopted by municipalities with widely ranging characteristics (from small areas with small population to large areas with large population).

Among the independent variables, those with strong explanatory power (in descending order) were the area class (range: 2.747), the population class (range: 1.095), and the region type (range: 0.994). Based on the low ratio of correct discrimination by geographical background, I can easily imagine other strong factors, such as the type of amalgamation, the attitudes of local people, the personal concepts of government systems of mayors, and the capacity of the buildings designated as headquarters' facilities.

13.3.2 Reformation of spatial government systems from the birth of new municipalities to 2009

In the same way, I identified the three spatial governmental systems of the 557 municipalities in 2009 and tabulated the transformations of each one in that period (Table 4). Note that their individual periods from their birth to 2009 varied from four to 10 years.

In 2009, the spatial governmental system with the largest share was the centralized headquarters system (municipalities: 300, share: 53.9%.) The multi-locational headquarters system was second (144, 25.8%) and comprehensive branch system was third (113, 20.3%.)

As shown in Table 4, among the 259 municipalities of the comprehensive branch system at their start, 139 changed to the centralized headquarters system to reduce their size and the functions of their branches. They decreased their branches to fewer than four divisions. According to my interviews with the officials of several merged municipalities, some had reformation plans in their formal agreements with a couple of stages (three and five years after their start) before their mergers. In spite of its operational inefficiency[12], almost all the municipali-

Table 4 Transformation among three spatial government systems in 557 municipalities

At start of new municipalities		In 2009		
	Total	Centralized	Comprehensive	Multi-locational
Centralized headquarters system	150	143	3	4
Comprehensive branch system	259	139	110	10
Multi-locational headquarters system	148	18	0	130
Total	557	300	113	144

Source: Author

Spatial Government Systems of Newly Merged Municipalities and Population Changes within
Municipalities Impacted by those Government Systems: Under a National Pro-merger Policy
of Municipalities in Post-Growth Societies

ties of the multi-locational headquarters system kept the same system in 2009. This suggests that sharing municipal government authorities is a critical areal framework of small and rural municipalities.

I repeated the same analysis on the relationships of the three spatial government systems and their municipal characteristics in 2009 (Tables 1 and 2). These relationships drastically changed. Among 443 municipalities of equal amalgamation, the number of municipalities of the comprehensive branch system drastically decreased to 83. Shown in Table 3, in 2009, even the municipalities of larger area classes were likely to adopt the centralized headquarters system. Among 70 municipalities whose areas exceeded 700 km², 34 adopted the centralized headquarters system and only 29 retained the comprehensive branch system (Table 3). Based on my interviews with the officials of several of those municipalities, this change reflected the larger cost of politically intra-autonomous systems and good public services for the local people in the merged and peripheral areas.

I also repeated Hayashi's discriminant analysis on the data in 2009. According to the result, the ratio of correct discrimination decreased to 49.0%. The most powerful explanatory variable was population class (range: 3.013), and the second was area class (range: 1.747). These results show the decrement of the total explanatory power and the decline of the importance of the area class for selecting a spatial government system. In other words, the municipalities were more likely to attach importance to factors other than the geographical background factors, with the exception of population class, for their selection of government systems.

I conducted an additional analysis on the allocation of the branch divisions of the 316 municipalities whose special detailed data were provided by their administrative organizations. The averaged number of branch divisions deployed at each branch decreased from 3.9 immediately at their start to 2.2 by 2009. The averages of the municipalities of the comprehensive branch system also decreased from 5.6 to 4.8. This phenomenon illustrates that even municipalities that kept the comprehensive branch systems reduced the size and the functions of their branches.

13.4 Impact on intra-area differences in population changes by allocations of headquarters/branches and branch types related to three spatial government systems

In this section, I examine the impact on the intra-area differences in the population changes caused by the allocation of the three spatial government systems. I chose population changes among various areal characteristic variables as an index of the intra-area differences because the population changes were a basic indicator of areal development and decline. I easily obtained the census data of 2000 and 2010 on the former municipal units of 2000 from the National Statistical Bureau.

The following were the procedures of this analysis. First, I concentrated on the 58 munici-

Table 5 Averages of population change rates by former municipalities between 2000 and 2010

	Areas	Population changes	
	2010	Change rate	Shared change rate
Headquarters areas	58	–2.0%	101.2%
Centralized headquarters system	34	–2.1%	101.6%
Comprehensive branch system	8	–2.4%	101.4%
Multi-locational headquarters system	16	–1.8%	100.4%
Branch areas	150	–7.8%	94.8%
Centralized headquaters system	81	–9.4%	94.1%
Comprehensive branch system			
- Largel branch	17	–2.7%	98.6%
Comprehensive branch system			
- Small branch*	30	–10.1%	91.4%
Sub Heaadquarters	22	–2.7%	99.3%

Note: * contains small branch without mayoral department
in the multi-locational headquarters system.

Source: 2000 and 2010 Population Census

palities in the Tokai region (Gifu, Shizuoka, Aichi and Mie Prefectures), which is in a geo-graphically central part of Japan. It contains one of the country's three major metropolitan regions (Nagoya) and one major manufacturing region as well as mountainous and depopu-lated regions. Therefore, the Tokai region is a typical example for municipal amalgamation studies. Second, I calculated the population change rates and the change rates of the popula-tion shares within municipalities between 2000 and 2010 by the allocation of headquarters/branches and branch types related to the three spatial government systems.

Before analyzing the population changes, I confirmed the municipalities' adoptions of the three spatial government systems in the Tokai region. The following are the numbers of the municipalities of the three systems in 2009: centralized headquarters system, 34, comprehen-sive branch system, 8, and multi-locational headquarters system, 16.

Table 5 shows the population change rates between 2000 and 2010 of the municipalities that were separated into 58 former municipalities with headquarters (headquarters areas) and 150 former municipalities with branches (branch areas). Their complete averaged population changes indicated minus values. However, there were quite large intra-differences between the headquarters areas (–2.0%) and the branch areas (–7.8%) by the former municipalities.

Discussing the details by the three spatial government systems, the rates of the headquar-ters areas varied from –1.8% in the multi-locational headquarters system, to –2.1% in the centralized headquarters system, to –2.4% in the comprehensive branch systems and were almost the same among the three systems.

On the contrary, I found large differences among the branch areas by the three systems. Strictly speaking, even in the comprehensive branch systems, there were two types of branches: large branches with four or more branch divisions and small branches with fewer than four divisions. In the multi-locational headquarters systems, there are also two types of branches. The first type has branches with a part of mayoral departments, sub-headquarters, and the second type only has branches without mayoral departments and fewer than four branch divisions. In Table 5, the second type of branches of the multi-locational headquarters system was tabulated operationally into a cetegory of 'Comprehensive branch system-Small branch'. Among the four types, there were large differences in the population change rates from -2.7% to -10.1%. Consequently, the four types of branches were classified into two groups: with small population decreasing rates that consisted of large comprehensive branches and the sub-headquarters. These branches shared larger parts of the municipal governments than the branches of the centralized headquarters system and the small branches of the comprehensive branch systems. In other words, larger branches of municipal government show smaller decrements in their populations.

When investigating the changing rates of the areas' population shares, I got almost the same results on the intra-differences of the population changes. Even under all situations where the populations decreased, the population shares of the headquarters areas only increased slightly. On the other hand, the shares of the areas of all the branch types decreased. In terms of the changing rates of the population shares, the four types of branches were also classified into two groups. The large comprehensive branches and the sub-headquarters experienced very small losses in their shares. The areas of the branches of the centralized headquarters system and the small branches of the comprehensive branch systems also lost large shares.

Finally, we conclude that the spatial population patterns within the municipalities were drastically affected by the amalgamations. As mentioned above, perhaps the allocations of the headquarters/branches and the types of branches related to the three government systems had strong relationships with the situations of the population changes. However, I could not accurately separate the impacts of the allocations of facilities related to the spatial government systems from other factors. Therefore, a strict examination must be continued, for example, using multi-regression analysis with independent variables of other regional characteristics and a comparative analysis on the population changes between merged and non-merged municipalities.

13.5 Concluding remarks

In the Heisei pro-merger policy, many newly established municipalities adopted not a centralized headquarters system but comprehensive branch and multi-locational headquarters systems to avoid negative impact on their peripheral areas that were caused by municipal amalgamation. Based on my interviews with about 25 municipalities from all over Japan, the latter two systems perhaps did not provide quite the same levels of public services but did meet the general expectations of the local citizens and eased their anxieties about the amalgamations.

However, almost all of the municipalities reduced their branches at the cost of the provision levels of public services in the peripheral areas. Seeking highly efficient management of their governments, half of the municipalities of the comprehensive branch system at the birth of the new municipalities reorganized them into the centralized headquarters system. As a result, especially in peripheral areas, the provision level of public services decreased and the local citizens were probably discouraged from getting involved in municipal politics.

During negotiations for new municipalities before the amalgamations, crucial decisions included what type of spatial government system to adopt, where to locate the headquarters within municipalities, and what types of branches to deploy in the peripheral areas. After the allocation of government facilities, quite large intra-differences emerged within municipalities, due to the allocation of headquarters/branches and branch types related to the three government systems. However, I cannot conclude that all of the intra-differences within the municipalities were caused by the spatial government systems. Strong geographical factors other than the allocation of municipal government facilities might have influenced the emergence of large intra-area differences. Various municipal government facilities were deployed based on the area-related importance of population, economic activities, etc.

Impacted by the amalgamations, the spatial population patterns within municipalities drastically changed. Through my analysis, I found serious population decrements in the branch areas, or the formerly merged municipal areas after the municipal amalgamations. We should look for ways to provide local people with an adequate quality of life in the branch areas of post-growth societies. One possible way might be a relocation plan of people from scattered and small settlements into places adjacent to such public service facilities as municipal branch offices, hospitals, post offices, and primary schools (Pacione 2012).

Notes:

1) Up to the present, the Japanese national government has implemented nationwide pro-merger actions of municipalities during periods of political change. The Meiji pro-merger policy promoted the establishment of municipal offices with municipal assemblies and primary schools in the modernization process of local administration after the Meiji Restoration (1868). The Showa pro-merger policy aimed at the reorganization of municipalities in order to provide full-fledged public services as well as the establishment of new middle schools for compulsory education after World War II (1941-45).

2) The prefectural percentage of municipalities that joined the amalgamations varied from 4.5% (Osaka Prefecture), 5.0% (Tokyo Prefecture), and 8.1% (Kanagawa Prefecture) at the lowest, to 97.1% (Ehime Prefecture), 93.0% (Hiroshima Prefecture), and 89.8% (Shimane

Prefecture) at the highest. Osaka, Tokyo, and Kanagawa Prefectures are included in Japan's two largest metropolitan regions. Almost all of the municipalities in these urbanized prefectures had no real need for the amalgamations, due to their overall good financial condition.

3) During the same period, many prefectural governments also published final reports on the results of the municipal amalgamations in their own prefectures. They pointed out their unique concerns related to their geographical characteristics and that almost the same problems had happened in the national government.

4) As a unique example to prevent from possibly areal declining, the two former municipalities of Toyo Town in Kochi Prefecture hosted their headquarters by turn every two years for 34 years after their amalgamation in 1959 during the Showa pro-merger policy.

5) In general, the administrative organizations of Japanese municipalities consist of a municipal assembly, mayoral departments, and several administrative boards, including educational boards, election boards, and agriculture boards. The departments of municipal government headquarters that are managed directly by mayors are called mayoral departments. The administrative boards, the members of which are nominated by the mayor with the consent of the assembly, have their own authority in their limited and specific areas.

6) Even though only a few years had passed, many of the shops and business services in the branch areas had closed, owing to the closure of the former municipal offices, as frequently reported by newspapers (i.e., April 22, 2004, Asahi News).

7) If residents have more than one purpose for dealing with their local government, they might have to visit more than one of the headquarters and the sub-headquarters, which are located at different sites. To ease such difficulty, a general receptionist system, or a 'one stop service system,' has been adopted into the headquarters and the sub-headquarters by many merged municipalities.

8) Strictly speaking, some municipalities contain branches with different levels of size. In my classification of the centralized headquarters and the comprehensive branch systems, I examined the largest among all of the branches of each municipalities. Here, I did not examine the functions of the headquarters and the branches based on the definitions of those systems; instead, I used operational criteria to classify those two levels' functions (almost the same services as before the mergers or primary services). Based on my criteria between the centralized headquarters and comprehensive branch systems, the optimal number of branch divisions is four. If the branches have four divisions (general affairs, management of resident documents, management of local roads, water, and sewage, and management of healthcare and welfare), they cannot quite provide the same level of service as before the mergers, but they can meet the general expectations of the local citizens.

9) The Japanese system has two types of municipal amalgamation. The first is called equal

amalgamation, which means that all the amalgamation participants closed their municipalities and were consolidated into new ones as equal partners. The second is absorbed
amalgamation, where one large municipality absorbed other smaller municipalities.

10) The Densely Inhabited Districts (DIDs) designated by the Statistical Bureau for the urbanized areas were used in my analysis. DIDs have provided the data of urban areas for
the census since 1960. The statistical bureau shows the criteria on its webpage (http://
www.stat.go.jp/english/data/chiri/did/1-1.htm, as of July 31, 2014). The criteria are as follows:

(1) Districts containing basic unit blocks for the statistics with a population density of
4,000 or more per square kilometer that are adjacent to each other in a municipality

(2) Districts consisting of the above adjacent basic unit blocks whose population is 5,000
or more

11) In Hayashi's discriminant analysis, a range means the absolute-valued intervals between
the minimum and maximum valued partial coefficients of the categorical items of each
independent variable. An explanatory variable, which has the largest range of value
among the explanatory variables, must have the largest explanatory power.

12) In this system, it is very difficult for officials to discuss important agenda items in a face-
to-face setting, especially with the mayor and executive officials. Based on my in-depth
questionnaire research with the municipality officials of the multi-locational headquarters
of Izu City, Shizuoka Prefecture, the annual total time cost of the trips by officials between headquarters and the two sub-headquarters was estimated to be about 120,000
Euros. Izu City's population was 35,115 (in 2005) and its area was 364 km^2, with about 350
officials in the city government.

References

Morikawa, H. 2011. Major mergers in the Heisei Era and the relationship with commuting
areas. *Geographical Review of Japan* 84: 432-441. (J)

Nishihara, J. 2005. New large municipalities and Japan's pro-merger policy: The Implications
of alternative administrative systems. In *Cities in global perspective: Diversity and transition*, ed. Y. Murayama and D. Guoqing, 521-529. Tokyo: College of Tourism, Rikkyo University with IGU Urban Commission.

Nishihara, J. 2007. Japan's pro-merger policy and new large municipalities: The impacts of
three spatial forms of administrative organization, In *Urban development, planning and
governance in globalization*, ed. X. Yan and D. Xue, 539-550. Guangzhou: Sun Yat-Sen
University Press.

Pacione, M. 2012. The urban geography of post-growth society. In Paper presented to *the Annual Conference of the Human Geographical Society of Japan* (17th-18th November 2012).

Tsutsumi, M. 1974. A study of the hierarchical systems of central places in Fukushima Prefecture. *Japanese Journal of Human Geography* 27 (3): 2-25. (J)

Volker, E. 2011. The impact of the Trinity reforms and the Heisei mergers on processes of peripherisation in Japan's mountain villages. *Japanese Journal of Human Geography* 63 (6): 44-56.

(J) means "written in Japanese" (with an English summary, in some cases).

224

14. Knowledge Spillover Effects on Agglomerations of Environment-related Industries: A Case in Japan

Jun YAMASHITA

Abstract

The number of environment-related technologies has increased remarkably over the past two decades, as these technologies received the public interests in effective resource use and ways to reduce the effects of global warming. Industries based on environment-related technologies are thus growing rapidly. Previous studies revealed that externalities derived from the population concentration in urban areas positively affect agglomerations of high-tech industries. Such externalities have been named the "knowledge spillover effects." The purposes of the present chapter are to (1) give a thumbnail sketch of the locations of environment-related industries around the world, using the Organisation for Economic Co-operation and Development environment-related patent statistics, and (2) explicate the effects of the Marshall-Arrow-Romer (MAR) externalities and the Jacobs externalities, which result from population concentrations in urban areas, on the agglomeration of environment-related industries in Japan. The analysis revealed that environment-related industries are located chiefly in urban areas across the globe because of the accumulation of existing industries, and that both externalities positively influenced the agglomeration of these industries in Japan.

Keywords

innovation, environment-related industry, externalities, knowledge spillover effects, OECD patent statistics

14.1 Introduction

When the relations between an economy and the environment are examined, the concept of sustainable development is often employed. In the Brundtland Report, the sustainable development is defined as follows: the development meets the needs of the present without compromising the ability of future generations (The United Nations World Commission on Environment and Development, 1987, p. 27). The main purpose of such development is to decouple the relation of environmental impacts, such as greenhouse gas emissions, with economic growth. At present, it is difficult to ensure the decoupling of economy and environment, or more specifically, the simultaneous decoupling of the maintenance of economic growth and the mitigation of environmental impacts. To address this decoupling, many theories that do not rely on sustainable development were proposed in recent years. These theories are not theoretically count on the economic growth upon which sustainable development relies, and they presented alternative societies (Federal Ministry for Agriculture, Forestry, Environment and Water Management, 2012). The alternative societies are based on less or not economic growth. These theories could be termed the "post-sustainable development theories," and they include the green growth, de-growth and post-growth theories.

Both the United Nations Development Programme (UNDP) and the Organisation for Economic Co-operation and Development (OECD) advocate the green growth. The main purpose of this growth is to make the economy green—that is, to convert economic and industrial structures into structures with lighter environmental loads. Environment-related industries, the focus of the present study, are also included in the category of green growth because the purpose of establishing such industries is to convert the structures of existing industries into environmentally friendly ones. By greening the economy, newly established environment-related industries create new jobs with continuous economic growth, and they utilize the natural environment in more efficient ways. Aside from differences in economic and industrial structures between conventional and green economies, the green growth theory affirms economic growth because of relying on the same conventional economic theory as the sustainable development has. In this affirmative perspective on the economic growth, sustainable development has the same alternative societies as the green growth.

Conversely, neither the de-growth theory nor the post-growth theory affirms economic growth. The main goal of the de-growth theory is to reduce production and/or consumption. The degrowth theory takes a negative stance against economic growth. This is because, from the viewpoint of macro-economics, the economic growth represented by a gross domestic product (GDP) is calculated using the production data of manmade capital resulting from the consumption of natural capital, and sometimes the over-consumption of natural capital beyond the environment's capacity. Nicholas Georgescu-Roegen coined the term "degrowth" (Bonaiuti, 2011), and Georgescu-Roegen's idea of degrowth was expanded into the "steady-state economy" by his colleague, Herman Daly. In a steady-state economy, it is assumed that the stock of natural capital is constant. In such an economic situation, no economic growth may occur.

The post-growth theory presents another economic society. In a post-growth society, people enjoy a high quality of life and prosperity within the environment's capacity and without economic growth. Time Jackson is at the forefront of the post-growth theory (Jackson, 2009). He stressed that a degrowth society is not sustainable in terms of the strong sustainability because the degrowth theory relies on macroeconomics which do not assume the finitude of natural resources, and because this theory depends solely upon the reduction of production and consumption. Thus, Jackson advocated the need for establishing a new theory based on the ecological economics, which assumes the environment capacity. On the basis of such a theory, he stated that the post-growth society is a new form of society whose goal is prosperity or the flourishing of human life as the alternative to economic growth. At present, however, it is difficult to say that either the degrowth or post-growth theory has presented a concrete (macro) economic theory. Based partly on the aforementioned concept of alternative societies that is not based on economic growth, I focus here on industry agglomeration, which contributes to green growth, in the following sections.

Most developed countries transformed from an industrial society based on labor or capital to a knowledge society, in which knowledge and technology are emphasized. For such a societal change to take place, innovation is essential to build new companies and to maintain the competitiveness of these companies, and in turn, to grow new industries and achieve national competitiveness in a country. In recent years, new knowledge and technologies that enhance innovation have received a great deal of societal and academic interest (Malmberg and Maskell, 1997; Tomozawa, 2000; Yamamoto, 2005; Matsubara, 2006). The growing interest in environment-related industries based on environmental technologies is an example of this attention. Since the collapse of the information technology (IT) bubble in the first half of the 2000s, many institutional investors have changed their investment focus from IT companies to environment-related industries. The start of the first commitment period of the Kyoto Protocol in 2008 also enhanced investment in environment-related industries. In line with the surging social interest in ways to protect the natural environment such as effective resource use and the prevention of global warming, environmental technologies designed to reduce environmental loads have developed rapidly in recent years, and in turn, environment-related industries have been growing markedly.

Under such circumstances, several metrics were developed to grasp the status of knowledge associated with various innovations and related environmental technologies. The OECD patent statistics and the new System of National Accounts, which was adopted by the United Nations in 2008, are examples, and they also became global standards.[1] According to OECD (2008), the number of environment-related patents almost doubled from 1998 to 2008, indicating an increase in the number of environmental technologies and environment-related industries based these technologies.[2] Other than the OECD (2008) report, which mentioned only limited categories of environmental technologies, there are only a limited number of studies providing an overview of the global development of the environmental industries.

In cities all over the world, the scale economies could be affected by the agglomeration of environmental industries. In a previous study I found that environmental industries were concentrated in large urban areas on a global scale (Yamashita 2013). Using the number of environment-related patents as an indicator of innovation, the results of that study indicated that the externalities of high population density can influence the agglomeration of high-tech industries. In other words, because companies and professionals are accumulated at high density in small spatial areas within cities, innovative knowledge, skills and technologies are shared among these companies and professionals, and as a result, the creation and growth of high-tech industries can be encouraged in urban environments. This type of externalities is referred to as a knowledge spillover effect (Jaffe et al., 1993).

Externalities that enhance industry agglomerations can be classified into two domains (Beaudry and Schiffauerova, 2009). One domain is the so-called Marshall-Arrow-Romer (MAR) externalities, and the other is the Jacobs externalities. In the MAR domain, it is assumed that a regional specialization of an industry or a specialization in industry agglomeration can promote regional economic growth. In the Jacobs domain, it is thought that rather than specialization, diversity in industries can enhance economic growth and technological innovation. Another type of externalities, the Porter externalities, is similar to the MAR externalities. In both, the regional specialization of industries or a specialization in industry agglomeration is thought to lead to regional economic growth. However, MAR and Porter externalities are different in the following way. In the MAR domain, it is emphasized that is an exclusive environment of a monopolized company or industry could result in industrial accumulation and regional economic growth. In the Porter externalities, in contrast, it is stressed that a competitive environment with a group of companies or industries can bring innovation or economic growth.

Based on their analysis of 67 peer-reviewed papers, Beaudry and Schiffauerova (2009) concluded that both MAR and Jacobs externalities have positively affected industry agglomeration and economic growth, and they summarized the characteristics of these two types of externalities as follows: (1) the MAR externalities were dominant in the analyses of industries categorized in the broad industrial classification, whereas the Jacobs externalities affected the articulated classification. Both influenced the medium classification. (2) Regarding combinations of industry classification and geographic units, neither the MAR nor the Jacobs externalities had an influence in analyses using the broad industry classification and disaggregated spatial units or when using the coarse industry classification and aggregated spatial units. Both externalities have effects in both industries classification and spatial units in between. (3) Regarding traditional and high-tech industries, the MAR externalities are somewhat more influential in traditional industries compared to the Jacobs externalities, whereas the Jacobs externalities have a greater impact on high-tech industries. Both externalities affect the intermediate industries between traditional and high-tech industries. (4) Concerning the life stage of industries, the Jacobs externalities are dominant at the early stage, and the MAR externalities has a greater effect at the final stage.

Neffke et al. (2012) confirmed these findings in their study of 12 Swedish manufacturers. They found that when researchers used innovation—which was represented by factors such as the total amount of research and development costs and the number of patents as the dependent variable instead of economic growth—the Jacobs externalities had greater influence than the MAR externalities in analyses using an articulated or less coarse industry classification, whereas the MAR externalities were more dominant in analyses using the broad industry classification.

Beaudry and Schiffauerova (2009) also summarized the effects of both externalities by country. On the basis of just one case, they reported that only the MAR externalities had a positive effect in Sweden. For Japan, using four cases, they indicated that only the MAR externalities were effective in one case, and that only the Jacobs externalities were effective in another case. Both types of externalities affected the other two cases. However, it remains difficult to conclude which externalities are dominant in Sweden and Japan, and further research on the effects of the MAR and Jacobs externalities on industry agglomeration in both countries is needed.

Moreover, regarding the effects of these two types of externalities on high-tech industries, studies of high-tech industries have focused mainly on information and communications technology (ICT) and biotechnology, and thus the accumulation of analyses using an environment-related industry or innovation as the dependent variable is not sufficient. Taking the aforementioned research circumstances into consideration, and using the OECD environment patent data, I conducted the present study to provide an overview of regional locations of environment-related industries across the globe, and to identify the effects of the MAR and Jacobs externalities—which resulted from population accumulations in urban areas—on the agglomeration of environment-related industries. Section 2 describes research methods for revealing the regional locations of environment-related industries across the world and effects of the two externalities. After the regional locations of environment-related industries are presented in Section 3, I examine the effects of the externalities in Section 4. The final section is a summary of both the regional locations of and the characteristics of the externality impacts on the environment-related industries, along with suggestions for further study directions.

14.2 Methods

As mentioned above, the environment-related industries are the focus of the present study. Using the number of environment-related patents aggregated by region, I examined the accumulation of environment-related industries. As Oltra et al. (2009) pointed out, these patents are good indicators for measuring environment-related innovations. I used the OECD patent statistics to gather the environment-related patents.[3] These statistics are aggregated by Territorial Level 3 (TL3), which is the OECD's unique regional statistic unit. I summed the total number of OECD patent statistic data issued between 1998 and 2008, and used the summed figures to examine the locations of the environment-related industries worldwide. To reveal effects of the MAR and Jacobs externalities, I also used the OECD's TL3 regions. These regions are equivalent to prefectures in Japan or to states in the U.S. There are 47 prefectures, i.e., TL3 regions, in Japan.

Using six of the seven categories of OECD environment technology patent statistics, I examined regional agglomerations of the environment-related industries and the effects of the

Table 1 Classifications of environment-related patents by OECD

A. GENERAL ENVIRONMENTAL MANAGEMENT

1. Air pollution abatement (from stationary sources)

2. Water pollution abatement

3. Waste management

   i. Solid waste collection

   ii. Material recycling

   iii. Fertilizers from waste

   iv. Incineration and energy recovery

   v. Landfilling [n.a.]

   vi. Not elsewhere classified

4. Soil remediation

5. Environmental monitoring

B. ENERGY GENERATION FROM RENEWABLE AND NON-FOSSIL SOURCES

1. Renewable energy generation

   i. Wind energy

   ii. Solar thermal energy

   iii. Solar photovoltaic (PV) energy

   iv. Solar thermal-PV hybrids

   v. Geothermal energy

   vi. Marine energy (excluding tidal)

   vii. Hydro energy - tidal, stream or damless

   viii. Hydro energy - conventional

2. Energy generation from fuels of non-fossil origin

   i. Biofuels

   ii. Fuel from waste (e.g. methane)

C. COMBUSTION TECHNOLOGIES WITH MITIGATION POTENTIAL (e.g. using fossil fuels, biomass, waste, etc.)

1. Technologies for improved output efficiency (Combined combustion)

   i. Heat utilisation in combustion or incineration of waste

   ii. Combined heat and power (CHP)

   iii. Combined cycles (incl. CCPP, CCGT, IGCC, IGCC+CCS)

2. Technologies for improved input efficiency (Efficient combustion or heat usage)

D. TECHNOLOGIES SPECIFIC TO CLIMATE CHANGE MITIGATION

1. Capture, storage, sequestration or disposal of greenhouse gases

   i. CO_2 capture and storage (CCS)

   ii. Capture or disposal of greenhouse gases other than carbon dioxide (N_2O, CH_4, PFC, HFC, SF_6)

E. TECHNOLOGIES WITH POTENTIAL OR INDIRECT CONTRIBUTION TO EMISSIONS MITIGATION

1. Energy storage

2. Hydrogen production (from non-carbon sources), distribution, and storage

3. Fuel cells

F. EMISSIONS ABATEMENT AND FUEL EFFICIENCY IN TRANSPORTATION

1. Technologies specific to propulsion using internal combustion engine (ICE) (e.g. conventional petrol/diesel vehicle, hybrid vehicle with ICE)
   i. Integrated emissions control (NOX, CO, HC, PM)
   ii. Post-combustion emissions control (NOX, CO, HC, PM)
2. Technologies specific to propulsion using electric motor (e.g. electric vehicle, hybrid vehicle)
3. Technologies specific to hybrid propulsion (e.g. hybrid vehicle propelled by electric motor and internal combustion engine)
4. Fuel efficiency-improving vehicle design (e.g. streamlining)

G. ENERGY EFFICIENCY IN BUILDINGS AND LIGHTING

1. Insulation (incl. thermal insulation, double-glazing)
2. Heating (incl. water and space heating; air-conditioning)
3. Lighting (incl. CFL, LED)

Source: OECD (2008), Compendium of Patent Statistics (Paris, OECD)

Table 2　Top 20 regions for agglomerations of high-tech industries

Rank	Region	No. of patents (1998-2008)	Share in the world (%)	Accumulated share in the world (%)
1	US146: San Jose-San Francisco-Oakland - CA	57,262.5	4.29	4.29
2	JPC13: Tokyo	55,680.0	4.17	8.47
3	US118: New York-Newark-Bridgeport - NY-NJ-CT-PA	43,729.8	3.28	11.75
4	US022: Boston-Worcester-Manchester - MA-NH	34,532.0	2.59	14.34
5	US097: Los Angeles-Long Beach-Riverside - CA	25,796.9	1.93	16.27
6	JPC14: Kanagawa	22,489.4	1.69	17.96
7	JPF27: Osaka	21,849.9	1.64	19.59
8	US145: San Diego-Carlsbad-San Marcos - CA	20,128.4	1.51	21.10
9	NL41: Noord-Brabant	19,911.2	1.49	22.60
10	US109: Minneapolis-St. Paul-St. Cloud - MN-WI	19,009.7	1.43	24.02
11	US032: Chicago-Naperville-Michigan City - IL-IN-WI	17,163.5	1.29	25.31
12	US127: Philadelphia-Camden-Vineland - PA-NJ-DE-MD	16,241.5	1.22	26.53
13	DE93: München	15,035.8	1.13	27.65
14	DE72: Stuttgart	13,999.9	1.05	28.70
15	US174: Washington-Baltimore-N.Virginia - DC-MD-VA-WV	13,743.9	1.03	29.73
16	KR011: Seoul	13,734.9	1.03	30.76
17	KR013: Gyeonggi-do	13,226.8	0.99	31.76
18	US075: Houston-Baytown-Huntsville - TX	12,468.4	0.93	32.69
19	US152: Seattle-Tacoma-Olympia - WA	11,913.9	0.89	33.58
20	JPE23: Aichi	11,832.7	0.89	34.47

Source: OECD Patent Database

MAR and Jacobs externalities (Table 1). Category E was excluded because of the lack of data. The seven categories are as follows. (1) Category A (General Environment Management) includes technologies of soil pollution control and sewage and waste-related treatments. (2) Category B (Energy Generation from Renewable and Non-Fossil Sources) consists of technologies for energy production associated with wind, solar, geothermal and other energy sources. (3) Category C (Combustion Technologies with Mitigation Potential) contains technologies related to cogeneration such as waste power generation. (4) Category D (Technologies Specific to Climate Change Mitigation) includes mainly technologies of carbon dioxide capture and storage (CCS) and other technologies concerning the capture and storage of different greenhouse gases. (5) Category E (Technologies with Potential or Indirect Contribution to Emissions Mitigation) comprises technologies related to fuel cells and the production, transportation and storage of hydrogen. (6) Category F (Emission Abatement and Fuel Efficiency in Transportation) encompasses the transport-related technologies including exhaust gas regulation systems and hybrid engines. (7) Category G (Energy Efficiency in Building and Lighting) consists of the technologies associated with the efficiency of heating and lighting in buildings.

Using the multiple regression model, I identified effects of the MAR and Jacobs externalities on agglomerations of the environment-related industries for each of the six categories (A, B, C, D, F, G). The dependent variables were the number of environment-related patents in the six categories.

The explanatory variables were three, representing the work force, the MAR and Jacobs externalities. The population of residents aged 16–64 years (*Employees*) was used as the workforce. As mentioned before, the MAR externalities imply the regional specialization of an industry or the specialization in an industrial agglomeration area. I therefore used the coefficient of specialization or location quotient ($LQir$), which is represented by the following equation, as the location quotient has been often used in previous studies as an indicator of the MAR externalities (Beaudry and Schiffauerova, 2009, p.321).

$$LQ_{ir} = (E_{ir} / E_r) / (E_{in} / E_n) \tag{1}$$

where E_{ir} is the number of employees in an industry sector i in a region r,

E_r is the total number of employees in a region r,

E_{in} is the total number of employees in an industry sector i at the national level, and

E_n is the total number of employees in the all industry sectors at the national level.

The high proportion of experts with professional knowledge within the total employees is crucial for the MAR externalities, and thus the location quotient was frequently calculated and used in many case studies using the total number of employees in each industry sector and in all of the industry sectors. Although the location quotients were used in this study, I did not use the number of employees because of the lack of employee data in the six categories of environment-related industries. Because of the constraints on the data, I evaluated the location quotients using the number of environment-related patents in each category and in all of the categories, and I used the total number of patents over all of the industries instead of the number of employees.

A location quotient higher than 1 indicates a high degree of agglomeration of environment-related industries in a region, whereas a location quotient lower than 1 indicates a low degree of agglomeration.

The Hirschman-Herfindahl index is often used as an index representing the Jacobs externalities (Beaudry and Schiffauerova, 2009, p.322). In the present study, however, Simpson's diversity index (D) was employed instead of the Hirschman-Herfindahl index. The Simpson's diversity index is expressed as the following equation.

$$D=1-\sum_{i=1}^{s} P_i^2 \qquad (2)$$

where P_i is the percentage of the number of a specie i in the total number of all of the species within a botanic community, and S is the number of species within a botanic community. I calculated the diversity index using the six categories of the environment-related industries as the species, and the 47 prefectures of Japan as the botanic communities. When the diversity index score is higher than 1, one industry monopolizes in a prefecture. In this case, the degree of diversity is very low. Conversely, when the score is close to null, the degree of diversity is very high.

Finally, regional agglomerations of the environment-related industries were examined using standard residuals derived from applications of the multiple regression analysis.

14.3 Locations of environment-related industries

The following subsections describe the regional locations of the environment-related industries observed for each of the six categories of environment-related technologies. Before identifying these locations, I briefly note the agglomerations of all of the high-tech industries and all of the environment-related industries.

14.3.1 All of the high-tech industries

The analysis of regional patent acquisitions, which indicate the locations of high-tech industries, such as ICT and biotechnology industries showed that large urban areas share the top spots on the list (Table 2). The San Jose-San Francisco area including Silicon Valley is first, and other large urban areas such as Tokyo, New York, Boston, Los Angeles, Kanagawa (Yokohama) and Osaka follow. Headquarters of globally expanding/expanded ICT, biotechnology and other high-tech multinational companies are situated. It is noteworthy that no Chinese cities are named in this top-20 list, although China is ranked at eighth place regarding the total number of all patents by country. Although large urban areas are dominant in this list, medium-sized urban areas such as Noord Brabant with Eindhoven in The Netherlands, where Philips' headquarters is located, also possess a large number of patents. This could be related to an agglomeration of the existing industries.

14.3.2 All environment-related patents

The regional acquisitions of all environment-related patents differ from those of all of the patents (Table 3). Regarding the acquisition of all environment-related patents, many regions in the U.S., where the ICT and biotechnology industries are accumulated, are at lower ranks compared to their ranks for all the patents. Conversely, areas in which there are transportation

Table 3   Top 20 regions for the total number of environment-related patents (six OECD categories)

Rank	Region	No. of patents (1998-2008)	Share in the world (%)	Accumulated share in the world (%)
1	DE72: Stuttgart	3,485.1	4.99	4.99
2	JPE23: Aichi	3,234.3	4.63	9.62
3	JPC13: Tokyo	2,387.6	3.42	13.03
4	JPC14: Kanagawa	1,434.8	2.05	15.09
5	US146: San Jose-San Francisco-Oakland - CA	1,344.2	1.92	17.01
6	US118: New York-Newark-Bridgeport - NY-NJ-CT-PA	1,204.2	1.72	18.73
7	JPF27: Osaka	1,101.5	1.58	20.31
8	US047: Detroit-Warren-Flint - MI	976.4	1.40	21.71
9	JPC11: Saitama	944.1	1.35	23.06
10	US097: Los Angeles-Long Beach-Riverside - CA	881.2	1.26	24.32
11	US022: Boston-Worcester-Manchester - MA-NH	869.1	1.24	25.56
12	NL41: Noord-Brabant	852.2	1.22	26.78
13	DE90: Regensburg	712.8	1.02	27.80
14	US109: Minneapolis-St. Paul-St. Cloud - MN-WI	665.4	0.95	28.76
15	DE93: München	659.1	0.94	29.70
16	US032: Chicago-Naperville-Michigan City - IL-IN-WI	656.1	0.94	30.64
17	US127: Philadelphia-Camden-Vineland - PA-NJ-DE-MD	568.5	0.81	31.45
18	US075: Houston-Baytown-Huntsville - TX	539.3	0.77	32.23
19	JPC08: Ibaraki	521.7	0.75	32.97
20	KR011: Seoul	506.8	0.73	33.70

Source: OECD Patent Database

Knowledge Spillover Effects on Agglomerations of Environment-related Industries: A Case in Japan   235

equipment companies related to Category E in the OECD classification rise in this ranking. Detroit, where the Big Three auto manufacturers are situated, Saitama (Honda), Regensburg (BMW), and Ibaraki (Hitachi Construction Machinery, or HCM) are examples.

14.3.3 Category A: General environment management

The locations of the Category A, environment-related patents are quite similar to those of all the environment-related patents (Table 4). There are slight changes in the high-ranking spots, but no replacement up to the 15th place. Below the 16th rank, only Gyeonggi-do, Atlanta and Gifu are new to the top 20. However, these areas each have less than one percent of the market share. Thus, these locations might contribute less to the global locations of environment-related industries in Category A.

Table 4   Top 20 regions for patents in OECD Category A: General Environment Management

Rank	Region	No. of patents (1998-2008)	Share in the world (%)	Accumulated share in the world (%)
1	JPC13: Tokyo	897.1	3.52	3.52
2	JPE23: Aichi	818.2	3.21	6.74
3	DE72: Stuttgart	540.8	2.12	8.86
4	US118: New York-Newark-Bridgeport - NY-NJ-CT-PA	525.4	2.06	10.93
5	US109: Minneapolis-St. Paul-St. Cloud - MN-WI	403.8	1.59	12.52
6	JPC14: Kanagawa	396.0	1.56	14.07
7	JPF27: Osaka	362.4	1.42	15.50
8	US022: Boston-Worcester-Manchester - MA-NH	325.0	1.28	16.77
9	US146: San Jose-San Francisco-Oakland - CA	320.3	1.26	18.03
10	US097: Los Angeles-Long Beach-Riverside - CA	314.7	1.24	19.27
11	US032: Chicago-Naperville-Michigan City - IL-IN-WI	311.6	1.22	20.49
12	JPC11: Saitama	292.4	1.15	21.64
13	US075: Houston-Baytown-Huntsville - TX	264.8	1.04	22.68
14	KR011: Seoul	248.3	0.98	23.66
15	US127: Philadelphia-Camden-Vineland - PA-NJ-DE-MD	221.5	0.87	24.53
16	DE44: Köln	213.3	0.84	25.36
17	KR013: Gyeonggi-do	211.8	0.83	26.20
18	US047: Detroit-Warren-Flint - MI	210.4	0.83	27.02
19	US011: Atlanta-Sandy Springs-Gainesville - GA-AL	175.6	0.69	27.71
20	JPE21: Gifu	173.8	0.68	28.40

Source: OECD Patent Database

14.3.4 Category B: Energy generation from renewable and non-fossil sources

Concerning the regional distributions of the Category B, environment-related patents, the regions situated at lower than the 10th rank differ from those of Category A and from the all-environment-related patents (Table 5). The four regions in the 10th, 13th, 17th and 19th ranks are located in the Jutland peninsula, Denmark. Cooke (2008) revealed that wind turbine clusters were established in these regions. It can be inferred that various technologies related to wind turbines have been created and shared among companies in these clusters. Although Spain and China share high ranks in the country patent profile (8th with 2.6 percent and 9th with 2.5 percent, respectively), it would not be concluded that the environment-related industries in Category B were regionally concentrated in Spain and China. In addition, similar to the Danish wind turbine clusters, it is surmised that environment-related technologies might be derived from the existing oil and gas industries when energy resources were diversified

Table 5   Top 20 regions for patents in OECD Category B: Energy Generation from Renewable and Non-Fossil Sources

Rank	Region	No. of patents (1998-2008)	Share in the world (%)	Accumulated share in the world (%)
1	US146: San Jose-San Francisco-Oakland - CA	725.0	5.20	5.20
2	JPC13: Tokyo	432.8	3.10	8.31
3	US097: Los Angeles-Long Beach-Riverside - CA	277.1	1.99	10.29
4	US022: Boston-Worcester-Manchester - MA-NH	272.9	1.96	12.25
5	JPF27: Osaka	250.4	1.80	14.05
6	JPC14: Kanagawa	203.1	1.46	15.51
7	US118: New York-Newark-Bridgeport - NY-NJ-CT-PA	192.7	1.38	16.89
8	US127: Philadelphia-Camden-Vineland - PA-NJ-DE-MD	154.3	1.11	18.00
9	US047: Detroit-Warren-Flint - MI	152.0	1.09	19.09
10	DK042: Østjylland	148.3	1.06	20.15
11	US045: Denver-Aurora-Boulder - CO	146.4	1.05	21.20
12	KR011: Seoul	129.5	0.93	22.13
13	DE12: Ost-Friesland	129.4	0.93	23.06
14	DE93: München	127.2	0.91	23.97
15	AU105: Sydney - NSW	113.2	0.81	24.78
16	US133: Raleigh-Durham-Cary - NC	106.5	0.76	25.55
17	DK032: Sydjylland	102.2	0.73	26.28
18	KR013: Gyeonggi-do	101.1	0.72	27.00
19	DK041: Vestjylland	94.2	0.68	27.68
20	US174: Washington-Baltimore-N.Virginia - DC-MD-VA-WV	92.7	0.66	28.34

Source: OECD Patent Database

from fossil fuel to renewable energy in Denver, Colorado (11th) and Sydney (15th).

14.3.5 Category C: Combustion technologies with mitigation potential

As regards the OECD Category C, the large urban areas situated in the higher places in Table 6 are rather similar to those in the case of all the environment-related patents, whereas the regions in the lower ranks in this table are different (Table 6). Regions in the top spots are located mainly in large urban areas, and their positions in this table are higher than their positions in Table 3. These regions include Tokyo, Houston, Los Angeles, Boston and Chicago. Hyogo (13th), Stockholm (14th) and Duisburg-Essen (16th) are newly entered as top-20 regions. KOBELCO's and Thyssen Krupp's headquarters are located in Hyogo (Kobe, Japan) and Duisburg-Essen, Germany, respectively. Metal industries, especially steel industries, are accumulated in these two areas. It may be suggested that cogeneration system-related technologies were established using waste heat from metal industry plants. In contrast, technolo-

Table 6 Top 20 regions for patents in OECD Category C: Combustion Technologies with Mitigation Potential

Rank	Region	No. of patents (1998-2008)	Share in the world (%)	Accumulated share in the world (%)
1	JPC13: Tokyo	94.4	4.98	4.98
2	US075: Houston-Baytown-Huntsville - TX	79.0	4.17	9.15
3	US118: New York-Newark-Bridgeport - NY-NJ-CT-PA	55.8	2.94	12.09
4	DE86: Industrieregion Mittelfranken	46.9	2.47	14.56
5	NL32: Noord-Holland	43.0	2.27	16.83
6	US097: Los Angeles-Long Beach-Riverside - CA	41.1	2.17	19.00
7	US022: Boston-Worcester-Manchester - MA-NH	32.6	1.72	20.72
8	US032: Chicago-Naperville-Michigan City - IL-IN-WI	31.1	1.64	22.36
9	US072: Hartford-West Hartford-Willimantic - CT	30.7	1.62	23.98
10	US146: San Jose-San Francisco-Oakland - CA	27.2	1.44	25.41
11	CH033: Aargau	25.8	1.36	26.77
12	JPC14: Kanagawa	24.8	1.31	28.08
13	JPF28: Hyogo	24.6	1.30	29.38
14	SE110: Stockholms län	19.7	1.04	30.42
15	US023: Buffalo-Niagara-Cattaraugus - NY	18.8	0.99	31.41
16	DE41: Duisburg/Essen	17.7	0.93	32.34
17	DE93: München	17.2	0.91	33.25
18	US174: Washington-Baltimore-N.Virginia - DC-MD-VA-WV	15.7	0.83	34.08
19	US121: Orlando-The Villages - FL	15.5	0.82	34.89
20	FR105: Hauts-de-Seine	15.4	0.81	35.71

Source: OECD Patent Database

gies concerned with district heating and power systems have accumulated in Stockholm. It is inferred that the accumulations of these technologies enabled these three regions to rise in the ranks of patents held.

14.3.6 Category D: Technologies specific to climate change mitigation

Just like locational trends in the case of all environment-related patents, the environment-related industries in Category D are mainly concentrated in large urban areas (Table 7). Moreover, industries in this category are highly concentrated in Paris and its surrounding regions: Paris (14th), Lorraine (16th) and Hauts-de-Seine (17th). This might be closely connected to the accumulation of French companies around Paris with high environmental-related technologies such as those concerning the collection and savings of greenhouse gases, especially carbon dioxide capture and storage (CCS).

Table 7   Top 20 regions for patents in OECD Category D: Technologies Specific to Climate Change Mitigation

Rank	Region	No. of patents (1998-2008)	Share in the world (%)	Accumulated share in the world (%)
1	US118: New York-Newark-Bridgeport - NY-NJ-CT-PA	87.7	5.53	5.53
2	US075: Houston-Baytown-Huntsville - TX	72.6	4.57	10.10
3	US146: San Jose-San Francisco-Oakland - CA	67.0	4.22	14.32
4	JPC13: Tokyo	51.4	3.24	17.56
5	US097: Los Angeles-Long Beach-Riverside - CA	44.2	2.78	20.34
6	NL32: Noord-Holland	36.3	2.29	22.62
7	US022: Boston-Worcester-Manchester - MA-NH	30.0	1.89	24.51
8	US127: Philadelphia-Camden-Vineland - PA-NJ-DE-MD	29.1	1.83	26.35
9	JPC14: Kanagawa	29.1	1.83	28.18
10	US032: Chicago-Naperville-Michigan City - IL-IN-WI	28.8	1.82	30.00
11	US023: Buffalo-Niagara-Cattaraugus - NY	27.3	1.72	31.72
12	JPE23: Aichi	27.0	1.70	33.41
13	US045: Denver-Aurora-Boulder - CO	26.1	1.64	35.05
14	FR101: Paris	22.1	1.39	36.45
15	DE66: Rheinpfalz	21.4	1.34	37.79
16	FR716: Rhône	20.4	1.28	39.08
17	FR105: Hauts-de-Seine	17.9	1.13	40.21
18	NL33: Zuid-Holland	17.7	1.11	41.32
19	JPF27: Osaka	16.6	1.04	42.36
20	US040: Columbus-Marion-Chillicothe - OH	15.7	0.99	43.35

Source: OECD Patent Database

14.3.7 Category F: Emission abatement and fuel efficiency in transportation

Unlike other categories, the distribution of the environment-related industries in Category F is closely related to the locations of the automobile industry and construction machinery (Table 8). Stuttgart (Daimler-Benz and Porsche), Aichi (Toyota), Regensburg (BMW), Peoria (Caterpillar), Västra Götalands län (Volvo), Hauts-de-Seine (Renault), Osaka (Daihatsu), Yvelines (Peugeot and Citroen), Braunschweig (Volkswagen), Ibaraki (Hitachi Construction Machinery) and Shizuoka (Honda, Yamaha and Suzuki) are examples of this category. It is thus evident that some Category F regions are classified into large urban areas, but some are not.

Table 8   Top 20 regions for patents in OECD Category F: Emissions Abatement and Fuel Efficiency in Transportation

Rank	Region	No. of patents (1998-2008)	Share in the world (%)	Accumulated share in the world (%)
1	DE72: Stuttgart	2,830.9	14.40	14.40
2	JPE23: Aichi	2,290.2	11.65	26.05
3	DE90: Regensburg	601.2	3.06	29.11
4	US047: Detroit-Warren-Flint - MI	543.0	2.76	31.88
5	JPC11: Saitama	489.0	2.49	34.36
6	JPC14: Kanagawa	476.2	2.42	36.79
7	JPC13: Tokyo	410.4	2.09	38.88
8	US126: Peoria-Canton - IL	273.3	1.39	40.27
9	SE232: Västra Götalands län	258.7	1.32	41.58
10	DE93: München	249.6	1.27	42.85
11	FR105: Hauts-de-Seine	227.8	1.16	44.01
12	DE79: Bodensee-Oberschwaben	217.5	1.11	45.12
13	JPF27: Osaka	213.9	1.09	46.21
14	US118: New York-Newark-Bridgeport - NY-NJ-CT-PA	211.8	1.08	47.28
15	FR103: Yvelines	204.7	1.04	48.32
16	DE22: Braunschweig	188.0	0.96	49.28
17	DE51: Rhein-Main	173.9	0.88	50.17
18	JPC08: Ibaraki	171.6	0.87	51.04
19	US032: Chicago-Naperville-Michigan City - IL-IN-WI	171.4	0.87	51.91
20	JPC22: Shizuoka	170.9	0.87	52.78

Source: OECD Patent Database

14.3.8 Category G: Energy efficiency in building and lighting

As for locations of the environment-related industries in Category G, they too are located chiefly in large urban areas (Table 9). Outside the large urban areas, regions with high agglomerations of electrical machinery industries are also present among the top 20 regions. Examples are Aachen (6th), Gyeonggi-do (12th), where Samsung's and LG's headquarters are located, Cambridge (16th), where IT industries are agglomerated, and Berlin (18th), where Siemens is situated.

The results in all six of the OECD categories revealed that the most of the existing environment-related industries are located in large urban areas. In the next section, the impacts of externalities derived from urban populations are examined in a case study of Japan.

Table 9 Top 20 regions for patents in OECD Category G: Energy Efficiency in Building and Lighting

Rank	Region	No. of patents (1998-2008)	Share in the world (%)	Accumulated share in the world (%)
1	NL41: Noord-Brabant	698.7	9.51	9.51
2	JPC13: Tokyo	501.6	6.83	16.35
3	JPC14: Kanagawa	305.5	4.16	20.51
4	JPF27: Osaka	245.7	3.35	23.85
5	JPC12: Chiba	218.8	2.98	26.83
6	DE45: Aachen	163.4	2.23	29.06
7	DE93: München	143.6	1.96	31.01
8	US118: New York-Newark-Bridgeport - NY-NJ-CT-PA	130.7	1.78	32.79
9	JPC08: Ibaraki	103.2	1.41	34.20
10	US022: Boston-Worcester-Manchester - MA-NH	101.4	1.38	35.58
11	JPC11: Saitama	98.9	1.35	36.93
12	KR013: Gyeonggi-do	92.8	1.26	38.19
13	US139: Rochester-Batavia-Seneca Falls - NY	92.6	1.26	39.45
14	US146: San Jose-San Francisco-Oakland - CA	82.2	1.12	40.57
15	US097: Los Angeles-Long Beach-Riverside - CA	80.8	1.10	41.67
16	UKH12: Cambridgeshire CC	77.9	1.06	42.73
17	US035: Cleveland-Akron-Elyria - OH	77.0	1.05	43.78
18	DE30: Berlin	76.8	1.05	44.83
19	KR011: Seoul	75.0	1.02	45.85
20	US127: Philadelphia-Camden-Vineland - PA-NJ-DE-MD	71.4	0.97	46.82

Source: OECD Patent Database

14.4 Knowledge spillover effects

The multiple regression analysis elucidated that the MAR externalities were dominant regarding agglomerations of the environment-related industries in Japan (Table 10). All of the coefficients of determination are more than 0.5, and except for Categories C and F, they are more than 0.7. All of the coefficients are significant at the 1 % level, indicating that this multiple regression consisting of three variables produced reliable results. Regarding the individual variables, it can be seen in the table that the number of employees representing the city size is significant at the 1 % level in all six categories. The work force had positive effects on accumulations of the environment-related industries, as all of the values are positive. Except for Categories A and C, the MAR externalities positively influenced agglomerations of the environment-related industries because the location quotient representing regional specialization is significant at the 5 % level at least in each category, and they have positive signs. Unlike the previous two variables, the Simpson's diversity indexes are significant at the 5 % level and have negative signs in only Categories A and F. Since a high score of this index indicates a low degree of diversity, the diversity, namely the Jacobs externalities, positively affected agglomeration of the environment-related industries in these two categories (A and C). In sum, both MAR and Jacobs externalities influenced the industry agglomeration in Category F only, whereas only one of them had a positive effect in the other categories except Category C.

The results of this analysis revealed that both or one of the MAR and Jacobs externalities had positive effects on agglomerations of the environment-related industries in Japan. This finding is consistent with two points made by Beaudry and Schiffauerova (2009): (1) the MAR externalities are dominant in analyses using the broad industry classification data, in cases in which innovation is used as a dependent variable, and (2) both the MAR and Jacobs externalities affect industry agglomerations in Japan, together and alone.

Table 10 Results of the multiple regression model examining the effects of the MAR and Jacobs externalities on agglomerations of environment-related industries for the OECD categories

Category	Employees		LQ		D		R^2	
A	9.160E-05	***	−78.353		−359.784	**	0.741	***
B	3.657E-05	***	6.272	***	18.244		0.724	***
C	6.084E-06	***	0.195		4.082		0.590	***
D	4.540E-06	***	0.229	**	−6.096		0.723	***
F	9.041E-05	***	358.980	***	−945.581	***	0.502	***
G	4.350E-05	***	1.801	**	39.642		0.769	***

LQ: Location quotient; D: Simpson's diversity index; R^2: Coefficient of determination.
*** $p < 0.01$; ** $p < 0.05$; * $p < 0.1$.

Table 11 Standardized residuals in the 47 prefectures of Japan by OECD category

Prefecture	Category A: General Environment Management	Category B: Energy Generation from Renewable and Non-Fossil Sources	Category C: Combustion Technologies with Mitigation Potential	Category D: Technologies Specific to Climate Change Mitigation	Category F: Emission Abatement and Fuel Efficiency in Transportation	Category G: Energy Efficiency in Building and Lighting
Hokkaido						
Aomori						
Iwate						
Miyagi						
Akita						
Yamagata						
Fukushima						
Ibaraki						
Tochigi						
Gumma						
Saitama						
Chiba						
Tokyo	2.378	3.680	5.088	3.319		3.419
Kanagawa				1.169		1.500
Yamanashi						
Nagano						
Shizuoka						
Niigata						
Toyama						
Ishikawa						
Fukui						
Gifu	1.287					
Aichi	3.847			1.618	5.300	
Mie						
Shiga	1.171	1.234				
Kyoto				1.658		
Osaka		1.316				
Hyogo						
Nara						
Wakayama						
Tottori						
Shimane						
Okayama						
Hiroshima						
Yamaguchi						
Tokushima						

Kagawa	
Ehime	
Kochi	
Fukuoka	
Saga	
Nagasaki	1.007
Kumamoto	
Oita	
Miyazaki	
Kagoshima	
Okinawa	

The standard residuals derived from the present multiple regression analysis revealed that the environment-related industries are concentrated in large urban areas in Japan. These areas are Keihin, Hanshin and Chukyo metropolises, the cores of which are Tokyo, Osaka, and Aichi Prefecture, respectively (Table 11). Only standard residuals with 1.0 and above are shown in this table. The Keihin metropolitan area has the maximum in Categories B, C and D, while the Chukyo metropolitan area has the maximum in Categories A and F. The Hanshin area has not the highest but a high score in Category B. It is thus clear that the environment-related industries are agglomerated in large urban areas in Japan. This finding indicates the externalities of population accumulation on the agglomeration of these industries.

14.5 Conclusion

Using the OECD patent statistic data, I attempted to identify the locations of the environment-related industries around the world, and to estimate the impacts of the MAR and Jacobs externalities on the agglomeration of these industries due to population accumulation in large urban areas. The findings can be summarized as follows. First, the locations of these industries tended to be concentrated in large urban areas including New York, Los Angeles and Chicago in the United States, Tokyo and Kanagawa (Yokohama) in Japan, and Munich and Stuttgart in Germany. However, there were also exceptions to this general trend, such as regions in the Danish Jutland peninsula where technologies related to wind turbine energy are situated.

It was also revealed that both MAR and Jacobs externalities had positive impacts on the agglomeration of environment-related industries. This result is consistent with findings of previous studies. Both or one of the MAR and Jacobs externalities affected the industry agglomerations in Japan. When innovation was used as the dependent variable and categorized in the broad industry classification, the MAR externalities dominated in the industry agglomerations.

Although the present study identified the locations of environment-related industries and determinates of agglomerations of these industries, some unsolved research objectives remain. First, the following were not taken into account regarding the agglomeration of environment-related industries: the agglomeration mechanisms of these industries, cooperation/competition among environment-related companies in the industry agglomerated areas, the effects of national and regional policies designed to encourage innovation, and cluster creations for these industries. In addition, methodological problems in evaluating the externalities were also left behind. One such problem is the limitations of the data, and another is the selection of the index/indicator. Here I used the number of patents in the calculations of the location quotients, although the number of employees was often used in previous studies. It might be possible to first recalculate the number of employees in the smallest industry classification into the aforementioned seven categories of the environment-related industries, and to then use the recalculated numbers to evaluate the location quotients.

Further research is needed to employ such data to completely grasp the effects of the knowledge spillover. Although the location quotient and Simpson's diversity index represented the MAR and Jacobs externalities, respectively, in this study, Beaudry and Schiffauerova (2009) also pointed out that differences in externalities indicators caused varied results of effects on the industry agglomeration (p. 334). Like the necessity of using various measures, it is the same for dependent variables. Although I used environment-related patents as the indicator representing innovation in this paper, research and development expenses in the environmental industry might be substitutable for this indicator. Future studies should solve the aforementioned problems as we continue to attempt to identify the effects of knowledge spillover on the agglomeration of environment industries.

Acknowledgment

I extend my gratitude for the financial support provided by the Grants-in-Aid for Scientific Research (A) No. 24242034 and (C) No. 24520893.

References

Beaudry, C. and Schiffauerova, A. 2009. Who's right, Marshall or Jacobs? The localization versus urbanization debate. *Research Policy* 38: 318–337.

Bonaiuti, M. 2011. *From Bioeconomics to degrowth: Georgescu-Roegen's 'New economics' in eight essays.* Routledge.

Cooke, P. 2008. Regional innovation systems, clean technology and Jacobian cluster-platform policies. *Regional Science Policy and Practice* 1: 23-45.

Federal Ministry for Agriculture, Forestry, Environment and Water Management. 2012. *Future dossier: Alternative economic and social concepts.* Vienna: Federal Ministry for Agriculture, Forestry, Environment and Water Management.

Jackson, T. 2009. Prosperity without growth: Economics for a finite planet. Earthscan.

Jaffe, A. B., Trajtenberg, M. and Henderson, R. 1993. Geographic localization of knowledge spillovers as evidenced by patent citations. In *Quarterly Journal of Economics* 108: 577–598.

Malmberg, A. and Maskell, P. 1997. Towards an explanation of regional specialization and industry agglomeration. *European Planning Studies* 5: 25-41.

Matsubara, H. 2006. Economic geography: Theories of location, region and city. Tokyo: Tokyo University Press. (J)

Neffke, F., Henning, M., Boschma, R., Lundquist, K. -J. and Olander, L. -O. 2011. The dynamics of agglomeration externalities along the life cycle of industries. *Regional Studies* 45: 49-65.

OECD .2008. Compendium of patent statistics. OECD.

Oltra, V., Kemp, R. and de Vries, F. P. 2009. Patents as a measure for eco-innovation. Working *Paper of GREThA*, 2009-05: 1-19.

The United Nations World Commission on Environment and Development. 1987. In *Our common future*. Oxford: Oxford University Press.

Tomozawa, K. 2000. From production systems to learning systems: Research trend of industrial geography in Europe and America in the 1990s. *Annals of the Association of Economic Geographers* 46: 323-336. (J)

Yamamoto, K. 2005. Economic geography of industrial agglomeration. Tokyo: Hosei University Press. (J)

Yamashita, J. 2013. A note on locations of clean technology industries over the globe. *Bulletin of the Graduate School of Social and Cultural Studies* 19: 65-72.

(J) means "written in Japanese" (with an English summary, in some cases).

Notes

(Endnotes)

[1]The United Nations Statistics Division relinquished the version of the System of National Account (93SNA) as it adopted a new version (08SNA). The 08SNA includes a classification of "innovation", which enhance to create knowledge.

[2]According to the OECD patent statistics, the number of environment-related patents increased from 71,680 to 148,974 during the aforementioned period.

[3]The data were obtained from the following web site:

http://www.oecd.org/sti/innovationinsciencetechnologyandindustry/oecdpatentdatabases. htm

246

15. Conclusion

This book has considered the characteristics of urban areas in the 'Post-Growth' society of Japan. In the introduction, Dr. Michael Pacione, a professor at the University of Strathclyde in the United Kingdom, provided an overview of the worldwide trend of shrinking cities, examined trends in Japan, and raised several urban geographical questions related to the Post-Growth society. Evaluating the quality of life and using maps to interpret regional differences of social status were regarded as particularly important. Here, we briefly examine some of the material from the various chapters from the point of view of Dr. Pacione's discussion in Chapter 1.

Dr. Pacione introduced a four-stage development model in which the final stage is 're-urbanization', where the population of the city core increases again after a decline. The city cores of two major metropolitan areas (Tokyo and *Kei-Han-Shin*) have experienced slight population increases since the mid 1990s. We call this phenomenon a 'regression of population distribution to the city core'. Until the 1980s, these city cores experienced serious population decreases as the metropolitan boundaries expanded during the process of suburbanization. In addition, gentrification issues have been raised as the number of high-rise condominiums increased in the city cores. From these points of view, the phenomena observed in these two large Japanese metropolitan areas could be representative of Pacione's concept of re-urbanization. However, population changes associated with re-urbanization in Japanese cities are quite different from those seen in cities of the United States and Europe (Chapters 2, 3, 4, and 9). Two major factors make Japan different: a rapidly declining birthrate combined with an aging population and a surge in the number of high-rise condominiums built in the city core driven by the sharp decrease in land prices due to the collapse of the Bubble economy. These phenomena could be considered to be partly the result of the globalization of finance that triggered re-urbanization in U.S. and European cities, but based on the analyses presented in this book, we think the ongoing phenomena found in Japan have different causes. One possible factor affecting these phenomena is the shift from an increasing to a decreasing population since 2005.

The expansion of metropolitan areas has already stopped in Japan, and even worse, suburban residential areas are beginning to experience declining populations. The most dominant factor affecting the trend of population shifts seems to be easy access to railway services (Chapters 4 and 7). When looking at the spatial pattern of growth, metropolitan areas are also dominated by access to railway services. This trend has not changed over the last several decades. The degree of dependence on railway services, which functions as a key means of daily transportation, is very high in Japan as compared to most U.S. and European cities, where a high dependence on automobiles can be seen.

Although the Japanese major metropolitan areas do yet appear to be entering the stage of depopulation that Dr. Pacione regards as the first phase of shrinking cities (Chapter 1), severe depopulation can be observed in many small cities throughout Japan. A key factor in triggering municipal consolidation, as examined in detail in Chapter 13, is the declining birthrate and the subsequent aging population, which has resulted in depopulation and increases in the cost of welfare services. Reacting to an aging population is an ongoing and common task, not only in major metropolitan areas, but also in small cities in Japan. Several types of problems derived from the aging population were considered in Chapters 6, 7 and 8. For example, the problem of food deserts, an ongoing and serious problem in Japanese metropolitan areas that is also common in other aging societies, was examined in Chapter 7. Currently, in the early 2010s, an imbalance in the demand–supply of infrastructure, generally considered to be a major problem related to aging populations, has not yet been observed in Japan. However, an abundance of vacant land and vacant houses (examined in Chapter 8) has become a serious concern in the suburbs of medium-sized Japanese cities. Creating and implementing countermeasures against vacant houses has become a major concern for urban planners.

Forming 'individual-city-centered' networks is a crucial strategy for future growth, especially for Regional Centre Cities (Sapporo, Sendai, Hiroshima and Fukuoka) in Japan (Chapter 11). Chapter 12 examines the vulnerability of the industrial infrastructure, which is the key element for growth, in these Regional Centre Cities. In addition, establishment of new Research-and-Development type firms has tended to be limited to the major metropolitan areas (Chapter 14). The concept of future growth requires more discussion and study.

Japanese urban planners, urban policymakers, and researchers who are engaged in urban studies (including urban geographers) have a common recognition that the urban population will decrease in the near future. Therefore, they are working on the 'compact-city' concept that would be preferable in future urban societies. The compact-city concept has been adopted in the revitalization schemes of many cities in Japan. In addition, further development is now partially restricted in some suburban areas, and the subsequent expansion of city boundaries is complete in most Japanese cities. At this point, Japan has already turned to face the Post-Growth society, but the term itself has not been commonly used in previous studies. This may be because the concept of Post-Growth may appear to implicitly be the opposite of growth. Many people think that simple growth is necessary for the revitalization of city centres and therefore hesitate to adopt the Post-Growth concept. As Dr. Pacione explained, the concept of Post-Growth is derived from the idea of urban sustainability rather than simple growth. He also pointed out that discussing the problems related to shrinking cities will provide a paradigm shift from simple growth-driven urban planning to a new type of urban planning based on urban sustainability. In this sense, monitoring Japan's urban experience since the 1990s and providing feedback to society are important activities.

Unfortunately, this book still has a shortcoming on map interpretation of the regional differences of social status. However, related issues of quality-of-life are examined in several chapters. The time–space budget of working mothers in central Tokyo examined in Chapter 5 is one example because it is related to the work–life balance debate. The viewpoint of universal design in urban infrastructure reflecting the needs of an aging population in a residential area in the suburbs of Osaka (Chapter 6) and discussions related to the food-desert problem (Chapter 7) are also good examples of the types of quality-of-life issues that Japan must consider in the future.

It is our hope that readers will find this book a good opportunity to become more engaged in the discussions of the Post-Growth concept.

Masateru Hino and Jun Tsutsumi

250

List of Contributors   *Editor

Part I

1. **PACIONE, Michael**
University of Strathclyde, UK
m.pacione@strath.ac.uk

2. **ABE, Takashi**
Japan Women's University
geo-tak@fc.jwu.ac.jp

3. **YAMAGAMI, Tatsuya**
Wakayama University
yamagami@center.wakayama-u.ac.jp

4. **KOIZUMI, Ryo**
Tokyo Metropolitan University
Ryo.Koizumi@gmail.com

5. **YABE, Naoto**
Joetsu University of Education
yabe@juen.ac.jp

6. **KAGAWA, Takashi**
Kyoto University of Education
kagawa@kyokyo-u.ac.jp

7. **ITO, Tetsuya**
Rissho University
tetsudeu@ris.ac.jp

IWAMA, Nobuyuki
Ibaraki Christian University

HIRAI, Makoto
Kanagawa University

8. **KUBO, Tomoko**
Gifu University
tmkkb@gifu-u.ac.jp

YUI, Yoshimichi
Hiroshima University

SAKAUE, Hiroaki
Graduate Student, Hiroshima University

9. **FUJITSUKA, Yoshihiro**
Osaka City University
fujitsuka@gscc.osaka-cu.ac.jp

Part II

10. **YAMADA, Hirohisa**
Yamagata University
hyamada@human.kj.yamagata-u.ac.jp

11. **HINO, Masateru ***
Tohoku University
masateru@m.tohoku.ac.jp

12. **TSUTSUMI, Jun ***
University of Tsukuba
jtsu@geoenv.tsukuba.ac.jp

13. **NISHIHARA, Jun**
Shizuoka University
nishihara@inf.shizuoka.ac.jp

14. **YAMASHITA, Jun**
Kyushu University
yamasita@scs.kyushu-u.ac.jp

252

Index

A

absolute population aging   93, 98

absorbed amalgamation   213, 214, 222

accompanied migration   38

activity diary   79, 80, 87

administrative board   210-212, 221

administrative organization   210, 212, 217, 221

aged society/ aged community   124

agglomeration   227

aging population   91, 92-94, 110, 113, 118, 120, 123, 124, 136, 184, 247, 248

aging society   2, 102, 107, 117, 120, 147, 148, 248

aging suburban neighborhoods   123, 142

Arakawa river   172

B

baby boomers   38, 62

barrier-free   101, 102

birth rate   46, 107, 108, 110, 112, 118, 120, 121, 148, 179, 184

blue-collar workers   68-70, 72-74, 150

branch office (economy)   181-185, 190, 194, 199

Brundtland Report   225

bubble economy   2, 62, 64, 66, 74, 126, 160, 183, 184

(collapse of the) bubble economy   38, 46, 61, 149, 150, 247

C

central area   32, 33, 38-40, 43, 62, 112, 135, 147,149, 150, 208, 210

central business district   148, 182, 198, 200-203, 205

central city   46, 48, 112, 180, 190, 191, 194, 210, 214

central Tokyo   79, 87, 109, 112, 136, 141, 160

centralisation   51, 52

centralized headquarters system   208, 212-214, 216-220

centripetal population movement   63

chika-koji   161

city centre   46, 50-53, 55, 57, 77-79, 82, 87, 107, 123, 125, 150, 151, 248

cohort share analysis   36, 43

commercial land price   160, 162, 163, 165

community   13, 14, 16, 18, 25, 26, 91, 102, 103, 107, 109, 114, 116, 120, 124, 127, 129, 135, 139, 141-143, 148, 151, 153, 156, 170, 205, 233

commuting   2, 46, 48, 54-58, 63, 73, 109

commuting time   77, 82, 86, 87

compact city   1, 13, 180, 248

competitive effects   68

competitiveness   148, 227

comprehensive branch system   210, 213, 218

concrete dwelling unit   40

conversion   32, 142, 155, 180

counter-urbanisation   8

D

(analysis of) daily activities   109

daily life activities   107, 118

de-growth   15, 226

death rate   36, 110, 179

decentralisation   45, 46, 51, 53, 57

decoupling   225

decreases in population   108

demographic changes   63, 109, 120

Den'en-toshi Line   70

Densely inhabited district (DID)   62, 214, 232

(era of) depopulation   46

density function   50, 51, 57

depopulated region   218

depopulating city   13

depopulation around the city centre   46

deregulation   149, 150, 156

designated city   180, 181, 208

discriminant analysis   215, 217, 222

displace   148, 155

distant (distance) decay effect   55

distribution center   150, 190

district below sea level   168, 170, 176

doughnut phenomenon   32, 46

E

ecological economics   226

Edogawa river   172

elderly population   91, 93, 94, 96, 98, 107, 109, 113, 114, 116, 131, 136

emergency urban development area   150

empty nesters   32

end of suburbanization   63

environment-related industry   229

equal amalgamation   214, 217, 221

extended shift-share analysis   61, 65, 68

externalities   228, 229

exurbanisation   8, 50

F

festival   188, 189, 190, 191, 193

field survey   19, 124, 129, 132

filtering process   74

financial crisis   160, 162, 165, 175

first-generation residents   93

flexibility of schedule   85

flourishing of human life   226

former central area   208, 210

freedom of construction   148, 154, 156

fringe (metropolitan fringe)   73, 107-110, 120, 121

Fukaya city   109

Fukuoka   180-182, 191

Fukushima Daiichi nuclear power plant   173

full time job   79, 80

G

garden city   92

gateway   190, 197

gentrification   78, 148, 150, 154, 156

geographical factor   220

gray-collar workers   68-70, 72, 73

Great east Japan earthquake   160-162, 167, 168, 170, 173, 175, 176

green growth   15, 226, 227

greenhouse gas emissions   225

greening the economy   226

gross national happiness (GNH)   15

H

height restrictions   201

high-rise condominium   32, 39, 74, 149-151, 153-156

high-tech industry (industries)   229

Hiroshima (city)   180, 181

Hiroshima prefecture   127

Hirschman-Herfindahl index   233

Hokkaido   198, 199, 203, 205

home ownership   125, 126

hot spot   174-176

housekeeping task   85, 86

housework   82, 87

housing estates 123-125, 129, 136, 141, 143, 170, 174, 186, 187

housing linkage program 149

housing market 74, 123, 124, 126, 135, 143, 154

housing preferences 39, 168

housing unit 96, 99, 100, 149, 151, 154, 156

husband 85

I

individual-city-centered network 193

information and communications technology (ICT) 229

innovation 227-229, 241, 243, 244

intercity linkage 190-193

(the) Internet 79, 83

intra-difference 209, 218-220

IT (information technology) related workers 205

J

Jacobs externalities 228, 229, 232, 233, 241, 243, 244

K

Kansai (Kinki) 47, 48, 52, 57, 92

Kanto region 33, 39, 40, 109, 112, 170, 173

Kashiwa 73, 173, 174

Keihanshin metropolitan area 47, 48, 50, 52-57, 92

knowledge society 227

knowledge spillover 228, 244

Kobe 45, 47, 48, 50, 52, 57, 180, 181, 190

Kohoku new town 70, 72

Kumagaya city 109

Kyoto 45, 47, 48, 50, 52, 57, 180, 181

Kyoto protocol 227

L

labour costs 205

land market value publication 161

liquefaction 160, 168, 170, 172, 174-176

local allocation tax 208

local communities 109, 114, 116, 117, 141, 142

local economy 13, 109, 198

location quotient 232, 233, 241, 244

M

Marshall-Arrow-Romer (MAR) externalities 228

mayoral department 210-212, 219, 221

metropolitan region 11, 14, 45, 124, 127, 208, 218, 221

Ministry of internal affairs 209, 210, 212

Momoyamadai district 95, 96

multi-locational headquarters system 211, 213, 218

municipal assembly 209-211, 221

Musashino line 69, 70

N

Nagoya 45, 107, 180, 181, 218

national development plan 184

need for urban policies 117

new-build gentrification 148, 154

NPO 119, 190

O

occupation composition 65

OECD patent statistics 227, 229

office building 149, 151, 185, 186, 200-202

office location 197, 200

office property crisis 202

office vacancy rate 201-204

Olympic Game 198

online shopping   79, 87

ordinance-designated (autonomous) city
  198, 208

Osaka   45, 46, 48, 50, 52, 57, 92, 94, 107,
  126, 129, 148-150, 153, 155, 156, 180, 181,
  183, 208, 233, 239, 242

P

parent   21, 24, 38, 39, 73, 82, 86, 87, 93, 96,
  98, 102, 124-126, 131, 135, 139, 165, 188

parking lot   148, 155

patent   227, 229

people's daily activities   208

phase of decreasing population   32

population change   33, 48, 74, 108-112,
  217-219

population decline   11, 12, 46, 53, 57, 109,
  110, 112, 120, 121

population decrement   220

population densities   9, 50, 51

population dispersion   45, 46, 50, 51, 57

population distribution   31, 42, 46, 48, 56,
  111

population recovery   46, 50, 51, 53, 57, 78,
  149

Porter externalities   228

preservation   14, 148, 156

private financial initiative act   93, 102

pro-merger policy   207-210, 219

producer service   185

prosperity   15, 226

provincial region   209

public transportation   101, 109, 148, 151,
  154, 156

Q

quality of life (QOL)   7, 8, 15, 17-22, 24,
  26, 28, 79, 87, 220, 226, 247-249

questionnaire   74, 79, 80, 98, 99, 102, 109,
  114, 118, 120, 186, 212

R

radiation   160, 168, 173-176

rapid economic growth   91, 107, 109, 162,
  182, 186

re-concentration   46, 53, 57

reformation of spatial government systems
  216

regional central city   180, 190, 191, 194

regional characteristics of population
  change   109

rehabilitation   13, 148

relative population aging   93, 98

rental cost   201, 202

rented public condominium   96, 98

residential environment   124, 129, 136,
  139, 140

residential land price   160, 162, 163, 165,
  167, 175

residential paradigm   32

return migration   32

S

Saikyo Line   70

Saitama prefecture   35, 109, 110, 113, 139

Sapporo   180-182, 197, 207

second-generation residents   93

Sendai   180-183, 185-190, 192, 193

senior care centre   103

Senri new town   103

shopping behaviors   114

shrinking city   7, 8, 14, 180, 193

shrinking metropolitan areas   109

shrinking phase   32

shrinking zone   33, 35, 42

Simpson's diversity index   233, 241, 244

small array   150

smart phone   87

Sobu line   170

social changes   94

social mix   74

social polarization   62-64, 74

social relationships   116

socio-economic changes   109, 120

socio-economic reconfiguration   109, 120

spatial data framework   198

spatial entrapment   77, 78

special merger bond   208

speculator   148

sport club   190

stagnation of economic and social activities
   109

Standard Metropolitan Statistical Area   48

statistical analysis   109, 120

steady-state economy   226

suburb   112, 113, 123-127, 129, 132, 134-
   137, 142, 143, 160, 170, 176, 186-188

suburban neighborhoods   123, 124, 132,
   135, 136, 142, 143

suburbanisation   8, 11, 31, 38, 43, 51, 63,
   74, 78, 123, 125, 126, 136

sustainability   15, 132, 226, 248

sustainable city   147

sustainable development   16, 94, 101, 225,
   226

sustainable society   15

T

Tama new town   69, 70, 94, 129

terraced house   150, 155

territorial level 3 (TL3)   229

the elderly   17, 21, 93, 94, 96, 98, 99,107-
   109, 114, 116-118, 120, 127, 131, 136, 148,
   151, 154, 156

time budget   79, 81

Tohoku region   168, 183

Tokyo   31, 45, 61, 77, 92, 107, 123, 148,
   159, 180, 198, 208, 233, 237

Tokyo station   33, 42, 43, 64-66, 162, 163,
   165, 167

Tonegawa river   170

Toyoko line   73

traditional house   148, 150, 155

Trinity reforms   208

tsunami   160, 168, 170, 172, 174-176

U

under-utilized site   148

universal design   102, 103

university   93, 98, 189, 192, 193, 204

unmarried people   39, 40, 43

urban development stage model   51

urban fringe   52, 53, 55-57

urban landscape   147, 148, 150, 154-156

urban policy challenges   109, 118, 120

urban regeneration   147, 148, 150, 151, 154

urban renewal   74

urban shrinkage   9, 28, 46, 56-58

urban sprawl   9, 91

urbanisation   8, 45, 51, 91, 92, 159, 179, 181

urbanized areas   45, 52, 109, 118, 120, 213,
   215

V

vacancy   42, 43, 134, 140, 151, 153, 156,
   185, 201-203

vacant house   42, 124, 127, 133-136,
   139-143

vacant plot   187

vitalization   188, 190, 194

volunteer   118, 188, 190, 191

W

waterfront   172, 176

white-collar workers   66, 68-74

working mother   79, 81, 87

Y

Yamanote line   72

Yokohama   35, 70, 72, 180, 181, 233, 243

Yorii town   109